ATLAS OF RUSSIAN HISTORY

OTHER BOOKS BY MARTIN GILBERT

The Churchill biography
Volume III, 'The Challenge of War', 1914–1916
Volume III, Documents, Parts I and II
Volume IV, 'The Stricken World', 1917–1922
Volume IV, Documents, Parts I, II and III
Volume V, 'The Prophet of Truth', 1922–1939
The Exchequer Years, Documents, 1922–1929
The Wilderness Years, Documents, 1929–1935
The Coming of War, Documents, 1936–1939
Volume VI, 'Finest Hour', 1939–1941
At the Admiralty, Documents, 1939–1940
Volume VII, 'Road to Victory', 1941–1945
Volume VIII, 'Never Despair', 1945–1965

Historical works
The Appeasers (with Richard Gott)
The European Powers, 1900–1945
The Roots of Appeasement
Britain and Germany Between the Wars (documents)
Plough My Own Furrow: the Life of Lord Allen of Hurtwood (documents)
Servant of India: Diaries of the Viceroy's Private Secretary (documents)
Sir Horace Rumbold: Portrait of a Diplomat
Churchill: a Photographic Portrait
Churchill's Political Philosophy
Auschwitz and the Allies
Exile and Return: the Struggle for Jewish Statehood
The Jews of Hope: the Plight of Soviet Jewry Today
Shcharansky: Hero of our Time
Jerusalem: Rebirth of a City, 1838–1898
Final Journey: the Fate of the Jews in Nazi Europe
The Holocaust: the Jewish Tragedy
The Second World War
Churchill, A Life

Atlases
Dent Atlas of American History
Dent Atlas of the Arab–Israeli Conflict
Dent Atlas of the First World War
Dent Atlas of the Holocaust
Dent Atlas of Jewish History
Dent Atlas of Recent History (*in preparation*)
Dent Atlas of Russian History
The Jews of Arab Lands: Their History in Maps
The Jews of Russia: Their History in Maps
Jerusalem: Illustrated History Atlas
Children's Illustrated Bible Atlas

ATLAS OF
RUSSIAN HISTORY

Second edition

Martin Gilbert

Fellow of Merton College, Oxford

New York

OXFORD UNIVERSITY PRESS

1993

First published in Great Britain by
The Orion Publishing Group Limited
5 Upper St. Martin's Lane, London WC2H 9EA

Published in the United States of America by
Oxford University Press, Inc.
200 Madison Avenue
New York, N.Y. 10016, U.S.A.

Oxford is a registered trademark of
Oxford University Press

Library of Congress
Cataloging-in-Publication Data
Gilbert, Martin, 1936–
     Atlas of Russian history / Martin Gilbert
        p.   cm.
     Rev. ed. of: Russian history atlas / Martin Gilbert. 1972
     Includes bibliographical references and index.
     ISBN 0–19–521041–7 (hardback)
     ISBN 0–19–521061–1 (paperback)
     1. Russia—Historical geography—Maps.   2. Soviet Union—
Historical geography—Maps.   I. Gilbert. Martin, 1936–   Russian
history atlas.
G2111.SIG52   1993   <G&M>
911.47—dc20
                                                    93–21920
                                                       CIP
                                                       MAP

Printing (last digit): 9 8 7 6 5 4 3 2

Printed in Great Britain

Preface

I have designed this Atlas in the hope that it is possible to present—within the span of 161 maps—a survey of Russian history from the earliest times to the present day. In drafting each map, I drew upon material from a wide range of published works—books, articles, atlases and single sheet maps—each of which I have listed in the bibliography.

On the maps themselves I have included much factual material not normally associated with historical geography, such as the text of one of Stalin's few surviving personal communications—the postcard to his sister-in-law (printed on map 54), and Lenin's telegram to the Bolsheviks in Sweden (printed on map 87). I have drafted each map individually, in such a way as to enable the maximum factual information to be included without making use of a separate page of text; and I have compiled the index in order that it may serve as a means of using the Atlas as if it were a volume of narrative.

I wish to acknowledge the help of many colleagues and friends. In 1962 I began research into Russian history under the supervision of Dr George Katkov, whose insatiable curiosity about elusive historical facts, and whose enthusiasm in tracking them down, have influenced all my subsequent work. I also benefitted from the teaching and encouragement of Mr David Footman, Mr Max Hayward, Dr Harry Willetts and the late Mr Guy Wint. When I was preparing the first sketches for this Atlas, the maps I had drawn and the facts I had incorporated on them were scrutinized by three friends—Mr Michael Glenny, Mr Dennis O'Flaherty and Dr Harry Shukman—to each of whom I am most grateful for many detailed suggestions, and for giving up much time to help me. At the outset of my research I received valuable bibliographical advice from Dr J. L. I. Simmons, and suggestions for specific maps from Mr Norman Davies, Dr Ronald Hingley, Mr John B. Kingston and Mr Ewald Uustalu. Jane Cousins helped me with bibliographical and historical research; Mr Arthur Banks transcribed my sketches into clear, printable maps, and Kate Fleming kept a vigilant eye on the cartography. Susie Sacher helped me to compile the index: Sarah Graham, as well as undertaking all the secretarial work, made many important suggestions, factual and cartographic.

The first 146 maps in this atlas were drawn by Arthur Banks and his team of expert cartographers, including the late Terry Bicknell, who subsequently drew more than six hundred historical maps for me. The last fifteen maps were drawn by Tim Aspden, who also drew the extra maps for several of my other books and historical atlases.

I am particularly grateful to Abe Eisenstat and Kay Thomson for their help over several months in enabling me to bring this atlas up to date for this new edition. The collapse of Soviet Communism and the disintegration of the Soviet Union before the end of its eighth decade, an event which was not conceivable (certainly not to this author) when the atlas was first published in 1972, has led me to prepare fifteen new maps. In designing them, I have tried to show in detail the sequence of events that shook both the Soviet Union and Eastern Europe within the space of a decade, creating new States and new perspectives as the territorial and ideological monolith dissolved.

MARTIN GILBERT
Merton College, Oxford

3 March 1993

Maps

SECTION THREE: THE SOVIET UNION

SECTION FOUR: THE END OF THE SOVIET UNION

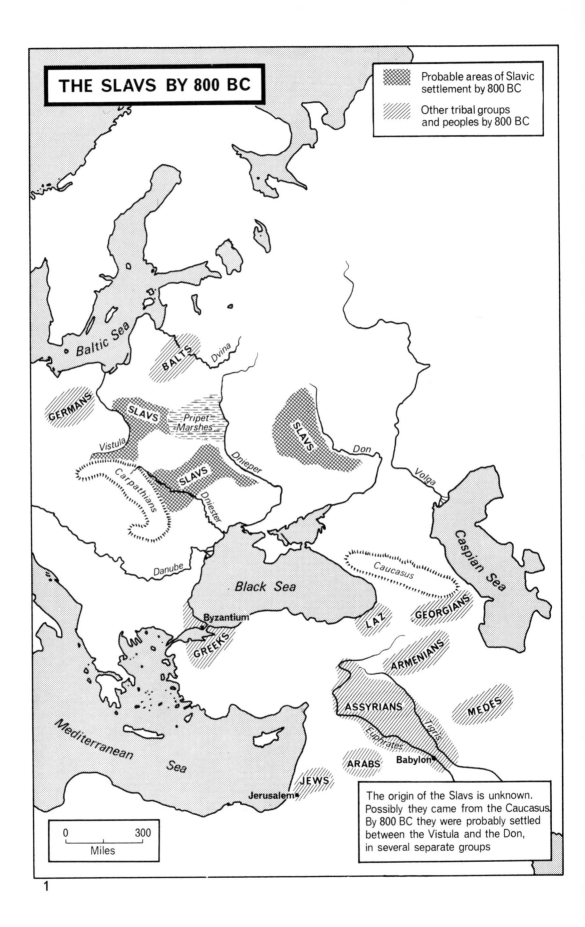

THE SLAVS BY 800 BC

Probable areas of Slavic settlement by 800 BC

Other tribal groups and peoples by 800 BC

Baltic Sea

BALTS

Dvina

GERMANS

SLAVS

Pripet Marshes

SLAVS

Don

Vistula

Carpathians

SLAVS

Volga

Dnieper

Dniester

Caspian Sea

Danube

Caucasus

Black Sea

Byzantium

LAZ

GEORGIANS

GREEKS

ARMENIANS

Mediterranean

MEDES

Sea

ASSYRIANS

Tigris

Euphrates

Babylon

ARABS

JEWS

Jerusalem

0	300

Miles

The origin of the Slavs is unknown. Possibly they came from the Caucasus. By 800 BC they were probably settled between the Vistula and the Don, in several separate groups

1

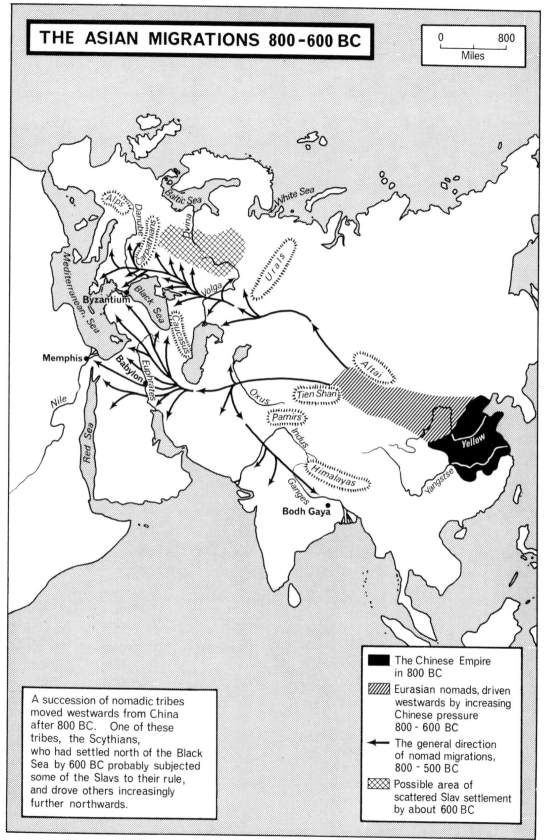

THE ASIAN MIGRATIONS 800-600 BC

0   800
Miles

Alps
Baltic Sea
Danube
Dvina
White Sea
Carpathians
Volga
Urals
Mediterranean Sea
Byzantium
Black Sea
Caucasus
Memphis
Babylon
Euphrates
Nile
Red Sea
Oxus
Pamirs
Tien Shan
Altai
Indus
Himalayas
Ganges
Bodh Gaya
Yellow
Yangtse

A succession of nomadic tribes
moved westwards from China
after 800 BC.   One of these
tribes, the Scythians,
who had settled north of the Black
Sea by 600 BC probably subjected
some of the Slavs to their rule,
and drove others increasingly
further northwards.

■ The Chinese Empire
  in 800 BC

▨ Eurasian nomads, driven
  westwards by increasing
  Chinese pressure
  800 - 600 BC

← The general direction
  of nomad migrations,
  800 - 500 BC

▩ Possible area of
  scattered Slav settlement
  by about 600 BC

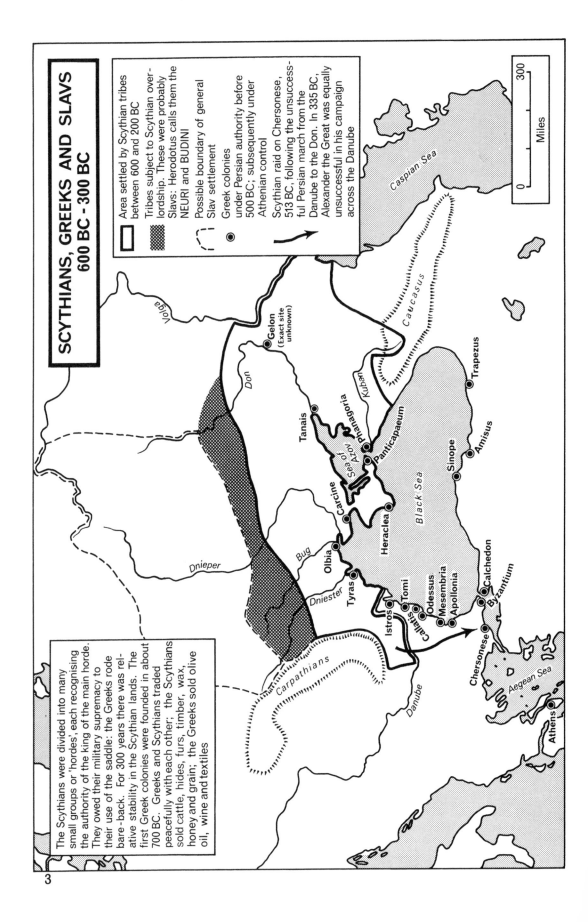

SCYTHIANS, GREEKS AND SLAVS 600 BC - 300 BC

Area settled by Scythian tribes between 600 and 200 BC

Tribes subject to Scythian over-lordship. These were probably Slavs: Herodotus calls them the NEURI and BUDINI

Possible boundary of general Slav settlement

Greek colonies under Persian authority before 500 BC; subsequently under Athenian control

Scythian raid on Chersonese, 513 BC, following the unsuccess-ful Persian march from the Danube to the Don. In 335 BC, Alexander the Great was equally unsuccessful in his campaign across the Danube

The Scythians were divided into many small groups or 'hordes', each recognising the authority of the king of the main horde. They owed their military supremacy to their use of the saddle: the Greeks rode bare-back. For 300 years there was rel-ative stability in the Scythian lands. The first Greek colonies were founded in about 700 BC. Greeks and Scythians traded peacefully with each other; the Scythians sold cattle, hides, furs, timber, wax, honey and grain; the Greeks sold olive oil, wine and textiles

300

Miles

Caspian Sea

Volga

Gelon (Exact site unknown)

Don

Tanais

Kuban

Caucasus

Sea of Azov

Phanagoria

Panticapaeum

Trapezus

Carcine

Black Sea

Sinope

Amisus

Heraclea

Bug

Dnieper

Olbia

Dniester

Tyras

Istros

Callatis

Tomi

Odessus

Mesembria

Apollonia

Calchedon

Byzantium

Chersonese

Aegean Sea

Carpathians

Danube

Athens

3

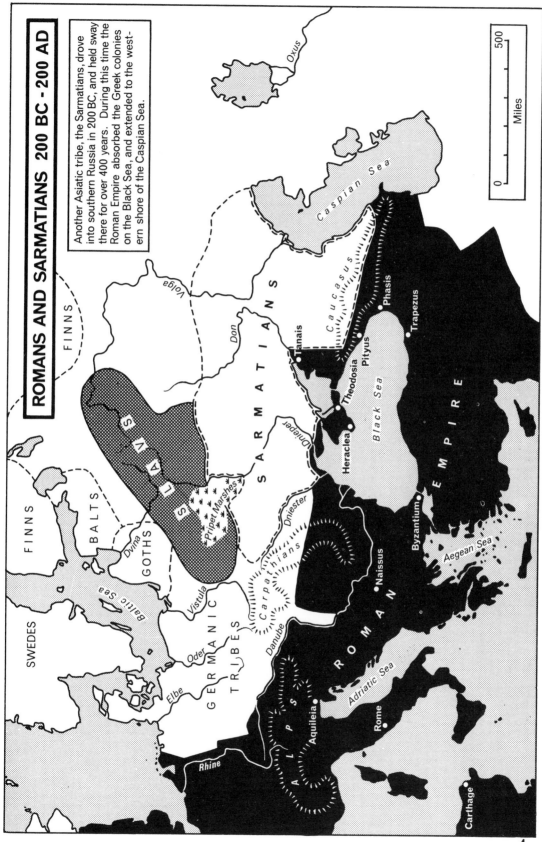

ROMANS AND SARMATIANS 200 BC - 200 AD

Another Asiatic tribe, the Sarmatians, drove into southern Russia in 200 BC, and held sway there for over 400 years. During this time the Roman Empire absorbed the Greek colonies on the Black Sea, and extended to the western shore of the Caspian Sea.

500

0

Miles

Oxus

Caspian Sea

Volga

FINNS

Caucasus

Don

SARMATIANS

Tanais

Phasis

Trapezus

Pityus

Theodosia

Dnieper

Black Sea

Heraclea

EMPIRE

SLAVS

Dniester

Pripet Marshes

Byzantium

Aegean Sea

SWEDES

FINNS

BALTS

Dvina

GOTHS

Vistula

Carpathians

Naissus

R O M A N

Baltic Sea

GERMANIC TRIBES

Oder

Danube

Elbe

A L P S

Adriatic Sea

Aquileia

Rome

Rhine

Carthage

4

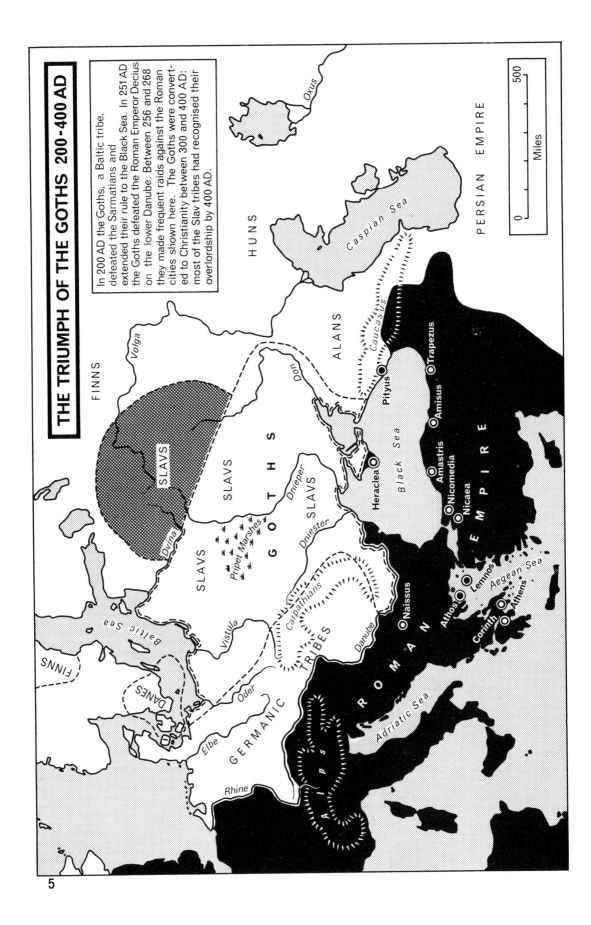

THE TRIUMPH OF THE GOTHS 200-400 AD

In 200 AD the Goths, a Baltic tribe, defeated the Sarmatians and extended their rule to the Black Sea. In 251 AD the Goths defeated the Roman Emperor Decius on the lower Danube. Between 256 and 268 they made frequent raids against the Roman cities shown here. The Goths were converted to Christianity between 300 and 400 AD: most of the Slav tribes had recognised their overlordship by 400 AD.

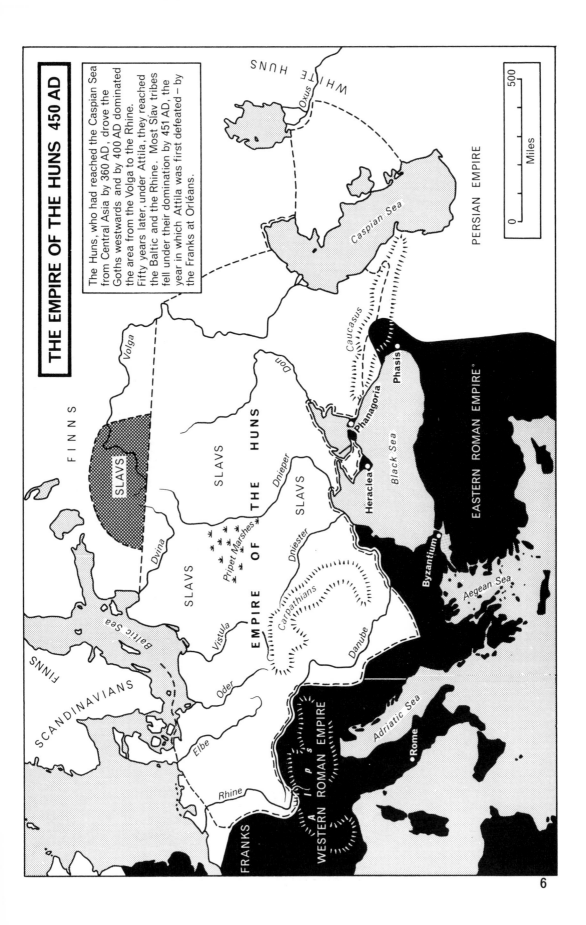

THE EMPIRE OF THE HUNS 450 AD

The Huns, who had reached the Caspian Sea from Central Asia by 360 AD, drove the Goths westwards and by 400 AD dominated the area from the Volga to the Rhine. Fifty years later, under Attila, they reached the Baltic and the Rhine. Most Slav tribes fell under their domination by 451 AD, the year in which Attila was first defeated – by the Franks at Orléans.

WHITE HUNS

Oxus

Caspian Sea

PERSIAN EMPIRE

0   500

Miles

Volga

FINNS

SLAVS

Don

SLAVS

Dnieper

SLAVS

Dvina

Caucasus

Phasis

EMPIRE OF THE HUNS

Pripet Marshes

SLAVS

Dniester

Phanagoria

Black Sea

Heraclea

SCANDINAVIANS

FINNS

Baltic Sea

Vistula

Carpathians

Danube

Byzantium

Aegean Sea

EASTERN ROMAN EMPIRE

Oder

Elbe

Rhine

FRANKS

A L P S

WESTERN ROMAN EMPIRE

Adriatic Sea

Rome

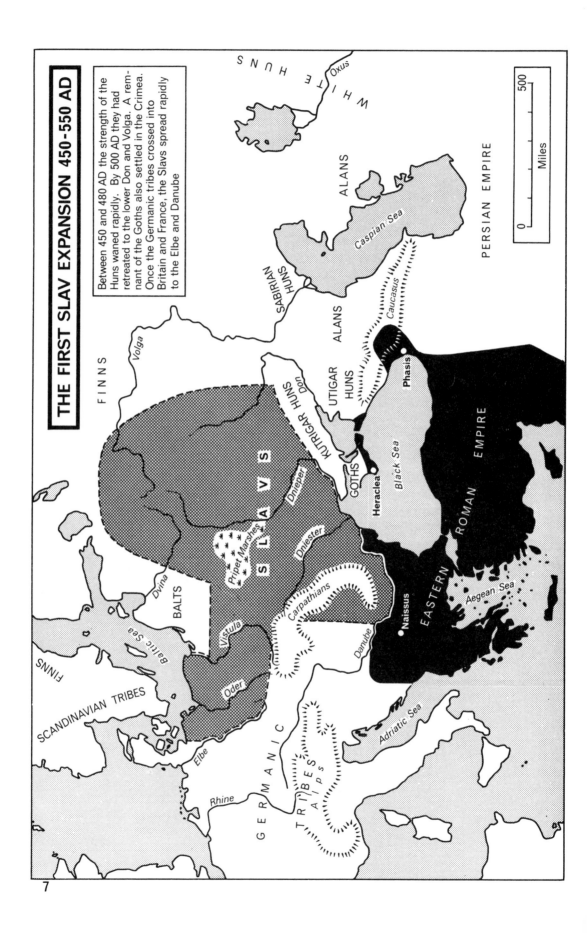

THE FIRST SLAV EXPANSION 450-550 AD

Between 450 and 480 AD the strength of the Huns waned rapidly. By 500 AD they had retreated to the lower Don and Volga. A remnant of the Goths also settled in the Crimea. Once the Germanic tribes crossed into Britain and France, the Slavs spread rapidly to the Elbe and Danube

500

Miles

WHITE HUNS

Oxus

ALANS

PERSIAN EMPIRE

Caspian Sea

SABIRIAN HUNS

ALANS

Caucasus

FINNS

Volga

UTIGAR HUNS

Phasis

KUTRIGAR HUNS

Don

GOTHS

Black Sea

Heraclea

S L A V S

Dnieper

Pripet Marshes

Dniester

Dvina

BALTS

Carpathians

Vistula

Danube

Naissus

EASTERN

ROMAN

EMPIRE

Aegean Sea

Baltic Sea

FINNS

SCANDINAVIAN TRIBES

Oder

Adriatic Sea

Elbe

G E R M A N I C

T R I B E S

Alps

Rhine

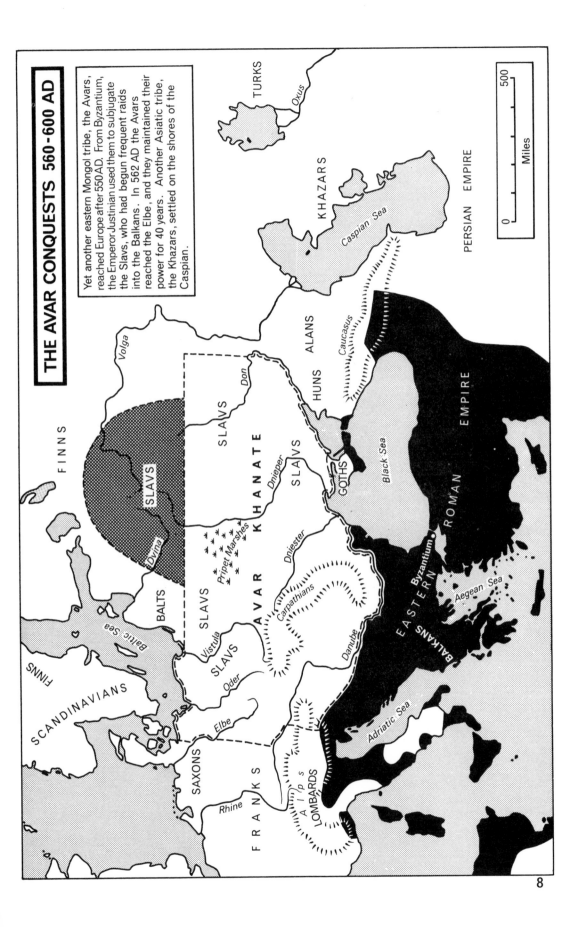

THE AVAR CONQUESTS 560-600 AD

Yet another eastern Mongol tribe, the Avars, reached Europe after 550AD. From Byzantium, the Emperor Justinian used them to subjugate the Slavs, who had begun frequent raids into the Balkans. In 562 AD the Avars reached the Elbe, and they maintained their power for 40 years. Another Asiatic tribe, the Khazars, settled on the shores of the Caspian.

500

0

Miles

TURKS

Oxus

KHAZARS

Caspian Sea

PERSIAN EMPIRE

Volga

FINNS

Don

SLAVS

HUNS ALANS

Caucasus

Dvina

SLAVS

Dnieper

SLAVS

GOTHS

Black Sea

BALTS

Baltic Sea

SLAVS

Pripet Marshes

AVAR KHANATE

SLAVS

Dniester

Byzantium

ROMAN

FINNS

SCANDINAVIANS

Vistula

Oder

SLAVS

Carpathians

Danube

EASTERN

BALKANS

EMPIRE

Aegean Sea

SAXONS

Elbe

FRANKS

Rhine

Alps

LOMBARDS

Adriatic Sea

8

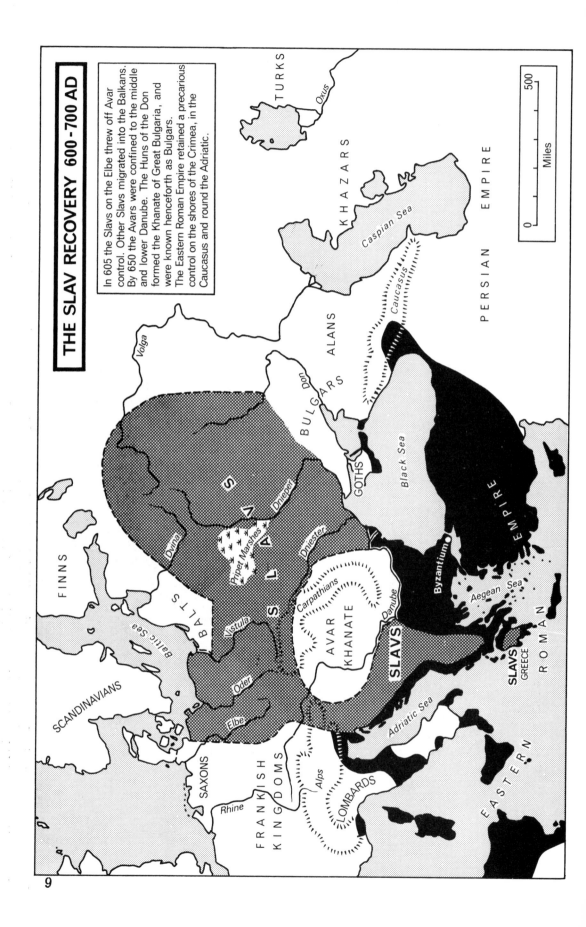

THE SLAV RECOVERY 600-700 AD

In 605 the Slavs on the Elbe threw off Avar control. Other Slavs migrated into the Balkans. By 650 the Avars were confined to the middle and lower Danube. The Huns of the Don formed the Khanate of Great Bulgaria, and were known henceforth as Bulgars. The Eastern Roman Empire retained a precarious control on the shores of the Crimea, in the Caucasus and round the Adriatic.

TURKS

Oxus

KHAZARS

Caspian Sea

PERSIAN EMPIRE

Volga

BULGARS

ALANS

Don

Caucasus

FINNS

Dvina

Dnieper

S L A V S

Pripet Marshes

Dniester

GOTHS

Black Sea

Byzantium

BALTS

Vistula

Carpathians

Danube

EASTERN

Byzantium

Aegean Sea

SCANDINAVIANS

Baltic Sea

Oder

AVAR KHANATE

SLAVS

Elbe

SLAVS

GREECE

ROMAN

SAXONS

FRANKISH KINGDOMS

Rhine

Alps

LOMBARDS

Adriatic Sea

EMPIRE

0   500

Miles

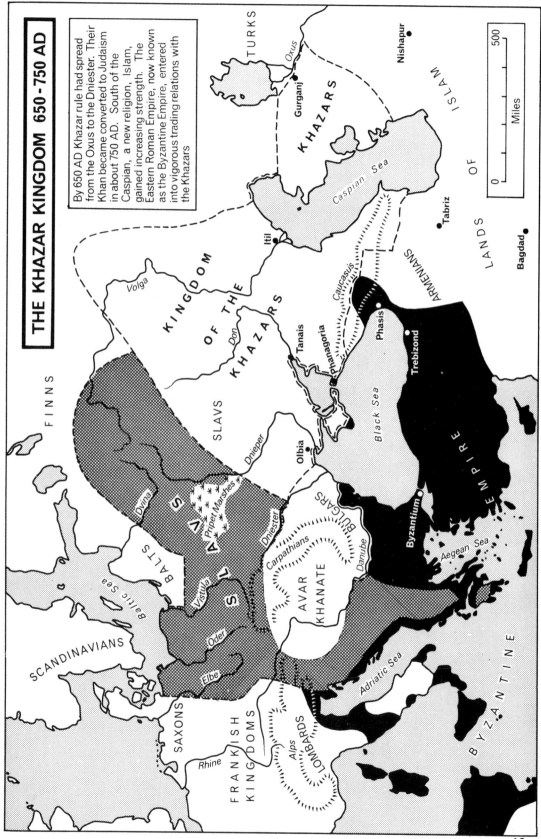

THE KHAZAR KINGDOM 650-750 AD

By 650 AD Khazar rule had spread from the Oxus to the Dniester. Their Khan became converted to Judaism in about 750 AD. South of the Caspian, a new religion, Islam, gained increasing strength. The Eastern Roman Empire, now known as the Byzantine Empire, entered into vigorous trading relations with the Khazars

500

0

Miles

TURKS

KHAZARS

Oxus

Gurganj

Nishapur

Caspian Sea

ISLAM

Tabriz

Itil

Bagdad

Volga

KINGDOM

OF

THE

KHAZARS

Don

LANDS

OF

Caucasus

ARMENIANS

FINNS

Tanais

Phanagoria

Phasis

SLAVS

Trebizond

Dnieper

Black Sea

Olbia

Dvina

Pripet Marshes

S

L

A

V

S

BALTS

Dniester

BULGARS

Byzantium

EMPIRE

Vistula

Carpathians

Danube

Aegean Sea

Baltic Sea

Oder

AVAR

KHANATE

Adriatic Sea

SCANDINAVIANS

Elbe

SAXONS

Alps

LOMBARDS

BYZANTINE

FRANKISH

KINGDOMS

Rhine

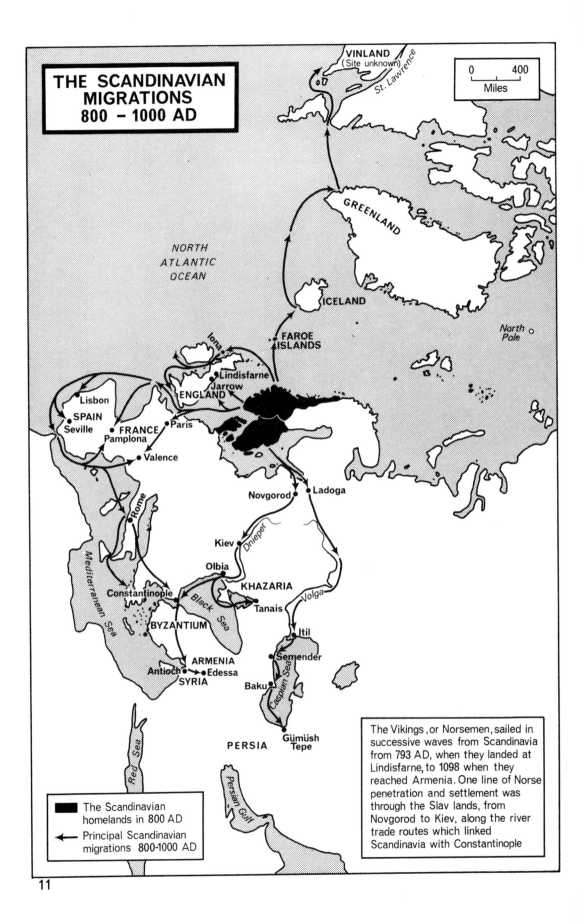

THE SCANDINAVIAN MIGRATIONS 800 – 1000 AD

0   400
Miles

VINLAND
(Site unknown)
St. Lawrence

GREENLAND

NORTH
ATLANTIC
OCEAN

ICELAND

North
Pole

FAROE
ISLANDS

Iona

Lindisfarne
Jarrow
ENGLAND

Lisbon
SPAIN
Seville
FRANCE   Paris
Pamplona
Valence

Rome

Novgorod   Ladoga

Kiev   Dnieper

Olbia

KHAZARIA

Mediterranean Sea

Constantinople   Black Sea   Tanais   Volga

BYZANTIUM

Itil

ARMENIA   Semender
Antioch   Edessa
SYRIA   Baku
Caspian Sea

Red Sea

PERSIA   Gümüsh
Tepe

Persian Gulf

The Scandinavian
homelands in 800 AD
Principal Scandinavian
migrations 800-1000 AD

The Vikings, or Norsemen, sailed in
successive waves from Scandinavia
from 793 AD, when they landed at
Lindisfarne, to 1098 when they
reached Armenia. One line of Norse
penetration and settlement was
through the Slav lands, from
Novgorod to Kiev, along the river
trade routes which linked
Scandinavia with Constantinople

11

THE SLAVS AND THE NORSEMEN BY 880 AD

Slav settlement by 880 AD
SERB Principal Slav tribes
BALTS Other tribes
'Kievan Rus', ruled by the Norsemen (Varangarians), who took tribute from the neighbouring Slavs, and protected them against Khazar and Pecheneg attacks

NORSE

SWEDES

DANES

FINNS

SLOVIANIANS
Novgorod

CHEREMESIANS

Visby

Baltic Sea

BALTS

VIATCHIANS

MORDVINS

Volga

OBODRICHI

POLOCHANE

Smolensk

POLES
MAZOVIANS
Pripet Marshes

KRIVICHIANS

RADIMICHIANS

Elbe

SILESIANS

GERMANS

CZECHS

DEREVLIANS

SEVERIANS

Don

MORAVIANS

Kiev

KHAZARS

SLOVAKS

POLIANIANS

VOLHYNIANS

Danube

SLOVENES

MAGYARS

PECHENEGS

Venice

VLACHS

CROATS

Tmutorokan

Caucasus

Adriatic Sea

SERBS

Black Sea

Preslav

ARMENIANS

BULGARS

Constantinople

Aegean Sea

Athens

GREEKS

The Norse settlers between Novgorod and Kiev quickly dominated the local Slavs, over whom they established political control. Known as "Varangarians", these Norse overlords moulded the Slavs into a coherent federation, "Kievan Rus". Originally Norse speaking, Kievan Rus, or Russia, saw a close mingling of Scandinavian and Slav culture; and the emergence of a strong Kievan, or Russian national consciousness. The first Varangarian ruler, Rurik, led an expedition against Constantinople in 860 AD. His successor Oleg established his capital at Kiev in about 880 AD.

0 ___ 300
Miles

12

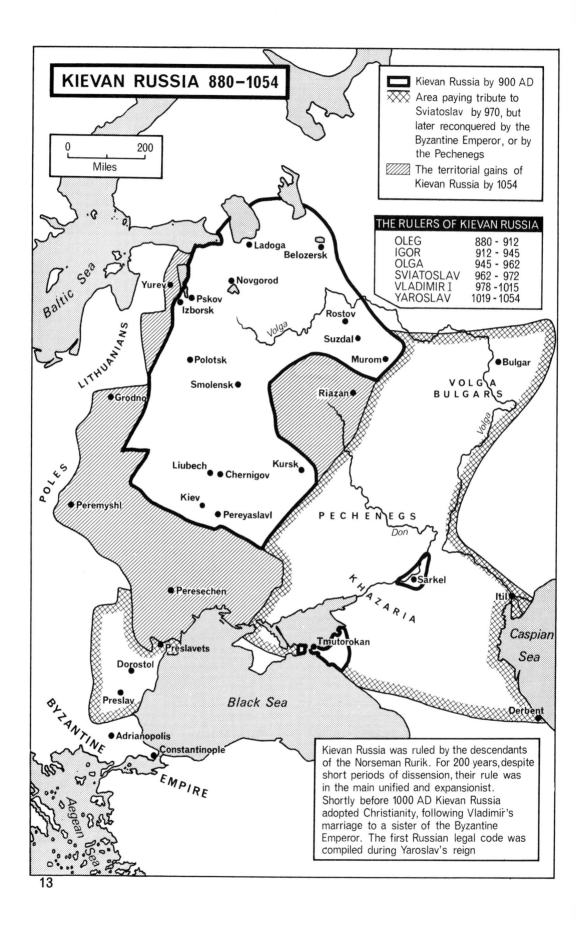

KIEVAN RUSSIA 880–1054

0	200

Miles

Legend:

- ☐ Kievan Russia by 900 AD
- ☒ Area paying tribute to Sviatoslav by 970, but later reconquered by the Byzantine Emperor, or by the Pechenegs
- ▨ The territorial gains of Kievan Russia by 1054

THE RULERS OF KIEVAN RUSSIA

OLEG	880 – 912
IGOR	912 – 945
OLGA	945 – 962
SVIATOSLAV	962 – 972
VLADIMIR I	978 – 1015
YAROSLAV	1019 – 1054

Baltic Sea

LITHUANIANS

POLES

• Ladoga
Belozersk

Yurev •
• Novgorod
• Pskov
Izborsk

Volga

• Rostov

Suzdal •

Murom •

• Polotsk

Smolensk •

Riazan •

VOLGA
BULGARS

• Bulgar

Volga

• Grodno

Liubech •
• Chernigov
Kursk •

Kiev •
• Peremyshl
• Pereyaslavl

PECHENEGS

Don

KHAZARIA

• Sarkel

Itil •

Caspian
Sea

• Peresechen

Tmutorokan

Black Sea

Derbent •

• Preslavets

Dorostol •

• Preslav

BYZANTINE

EMPIRE

• Adrianopolis
• Constantinople

Aegean Sea

Kievan Russia was ruled by the descendants of the Norseman Rurik. For 200 years, despite short periods of dissension, their rule was in the main unified and expansionist. Shortly before 1000 AD Kievan Russia adopted Christianity, following Vladimir's marriage to a sister of the Byzantine Emperor. The first Russian legal code was compiled during Yaroslav's reign

13

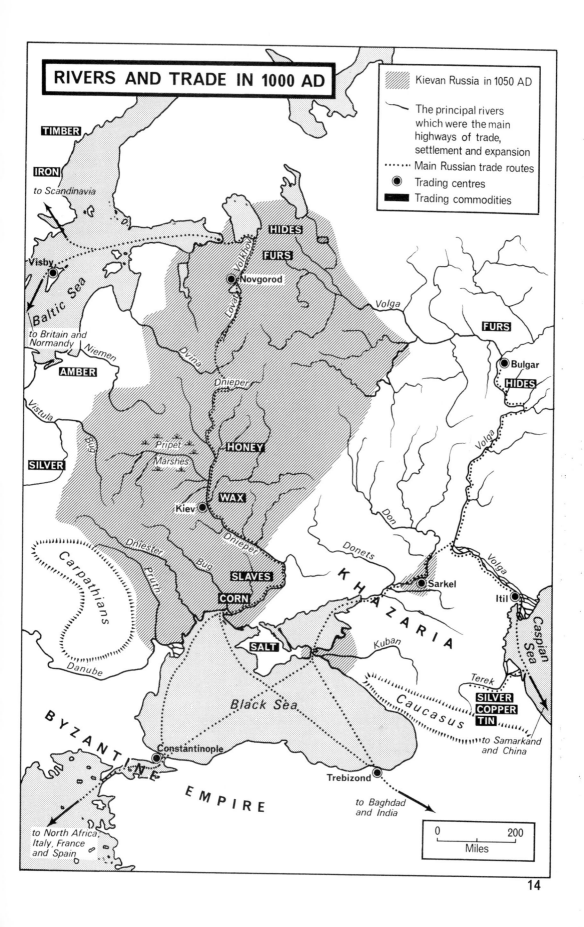

RIVERS AND TRADE IN 1000 AD

Kievan Russia in 1050 AD

The principal rivers which were the main highways of trade, settlement and expansion

Main Russian trade routes

Trading centres

Trading commodities

TIMBER

IRON

to Scandinavia

HIDES

FURS

Visby

Novgorod

Volga

Baltic Sea

FURS

to Britain and Normandy

Niemen

Bulgar

AMBER

HIDES

Dvina

Dnieper

Vistula

Bug

Volga

SILVER

Pripet

Marshes

HONEY

WAX

Kiev

Don

Dniester

Dnieper

Donets

Pruth

Bug

Carpathians

KHAZARIA

Sarkel

Volga

SLAVES

Itil

CORN

Caspian Sea

Danube

SALT

Kuban

Terek

Black Sea

Caucasus

SILVER

COPPER

TIN

B Y Z A N T I N E

to Samarkand and China

Constantinople

E M P I R E

Trebizond

to Baghdad and India

to North Africa, Italy, France and Spain

0	200

Miles

CHRISTIANITY AND THE SLAVS BY 1000 AD

The spread of Christianity led to the division of the Slav world. The Croats (in 700 AD) and the Poles (in 999 AD) were converted to Roman Catholicism. The Serbs (in 700 AD), Bulgars (865 AD) and Russians (988 AD) were converted to Eastern (Orthodox) Catholicism. This led in particular to strong antipathy between Russians and Poles, and also between Serbs and Croats

NORSE

SWEDES

North Sea

Baltic Sea

•Novgorod

•Smolensk

RUSSIANS

GERMANS

POLES

Oder

Rhine

•Paris

FRANKS

•Kiev

Volga

Don

Carpathians

Danube

MAGYARS

Dniester

Alps

Milan•

CROATS

ALANS

Caucasus

Caspian Sea

Adriatic Sea

SERBS

Black Sea

Tiflis

Rome•

BULGARS

•Ochrid

Constantinople

ARMENIANS

•Tabriz

GREEKS

Tarsus
•

Tigris

Kairouan•

Athens

•Aleppo

•Bagdad

Mediterranean Sea

Euphrates

Jerusalem•

Alexandria•

Dead Sea

Nile

Red Sea

The spread of Eastern, or Orthodox, Catholicism, under Constantinople's authority by 1000 AD

Western, or Roman, Catholicism

Areas under Muslim, or Islamic, rule

0   400
Miles

THE FLOURISHING OF RUSSIAN MONASTICISM 1200-1600

Urals

White Sea

Solovetski monastery

KINGDOM OF SWEDEN

ZIRIANS

Siskoi monastery

Valaam

Ustiug

PERMIAKS

Belozersk

Ladoga

Spaso-Kamenni monastery

Baltic Sea

Galich

Novgorod

TEUTONIC KNIGHTS

Kostroma

Pskov

Rostov

Nizhni Novgorod

Tver

Pereyaslavl

Suzdal

Volokolamsk

Troitski-Sergievski monastery

Vladimir

Volga

Polotsk

Moscow

GRAND DUCHY OF LITHUANIA

Smolensk

MONGOL KHANATES

Chernigov

Volga

Kiev

The foundation of urban monasteries was most intense between 1200 and 1350. By 1400 the majority of monasteries being founded were rural or "desert" monasteries. Between 1350 and 1450 over 150 new monasteries were established, and by 1500 many monastic colonies had been set up in the predominantly pagan areas between Galich and the Urals. In 1588 the English Ambassador to Moscow wrote of the monasteries owning all the best land in Russia and being among the principal landowners

Caspian Sea

◉ Principal Orthodox monasteries established by 1500

/// Area of most active monastic colonization before 1500

■ Nomadic and heathen tribes among whom monastic missionary work was most active 1400-1500

-·-·- National frontiers in 1500

0 ———— 200

Miles

THE FRAGMENTATION OF KIEVAN RUSSIA 1054–1238

0   200
Miles

DEPENDENCIES OF NOVGOROD

FINNS

Ladoga

Belozersk
Ustiug

REPUBLIC
OF NOVGOROD
Novgorod

VLADIMIR–SUZDAL

Reval

Kostroma
Yaroslavl
Rostov

VOLGA
BULGARS

Pskov

Torzhok

Suzdal

Tver
Moscow

Vladimir

Riga

Dvina

Izborsk

Murom

SMOLENSK

Riazan

LITHUANIA

Polotsk

Vitebsk

Viazma

MUROM–
RIAZAN

Kovno

Smolensk

POLOTSK

Minsk

CHERNIGOV

Bialystok

TUROV
Pinsk

NOVGOROD–
SEVERSK

Vistula

Turov

Chernigov

POLAND

VOLHYNIA

KIEV
Kiev
Zhitomir

PEREYASLAVL
Pereyaslavl

Cracow

GALICIA
Galich

Don

Carpathians

Dniester

CUMANS or POLOVTSI

HUNGARY

Black
Sea

Constantinople

The twelve Principalities
of Russia in 1100

On the death of Yaroslav in 1054, Kievan Russia
was divided among his sons. Their constant
feuds led to the fragmentation of the once
powerful kingdom. United briefly from 1113 to 1125
by Vladimir Monomakh, the Russian lands were again
divided and in conflict during the hundred years
before the Mongol invasion of 1238. In 1199 Galicia
and Volhynia were united, and in 1254 recognised
by the Pope as an independent kingdom. In
1307 Polotsk came under Lithuanian suzerainty

Baltic Sea

THE REPUBLIC OF NOVGOROD
997-1478

The Republic of Novgorod obtained self-government from Kievan Russia in 997, and complete independence in 1136. The Republic styled itself "Sovereign Great Novgorod" and was governed by a Grand Prince and an Assembly of citizens. Novgorod was for over three hundred years a flourishing trading and cultural centre, and successfully fought off attacks by the Teutonic Knights, the Swedes, the Lithuanians and the Mongols. In 1478 it was finally crushed into complete submission by Ivan the Terrible, and annexed to Moscow. The town itself was largely destroyed by fire in 1695.

Ponoy

White Sea

Pogost-na-more

Spasskoi

FINNS

Ilomanets

Lake Onega

Onega

Pudozhskoi

Lake Ladoga

Olonets

1396

Baltic Sea

1295

1284

1313

SWEDES

Vyborg

1240, 1348

Gulf of Finland

Kopore

Oreshek

Ladoga

Vologda

Reval

1223

Yama

Volkhov

Nebolchi

Dorpat

NOVGOROD

TEUTONIC KNIGHTS

1242

1253

Pskov

Staraya Rusa

Izborsk

Porkhov

Torzhok

Volga

1238

Riga

1269

1298

1323

Tver

MONGOLS

Opochka

1238

Dvina

Velikie Luki

1213

Volokolamsk

Moscow

LITHUANIANS

Polotsk

1245

1253

0   100
Miles

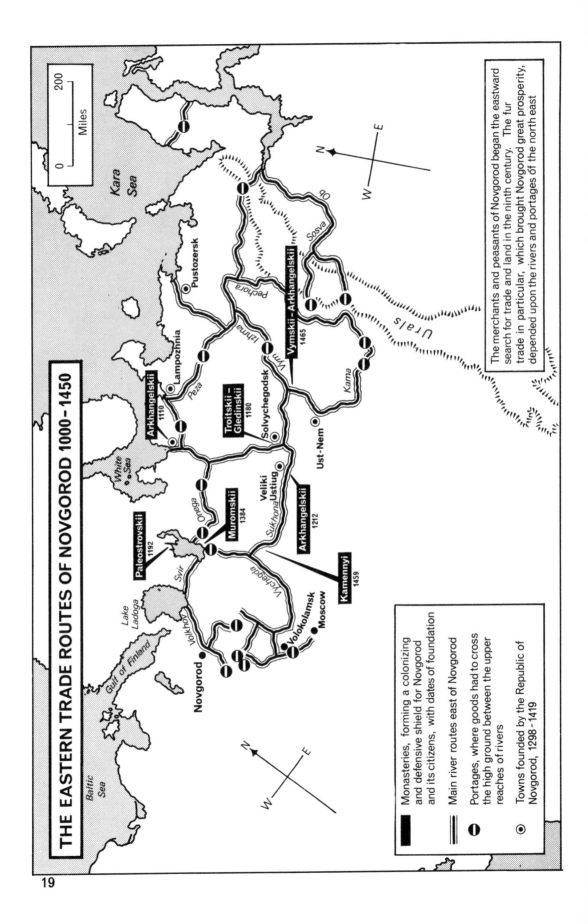

THE EASTERN TRADE ROUTES OF NOVGOROD 1000–1450

Kara Sea

Baltic Sea

Gulf of Finland

Lake Ladoga

White Sea

Arkhangelskii 1110

Lampozinia

Pustozersk

Peza

Izhma

Pechora

Sosva

Ob

Urals

Vymskii – Arkhangelskii 1465

Vym

Kama

Ust-Nem

Solvychegodsk

Troitskii – Gledinskii 1180

Onega

Svir

Volkhov

Paleostrovskii 1192

Muromskii 1384

Veliki Ustiug

Sukhona

Vychegda

Arkhangelskii 1212

Kamennyi 1459

Volokolamsk

Moscow

Novgorod

The merchants and peasants of Novgorod began the eastward search for trade and land in the ninth century. The fur trade in particular, which brought Novgorod great prosperity, depended upon the rivers and portages of the north east

Monasteries, forming a colonizing and defensive shield for Novgorod and its citizens, with dates of foundation

Main river routes east of Novgorod

Portages, where goods had to cross the high ground between the upper reaches of rivers

Towns founded by the Republic of Novgorod, 1298 - 1419

200

Miles

0

N

E

W

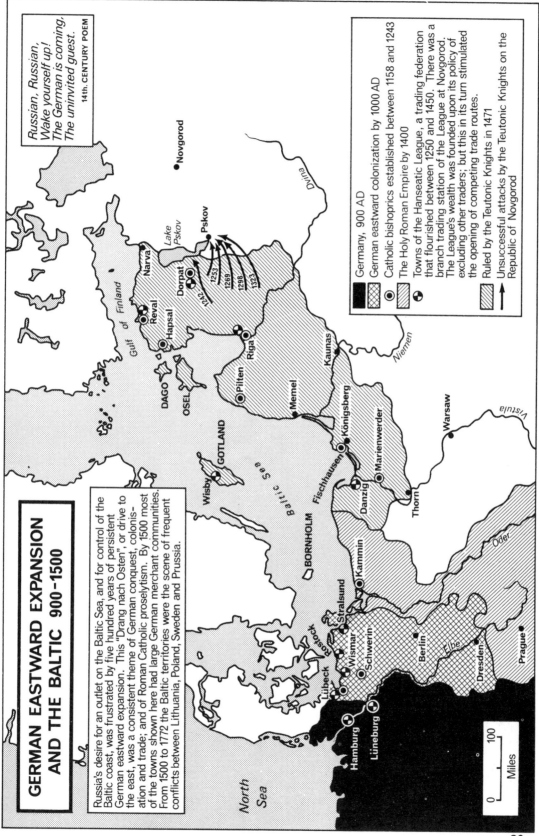

GERMAN EASTWARD EXPANSION AND THE BALTIC 900-1500

Russia's desire for an outlet on the Baltic Sea, and for control of the Baltic coast, was frustrated by five hundred years of persistent German eastward expansion. This "Drang nach Osten", or drive to the east, was a consistent theme of German conquest, colonis- ation and trade; and of Roman Catholic proselytism. By 1500 most of the towns shown here had large German merchant communities. From 1500 to 1772 the Baltic territories were the scene of frequent conflicts between Lithuania, Poland, Sweden and Prussia.

Russian, Russian,
Wake yourself up!
The German is coming.
The uninvited guest.

14th. CENTURY POEM

Germany, 900 AD

German eastward colonization by 1000 AD

Catholic bishoprics established between 1158 and 1243

The Holy Roman Empire by 1400

Towns of the Hanseatic League, a trading federation that flourished between 1250 and 1450. There was a branch trading station of the League at Novgorod. The League's wealth was founded upon its policy of excluding other traders; but this in turn stimulated the opening of competing trade routes.

Ruled by the Teutonic Knights in 1471

Unsuccessful attacks by the Teutonic Knights on the Republic of Novgorod

Novgorod

Pskov
Lake Pskov
1253
1269
1298
1323
1242

Narva
Dorpat
Reval
Hapsal
Riga
Pilten
DAGO
OSEL
Memel
Kaunas
Königsberg
Marienwerder
Warsaw
Fischhausen
Danzig
Thorn
GOTLAND
Wisby
BORNHOLM
Kammin
Stralsund
Rostock
Wismar
Schwerin
Lübeck
Berlin
Dresden
Prague
Hamburg
Lüneburg

Gulf of Finland
Baltic Sea
North Sea
Dvina
Niemen
Vistula
Oder
Elbe

0   100
Miles

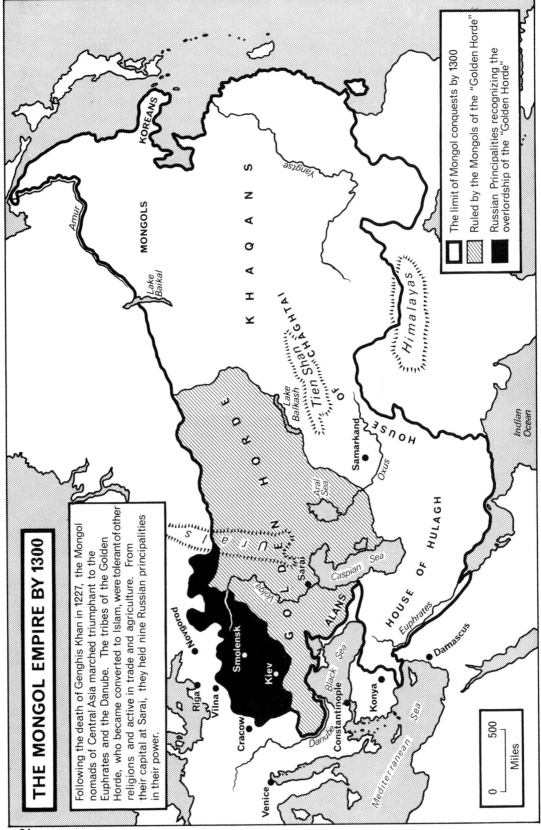

THE MONGOL EMPIRE BY 1300

Following the death of Genghis Khan in 1227, the Mongol nomads of Central Asia marched triumphant to the Euphrates and the Danube. The tribes of the Golden Horde, who became converted to Islam, were tolerant of other religions and active in trade and agriculture. From their capital at Sarai, they held nine Russian principalities in their power.

The limit of Mongol conquests by 1300

Ruled by the Mongols of the "Golden Horde"

Russian Principalities recognizing the overlordship of the "Golden Horde"

KOREANS

MONGOLS

Amur

Lake Baikal

KHAQANS

Yangtse

Himalayas

Tien Shan

CHAGHTAI

OF

Lake Balkash

Samarkand

Oxus

HOUSE

Aral Sea

Indian Ocean

G O L D E N   H O R D E

Urals

Sarai

Caspian Sea

HOUSE OF HULAGH

Volga

ALANS

Euphrates

Novgorod

Smolensk

Kiev

Black Sea

Damascus

Riga

Vilna

Cracow

Constantinople

Konya

Danube

Venice

Mediterranean Sea

0   500
Miles

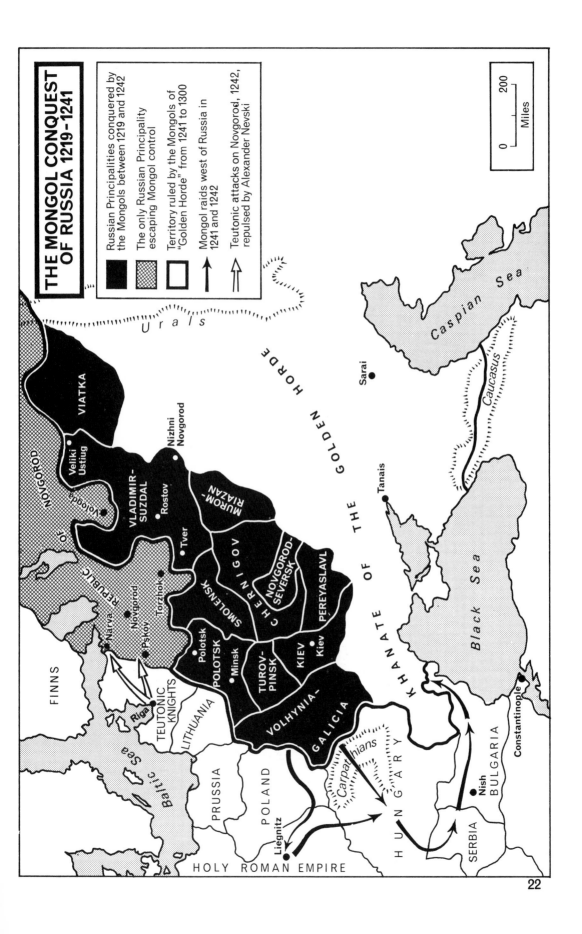

THE MONGOL CONQUEST OF RUSSIA 1219–1241

Russian Principalities conquered by the Mongols between 1219 and 1242

The only Russian Principality escaping Mongol control

Territory ruled by the Mongols of "Golden Horde" from 1241 to 1300

Mongol raids west of Russia in 1241 and 1242

Teutonic attacks on Novgorod, 1242, repulsed by Alexander Nevski

200

0

Miles

Caspian Sea

U r a l s

VIATKA

Sarai

Caucasus

NOVGOROD

Veliki Ustiug

Nizhni Novgorod

Vologda

VLADIMIR-SUZDAL

Rostov

MUROM-RIAZAN

OF

Tanais

Tver

REPUBLIC

CHERNIGOV

NOVGOROD-SEVERSK

PEREYASLAVL

Black Sea

Narva

Novgorod

Torzhok

SMOLENSK

THE

Pskov

Polotsk

KIEV

Kiev

KHANATE

FINNS

Minsk

POLOTSK

TUROV-PINSK

OF

Constantinople

Riga

TEUTONIC KNIGHTS

LITHUANIA

VOLHYNIA-

GALICIA

GOLDEN

HORDE

Baltic

Sea

PRUSSIA

POLAND

Carpathians

H U N G A R Y

BULGARIA

Nish

SERBIA

Liegnitz

HOLY ROMAN EMPIRE

THE LITHUANIAN CONQUESTS 1240-1462

Baltic Sea

ROSTOV

NOVGOROD

TVER

Riga

PSKOV

TEUTONIC   KNIGHTS

MOSCOW

Polotsk

Viazma

Kovno

Vitebsk

Smolensk

Vilna

TEUTONIC
KNIGHTS

Minsk

RIAZAN

Grodno

Brit Briansk

Warsaw

Slonim

Brest-
Litovsk

Turov

Pinsk

Chernigov

KINGDOM

Vladimir

OF

Kiev

POLAND

Zhitomir

Lvov

Poltava

CRIMEAN KHANATE
Mongols

CRIMEAN KHANATE
Mongols

Haji-bey

Sea of
Azov

0   150

Black
Sea

Miles

Grand Principality of Lithuania, 1240

Lithuanian conquests by 1340, including
the Russian Principalities of Polotsk
and Pinsk-Turov

Ruled by Lithuania in 1462

Russian Principalities unconquered
by Lithuania

Shattered by Mongol invasions, and
divided among themselves, the Russian
Principalities fell easy victims to Lithuanian
expansion after 1240.
In 1386, Lithuania and the Kingdom of
Poland united under a single king. The
Catholicism of this powerful kingdom was
an extra cause of conflict with Russia.

THE EASTWARD SPREAD OF CATHOLICISM BY 1462

Simultaneously with the Mongol invasions from the east, Russia was subjected to the continual westward movement of Roman Catholicism. Under Swedish and Lithuanian pressure, Russian Orthodoxy was pushed back almost to Moscow. Roman Catholicism also made advances against the Orthodox Bulgars in the Balkans, and against the Muslim lands in the eastern Mediterranean.

LAPLAND
1300

NORWAY

SWEDEN

DENMARK

Baltic Sea

Vyborg
1293

RUSSIA

Reval
1219

Novgorod

Pskov

Tver

Moscow

Mitava
1271

Kaluga

Danzig
1200

PRUSSIA

Vilna
1386

Smolensk
1450

Warsaw

LITHUANIA

THE

POLAND

Kiev
1385

HOLY

Prague

GALICIA

BOHEMIA

Lvov
1340

UKRAINE

ROMAN

Vienna

EMPIRE

HUNGARY

Tana
1261

CROATIA

TRANSYLVANIA

Kaffa
1261

Black   Sea

Rome

BALKANS

Constantinople
1261

Amastris
1310

Samsun
1310

Aegean Sea

Athens
1305

Edessa
1098

Antioch
1098

| | The Roman Catholic world in 1000 AD |
| | Conquered between 1000 and 1462 AD by Roman Catholic rulers, and forming part of Catholic kingdoms |

0   300

Miles

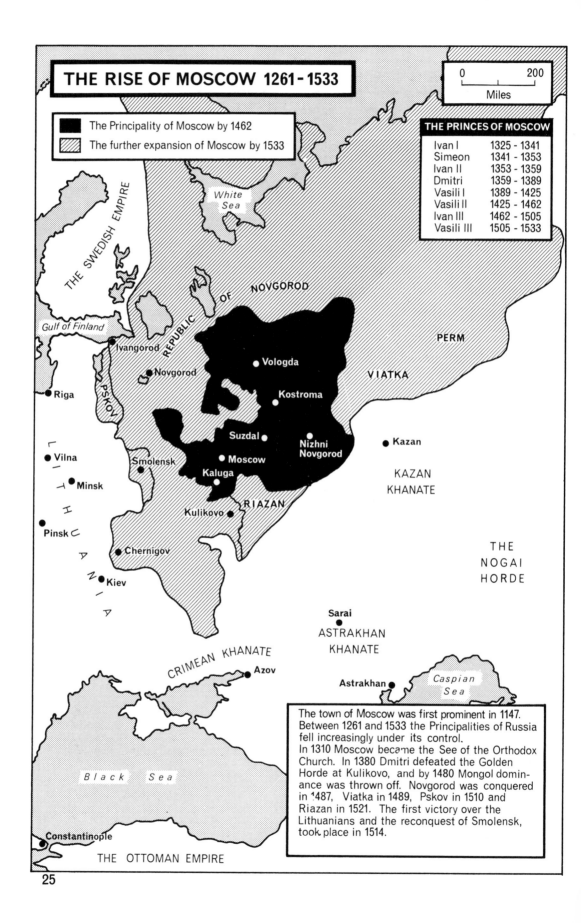

THE RISE OF MOSCOW 1261-1533

0   200

Miles

■ The Principality of Moscow by 1462

▨ The further expansion of Moscow by 1533

THE PRINCES OF MOSCOW

Ivan I	1325 - 1341
Simeon	1341 - 1353
Ivan II	1353 - 1359
Dmitri	1359 - 1389
Vasili I	1389 - 1425
Vasili II	1425 - 1462
Ivan III	1462 - 1505
Vasili III	1505 - 1533

THE SWEDISH EMPIRE

White Sea

Gulf of Finland

REPUBLIC OF NOVGOROD

PERM

Ivangorod

Vologda

VIATKA

Novgorod

PSKOV

Kostroma

Riga

Suzdal

Nizhni Novgorod

Kazan

Vilna

Moscow

KAZAN KHANATE

Smolensk

Kaluga

Minsk

L I T H U A N I A

RIAZAN

Kulikovo

Pinsk

THE NOGAI HORDE

Chernigov

Kiev

Sarai

ASTRAKHAN KHANATE

CRIMEAN KHANATE

Azov

Astrakhan

Caspian Sea

Black Sea

The town of Moscow was first prominent in 1147.
Between 1261 and 1533 the Principalities of Russia
fell increasingly under its control.
In 1310 Moscow became the See of the Orthodox
Church. In 1380 Dmitri defeated the Golden
Horde at Kulikovo, and by 1480 Mongol domin-
ance was thrown off. Novgorod was conquered
in 1487, Viatka in 1489, Pskov in 1510 and
Riazan in 1521. The first victory over the
Lithuanians and the reconquest of Smolensk,
took place in 1514.

Constantinople

THE OTTOMAN EMPIRE

THE EXPANSION OF RUSSIA 1533-1598

Russia in 1533

Unsuccessful military expedition against the Mongols of the Crimea 1556-1559

Russian conquests by 1598

Cities founded 1584-1594, with dates

Arctic Sea

SWEDISH EMPIRE

Baltic Sea

Kexholm

INGRIA

Pskov

Polotsk

LITHUANIA

Smolensk

Chernigov

Kiev

Archangel 1584

Dvina

Volga

Moscow

Kazan

Urals

Ob

Surgut 1594

Obski Gorodok 1585

SIBERIA

Tobolsk 1587

Tiumen 1586

Samara 1586

Voronezh 1586

Saratov 1590

Volga

THE NOGAI HORDE

Tsaritsyn 1589

CRIMEAN

Astrakhan

Bakhchisaray

KHANATE

Black Sea

Terek

Caspian Sea

Caucasus

OTTOMAN   EMPIRE

0	400

Miles

Ivan IV became Grand Duke of Moscow in 1533. In 1547 he was crowned "Tsar of All the Russias". He conquered the Mongol Khanate of Kazan in 1552, the Khanate of Astrakhan in 1556, and the Mongols east of the Urals in 1584. In 1583 the Swedes conquered Ingria and Russia lost all access to the Baltic Sea; but this was regained under Tsar Fedor, 1584-1598.

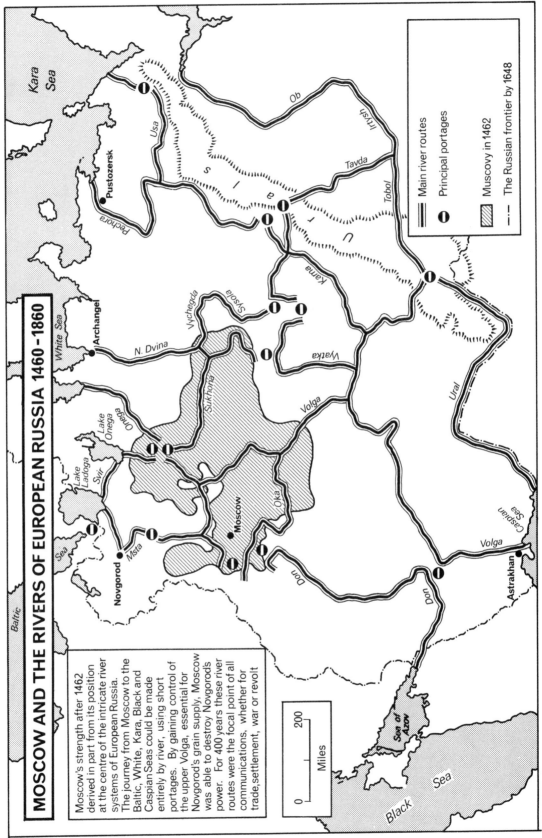

MOSCOW AND THE RIVERS OF EUROPEAN RUSSIA 1460–1860

Moscow's strength after 1462 derived in part from its position at the centre of the intricate river systems of European Russia. The journey from Moscow to the Baltic, White, Kara, Black and Caspian Seas could be made entirely by river, using short portages. By gaining control of the upper Volga, essential for Novgorod's grain supply, Moscow was able to destroy Novgorods power. For 400 years these river routes were the focal point of all communications, whether for trade, settlement, war or revolt

Main river routes

Principal portages

Muscovy in 1462

The Russian frontier by 1648

Kara Sea

Pustozersk

Ob

Usa

Pechora

Irtysh

Tavda

Tobol

Siberia

Urals

Kama

Archangel

White Sea

Vychegda

Sysola

N. Dvina

Vyatka

Sukhona

Ural

Lake Onega

Onega

Volga

Lake Ladoga

Svir

Moscow

Oka

Caspian Sea

Baltic Sea

Novgorod

Msta

Don

Volga

Astrakhan

Don

Sea of Azov

Black Sea

Miles

0   200

27

THE EXPROPRIATION OF LAND BY IVAN IV 1565–1571

In 1565 Ivan IV, "the Terrible", set up an independent state within Tsardom, which he ruled personally as its proprietor. This was known as the Oprichnina. By 1572 this area covered over half the Russian lands north of Moscow, as well as certain streets and suburbs in Moscow and Novgorod. Ivan settled 6,000 specially chosen guards and supporters in the land, which he had seized arbitrarily from its owners. In seven years he had driven 12,000 landowners from their estates. Their expropriated lands gave him a personal source of wealth and patronage, and destroyed completely the power of a large section of the landed gentry, the boyars.

The frontiers of Russia in 1565
Lands seized by Ivan IV in 1565
Lands seized 1566–1568
Lands seized 1569–1571
The general direction of the flight of the dispossessed

White Sea
Baltic Sea
Lake Ladoga

Varzuga
Pinega
Kholmogory
Dvina
Shenkursk
Kargopol
Veliki Ustiug
Totma
Vologda
Galich
Belozersk
Sol Vychegodskaya
Kergedan
Kama
Pechora
Ladoga
Novgorod
Loval
Staritsa
Viazma
Medyn
Kozelsk
Briansk
Starodub
Orel
Tula
Mozhaisk
Moscow
Alexandrovsk
Suzdal
Gus
Oka
Nizhni-Novgorod
Kazan
Volga

Miles
0   200

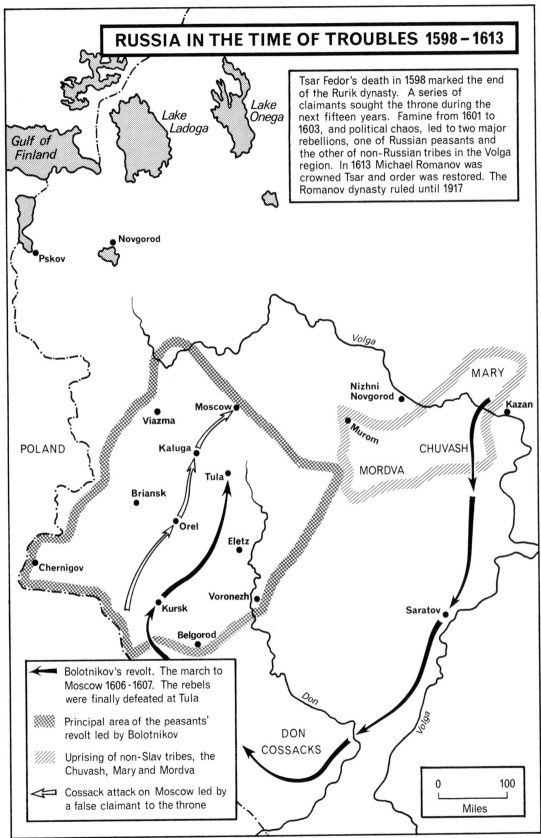

RUSSIA IN THE TIME OF TROUBLES 1598–1613

Tsar Fedor's death in 1598 marked the end of the Rurik dynasty. A series of claimants sought the throne during the next fifteen years. Famine from 1601 to 1603, and political chaos, led to two major rebellions, one of Russian peasants and the other of non-Russian tribes in the Volga region. In 1613 Michael Romanov was crowned Tsar and order was restored. The Romanov dynasty ruled until 1917

Gulf of Finland

Lake Ladoga

Lake Onega

● Pskov

● Novgorod

Volga

MARY

Nizhni Novgorod ●

● Kazan

● Moscow

Viazma ●

● Murom

CHUVASH

Kaluga ●

MORDVA

POLAND

Tula ●

Briansk ●

● Orel

Eletz ●

● Chernigov

Voronezh ●

Saratov ●

● Kursk

Belgorod ●

Don

Volga

⬅ Bolotnikov's revolt. The march to Moscow 1606-1607. The rebels were finally defeated at Tula

▓ Principal area of the peasants' revolt led by Bolotnikov

▨ Uprising of non-Slav tribes, the Chuvash, Mary and Mordva

⬅ Cossack attack on Moscow led by a false claimant to the throne

DON COSSACKS

| 0 | 100 |

Miles

29

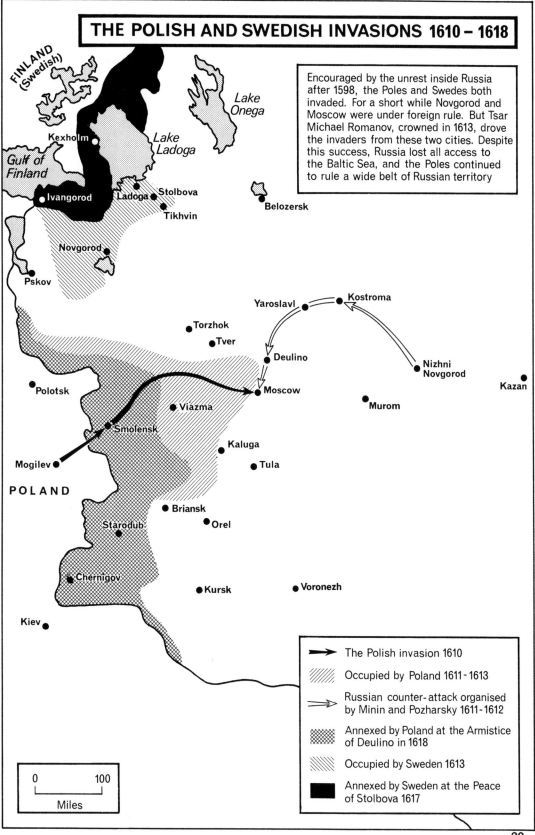

THE POLISH AND SWEDISH INVASIONS 1610 – 1618

Encouraged by the unrest inside Russia after 1598, the Poles and Swedes both invaded. For a short while Novgorod and Moscow were under foreign rule. But Tsar Michael Romanov, crowned in 1613, drove the invaders from these two cities. Despite this success, Russia lost all access to the Baltic Sea, and the Poles continued to rule a wide belt of Russian territory

FINLAND (Swedish)

Lake Onega

Kexholm

Lake Ladoga

Gulf of Finland

Ivangorod

Ladoga

Stolbova

Tikhvin

Belozersk

Novgorod

Pskov

Yaroslavl

Kostroma

Torzhok

Tver

Deulino

Nizhni Novgorod

Kazan

Polotsk

Viazma

Moscow

Murom

Smolensk

Kaluga

Mogilev

Tula

POLAND

Br
iansk

Orel

Starodub

Chernigov

Kursk

Voronezh

Kiev

➤	The Polish invasion 1610
▨	Occupied by Poland 1611 - 1613
→	Russian counter-attack organised by Minin and Pozharsky 1611-1612
▩	Annexed by Poland at the Armistice of Deulino in 1618
▨	Occupied by Sweden 1613
■	Annexed by Sweden at the Peace of Stolbova 1617

0   100

Miles

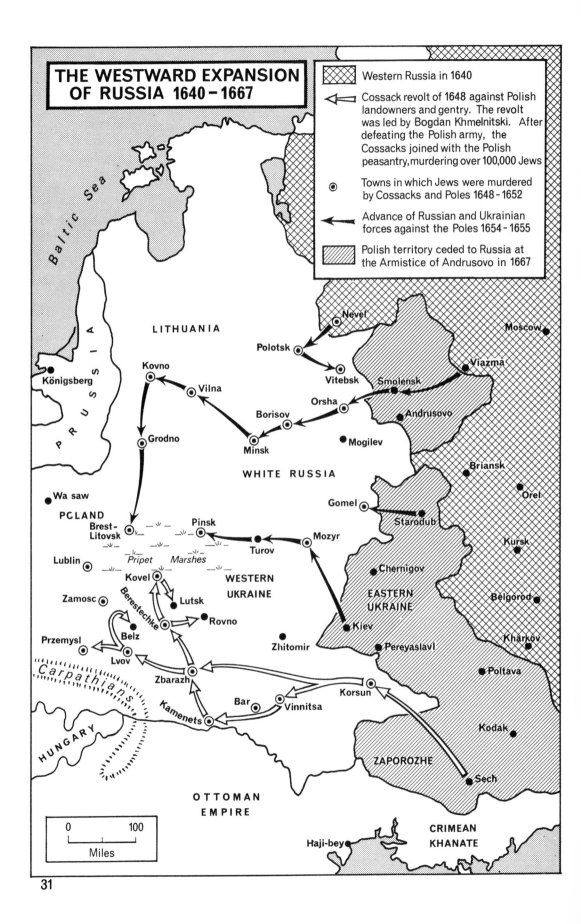

THE WESTWARD EXPANSION OF RUSSIA 1640-1667

Western Russia in 1640

Cossack revolt of 1648 against Polish landowners and gentry. The revolt was led by Bogdan Khmelnitski. After defeating the Polish army, the Cossacks joined with the Polish peasantry, murdering over 100,000 Jews

Towns in which Jews were murdered by Cossacks and Poles 1648-1652

Advance of Russian and Ukrainian forces against the Poles 1654-1655

Polish territory ceded to Russia at the Armistice of Andrusovo in 1667

Baltic Sea

PRUSSIA

LITHUANIA

Moscow

Nevel

Polotsk

Viazma

Königsberg

Kovno

Vilna

Vitebsk

Smolensk

Orsha

Andrusovo

Borisov

Grodno

Mogilev

Briansk

Minsk

WHITE RUSSIA

Orel

Wa saw

Gomel

POLAND

Starodub

Brest-Litovsk

Pinsk

Kursk

Mozyr

Turov

Lublin

Pripet Marshes

Kovel

WESTERN UKRAINE

Chernigov

Belgorod

Zamosc

Lutsk

Berestechke

Rovno

EASTERN UKRAINE

Przemysl

Belz

Zhitomir

Kiev

Kharkov

Lvov

Zbarazh

Pereyaslavl

Carpathians

Kamenets

Bar

Vinnitsa

Korsun

Poltava

HUNGARY

Kodak

ZAPOROZHE

OTTOMAN EMPIRE

Sech

0   100

Miles

Haji-bey

CRIMEAN KHANATE

SOCIAL UNREST 1648 and 1670

In 1648 uprisings took place in many of the principal Russian towns. As a result, a new code of laws was drawn up, protecting the rights of traders and town-dwellers. In 1670 a Don Cossack, Stenka Razin, led a widespread revolt of Cossacks, peasants, small traders, minor officials and the dispossessed of the Volga, Don and Donets river valleys. The revolt was crushed in 1671 and Razin broken on the wheel in Moscow.

Kargopol

Solvychegodsk

Veliki Ustiug   Cherdin

Olonets

Totma   Solikamsk

Gdov

Novgorod

Pskov

Ostrov

Romanov

Volga

Vladimir

Ruza

Moscow   Yadrin

Simbirsk

Koslov

Penza

Donets

Tambov   *Samara*

Kursk

Voronezh   Saratov

Don

Tsaritsyn

D O N
CO SSACKS

Gurev

Sea of Azov

Astrakhan

Black Sea

Terski Gorodok

Caspian Sea

◉   Urban uprisings of 1648-1650

▮   The peasants' revolt led by Stenka Razin 1670-1671

—   The Russian frontier in 1670

0   500

Miles

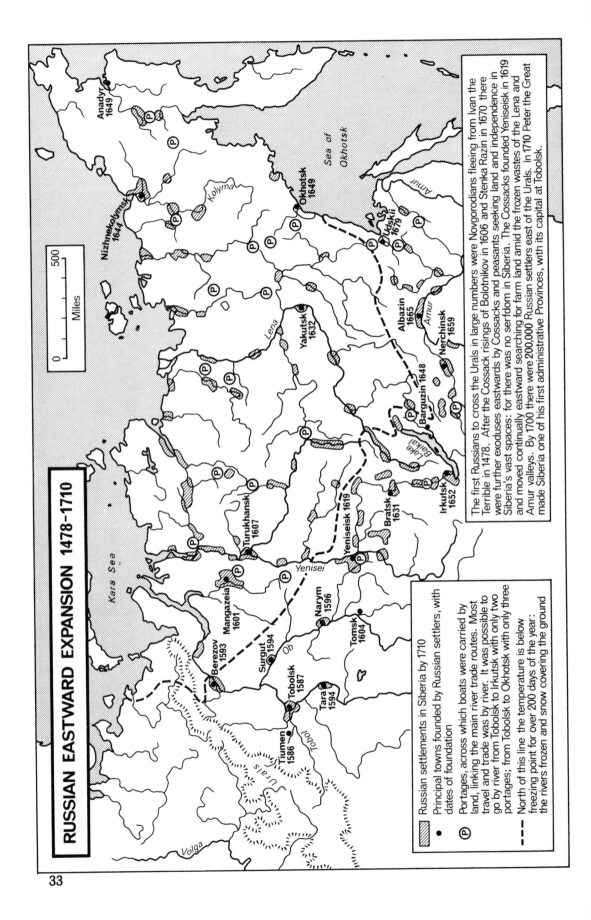

RUSSIAN EASTWARD EXPANSION 1478–1710

Kara Sea

Volga

Urals

Tiumen 1586

Tobol

Tobolsk 1587

Tara 1594

Berezov 1593

Surgut 1594

Ob

Narym 1596

Tomsk 1604

Mangazeia 1601

Yenisei

Turukhansk 1607

Yeniseisk 1619

Bratsk 1631

Irkutsk 1652

Lake Baikal

Barguzin 1648

Nerchinsk 1659

Albazin 1665

Amur

Lena

Yakutsk 1632

Kolyma

Nizhnekolymsk 1644

Anadyr 1649

Okhotsk 1649

Sea of Okhotsk

Udskii 1679

Amur

500

Miles

0

The first Russians to cross the Urals in large numbers were Novgorodians fleeing from Ivan the Terrible in 1478. After the Cossack risings of Bolotnikov in 1606 and Stenka Razin in 1670 there were further exoduses eastwards by Cossacks and peasants seeking land and independence in Siberia's vast spaces: for there was no serfdom in Siberia. The Cossacks founded Yeniseisk in 1619 and moved continually eastward searching for farm land amid the frozen wastes of the Lena and Amur valleys. By 1700 there were 200,000 Russian settlers east of the Urals. In 1710 Peter the Great made Siberia one of his first administrative Provinces, with its capital at Tobolsk.

Russian settlements in Siberia by 1710

● Principal towns founded by Russian settlers, with dates of foundation

Ⓟ Portages, across which boats were carried by land, linking the main river trade routes. Most travel and trade was by river. It was possible to go by river from Tobolsk to Irkutsk with only two portages; from Tobolsk to Okhotsk with only three

- - - North of this line the temperature is below freezing point for over 200 days of the year: the rivers frozen and snow covering the ground

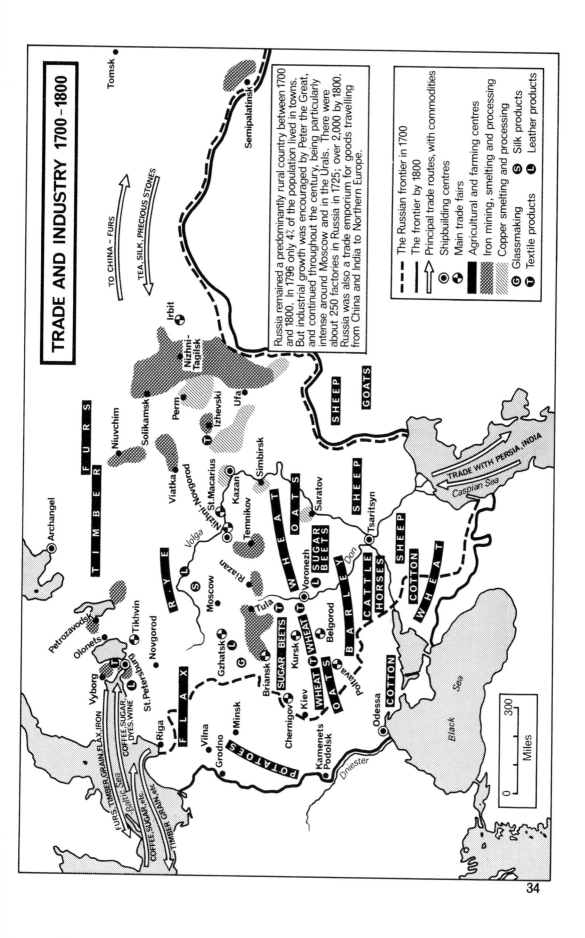

TRADE AND INDUSTRY 1700–1800

Russia remained a predominantly rural country between 1700 and 1800. In 1796 only 4% of the population lived in towns. But industrial growth was encouraged by Peter the Great, and continued throughout the century, being particularly intense around Moscow and in the Urals. There were about 250 factories in Russia in 1725; over 2,000 by 1800. Russia was also a trade emporium for goods travelling from China and India to Northern Europe.

The Russian frontier in 1700
The frontier by 1800
Principal trade routes, with commodities
Shipbuilding centres
Main trade fairs
Agricultural and farming centres
Iron mining, smelting and processing
Copper smelting and processing
Glassmaking   Silk products
Textile products   Leather products

TO CHINA – FURS

TEA, SILK, PRECIOUS STONES

TRADE WITH PERSIA, INDIA

Tomsk

Semipalatinsk

Irbit

Nizhni-Tagilsk

Perm

Niuvchim

Solikamsk

Izhevski

Ufa

SHEEP

GOATS

Viatka

Simbirsk

Kazan

St. Macarius

Nizhni-Novgorod

Temnikov

SHEEP

Saratov

WHEAT

OATS

SUGAR BEETS

Voronezh

Tsaritsyn

SHEEP

Volga

Riazan

Don

CATTLE

HORSES

SHEEP

COTTON

WHEAT

Archangel

TIMBER

FURS

RYE

Moscow

Tula

BARLEY

Belgorod

Caspian Sea

Petrozavodsk

Olonets

Tikhvin

Novgorod

Gzhatsk

Briansk

Kursk

SUGAR BEETS

WHEAT

OATS

WHEAT

Poltava

St. Petersburg

FLAX

Kiev

Chernigov

COTTON

Vyborg

Riga

Vilna

Minsk

Grodno

Kamenets Podolsk

POTATOES

Odessa

COTTON

Dniester

Black Sea

FURS, TIMBER, GRAIN, FLAX, IRON

COFFEE, SUGAR, DYES, WINE

COFFEE, SUGAR, etc.

TIMBER, GRAIN, etc.

Baltic Sea

0   300

Miles

34

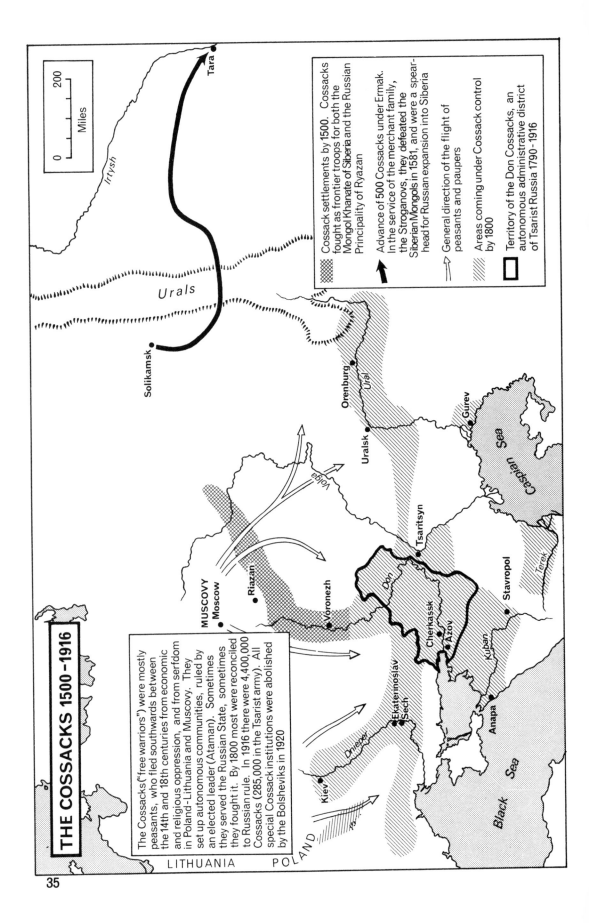

THE COSSACKS 1500–1916

The Cossacks ("free warriors") were mostly peasants, who fled southwards between the 14th and 18th centuries from economic and religious oppression, and from serfdom in Poland-Lithuania and Muscovy. They set up autonomous communities, ruled by an elected leader (Ataman). Sometimes they served the Russian State, sometimes they fought it. By 1800 most were reconciled to Russian rule. In 1916 there were 4,400,000 Cossacks (285,000 in the Tsarist army). All special Cossack institutions were abolished by the Bolsheviks in 1920

Cossack settlements by 1500. Cossacks fought as frontier troops for both the Mongol Khanate of Siberia and the Russian Principality of Ryazan

Advance of 500 Cossacks under Ermak. In the service of the merchant family, the Stroganovs, they defeated the Siberian Mongols in 1581, and were a spearhead for Russian expansion into Siberia

General direction of the flight of peasants and paupers

Areas coming under Cossack control by 1800

Territory of the Don Cossacks, an autonomous administrative district of Tsarist Russia 1790-1916

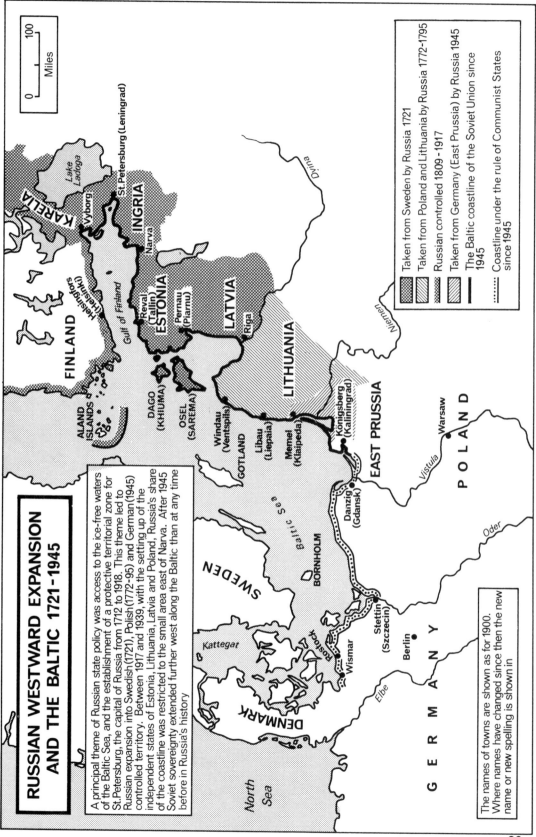

RUSSIAN WESTWARD EXPANSION AND THE BALTIC 1721-1945

A principal theme of Russian state policy was access to the ice-free waters of the Baltic Sea, and the establishment of a protective territorial zone for St.Petersburg, the capital of Russia from 1712 to 1918. This theme led to Russian expansion into Swedish (1721), Polish (1772-95) and German (1945) controlled territory. Between 1917 and 1939, with the setting up of the independent states of Estonia, Lithuania, Latvia and Poland, Russia's share of the coastline was restricted to the small area east of Narva. After 1945 Soviet sovereignty extended further west along the Baltic than at any time before in Russia's history

Taken from Sweden by Russia 1721

Taken from Poland and Lithuania by Russia 1772-1795

Russian controlled 1809 - 1917

Taken from Germany (East Prussia) by Russia 1945

The Baltic coastline of the Soviet Union since 1945

Coastline under the rule of Communist States since 1945

The names of towns are shown as for 1900. Where names have changed since then the new name or new spelling is shown in

North Sea

Kattegat

DENMARK

SWEDEN

FINLAND

Helsingfors (Helsinki)

ALAND ISLANDS

Lake Ladoga

KARELIA

Vyborg

St.Petersburg (Leningrad)

INGRIA

Narva

Gulf of Finland

Reval (Tallin)

ESTONIA

Pernau (Piarnu)

DAGO (KHIUMA)

OSEL (SAREMA)

LATVIA

Riga

Dvina

Windau (Ventspils)

GOTLAND

Libau (Liepaia)

Memel (Klaipeda)

LITHUANIA

Niemen

Königsberg (Kaliningrad)

EAST PRUSSIA

Baltic Sea

BORNHOLM

Danzig (Gdansk)

Vistula

Warsaw

P O L A N D

Oder

ROSTOCK

Wismar

Stettin (Szczecin)

Berlin

G E R M A N Y

Elbe

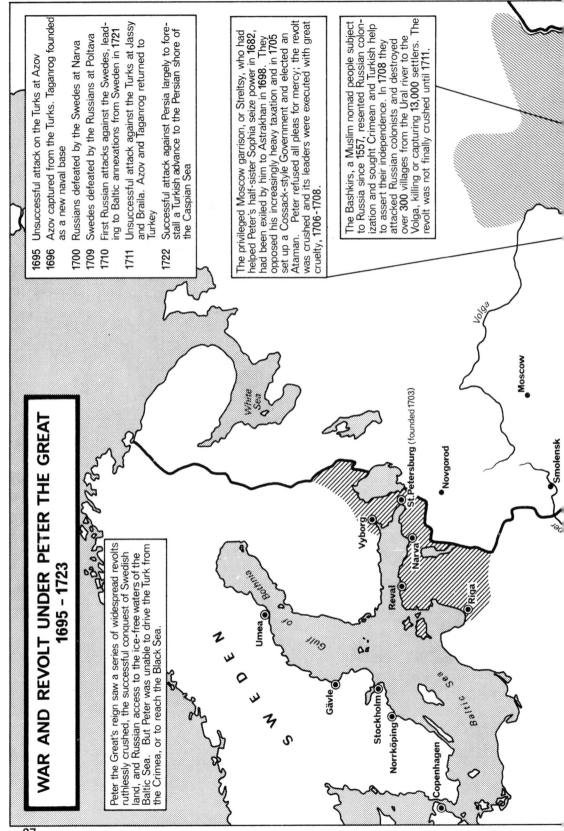

WAR AND REVOLT UNDER PETER THE GREAT
1695 – 1723

Peter the Great's reign saw a series of widespread revolts ruthlessly crushed, the successful conquest of Swedish land, and Russian access to the ice-free waters of the Baltic Sea. But Peter was unable to drive the Turk from the Crimea, or to reach the Black Sea.

1695 Unsuccessful attack on the Turks at Azov

1696 Azov captured from the Turks. Taganrog founded as a new naval base

1700 Russians defeated by the Swedes at Narva

1709 Swedes defeated by the Russians at Poltava

1710 First Russian attacks against the Swedes, leading to Baltic annexations from Sweden in 1721

1711 Unsuccessful attack against the Turks at Jassy and Braila. Azov and Taganrog returned to Turkey

1722 Successful attack against Persia largely to forestall a Turkish advance to the Persian shore of the Caspian Sea

The privileged Moscow garrison, or Streltsy, who had helped Peter's half-sister Sophia seize power in 1682, had been exiled by him to Astrakhan in 1698. They opposed his increasingly heavy taxation and in 1705 set up a Cossack-style Government and elected an Ataman. Peter refused all pleas for mercy; the revolt was crushed and its leaders were executed with great cruelty, 1706-1708.

The Bashkirs, a Muslim nomad people subject to Russia since 1557, resented Russian colonization and sought Crimean and Turkish help to assert their independence. In 1708 they attacked Russian colonists and destroyed over 300 villages from the Ural river to the Volga, killing or capturing 13,000 settlers. The revolt was not finally crushed until 1711.

SWEDEN

White Sea

Gulf of Bothnia

Gulf of Finland

Baltic Sea

Volga

Umeå

Gävle

Stockholm

Norrköping

Copenhagen

Vyborg

St. Petersburg (founded 1703)

Narva

Reval

Riga

Novgorod

Moscow

Smolensk

37

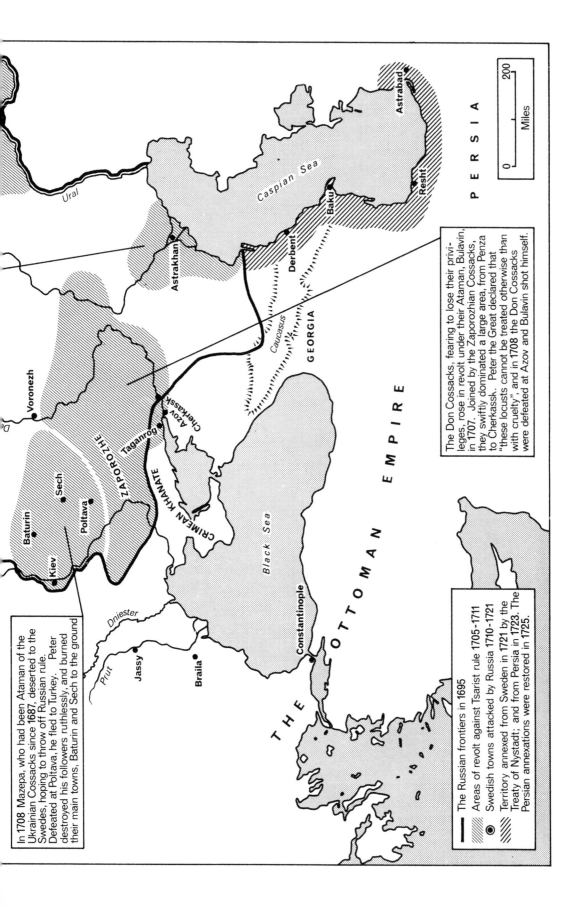

In 1708 Mazepa, who had been Ataman of the Ukrainian Cossacks since 1687, deserted to the Swedes, hoping to throw off Russian rule. Peter Defeated at Poltava, he fled to Turkey. Peter destroyed his followers ruthlessly, and burned their main towns, Baturin and Sech to the ground

The Don Cossacks, fearing to lose their privileges, rose in revolt under their Ataman, Bulavin, in 1707. Joined by the Zaporozhian Cossacks, they swiftly dominated a large area, from Penza to Cherkassk. Peter the Great declared that "these locusts cannot be treated otherwise than with cruelty", and in 1708 the Don Cossacks were defeated at Azov and Bulavin shot himself.

Voronezh

Baturin
Sech
Poltava
Kiev

ZAPOROZHE

Taganrog
Azov
Cherkassk

CRIMEAN KHANATE

Dniester

Jassy

Braila

Prut

Black Sea

Constantinople

THE   OTTOMAN   EMPIRE

GEORGIA

Caucasus

Astrakhan

Derbent

Baku

Resht

Caspian Sea

Astrabad

P E R S I A

Ural

Don

—— The Russian frontiers in 1695

///// Areas of revolt against Tsarist rule 1705-1711

●⊙ Swedish towns attacked by Russia 1710-1721

//// Territory annexed from Sweden in 1721 by the Treaty of Nystadt; and from Persia in 1723. The Persian annexations were restored in 1725.

0   200
Miles

THE PROVINCES AND POPULATION OF RUSSIA IN 1724

0   300
Miles

St. Petersburg

Selected as the site of a new town by Peter the Great in 1703, and built at great cost in human life by serf labour, St. Petersburg became the seat of the Russian Government in 1712. Courtiers and noble families were compelled by law to live there from 1725. The city had a population of 200,000 by 1788.

White Sea

Archangel

A R C H A N G E L

Dvina

S I B E R I A

Gulf of Finland

St. Petersburg

Novgorod

Vologda

Viatka

Perm

S T. P E T E R S B U R G

Pskov

Kostroma

Tver

Volga

Kazan

Moscow

Nizhni Novgorod

K A Z A N

Smolensk

M O S C O W

Simbirsk

Mogilev

S M O L E N S K

Riazan

Samara

Tula

Orel

Penza

Orenburg

Tambov

Saratov

Ural

Chernigov

A Z O V

Dnieper

K I E V

Voronezh

C O S S A C K S

Kiev

Kharkov

Poltava

Don

Volga

Dniester

C O S S A C K S

Azov

Caspian Sea

COSSACKS

C O S S A C K S

Black Sea

It was Peter the Great who first divided Russia into Provinces (known as "Gubernii" or "Governments"). These administrative divisions served a military, financial and judicial purpose. They enabled Peter to supervise the whole kingdom by means of Governors responsible directly to himself. Catherine the Great later divided these Provinces into smaller units. The establishment of Provincial administrations led to a rapid growth of bureaucracy, and a complex hierarchy of local seniority. The population of Russia in 1724 was just over 15 million, of whom only ½ million lived in towns.

—·— Russia's frontiers by 1725

▬▬ Provinces established by Peter the Great

▨ Area with over 20 inhabitants in every square verst. (One verst = two-thirds of a mile)

▧ Area with between 10 and 20 inhabitants per square verst

Russian territory with less than 10 inhabitants per square verst is not shaded

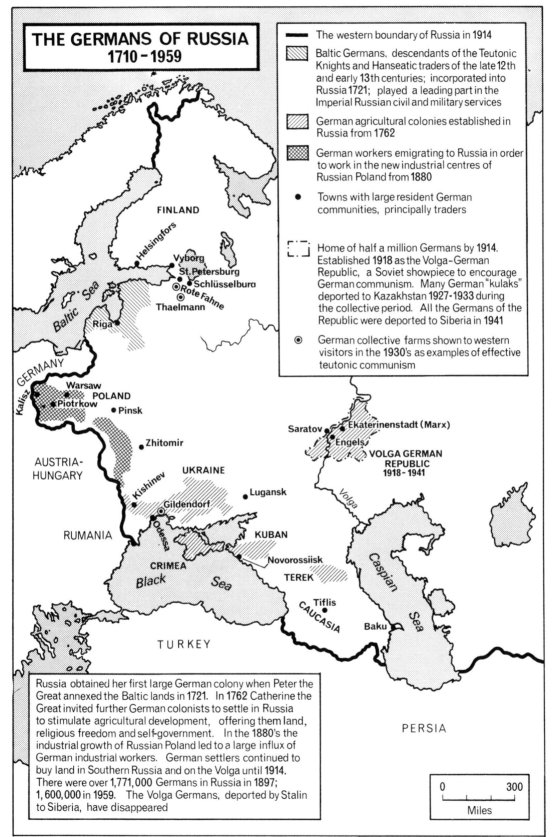

THE GERMANS OF RUSSIA 1710 – 1959

— The western boundary of Russia in 1914

Baltic Germans, descendants of the Teutonic Knights and Hanseatic traders of the late 12th and early 13th centuries; incorporated into Russia 1721; played a leading part in the Imperial Russian civil and military services

German agricultural colonies established in Russia from 1762

German workers emigrating to Russia in order to work in the new industrial centres of Russian Poland from 1880

● Towns with large resident German communities, principally traders

⌐ ⌐ Home of half a million Germans by 1914. Established 1918 as the Volga-German Republic, a Soviet showpiece to encourage German communism. Many German "kulaks" deported to Kazakhstan 1927-1933 during the collective period. All the Germans of the Republic were deported to Siberia in 1941

◉ German collective farms shown to western visitors in the 1930's as examples of effective teutonic communism

FINLAND

Helsingfors

Vyborg
St.Petersburg
Schlüsselbura
Rote Fahne
Thaelmann

Baltic Sea

Riga

GERMANY

Warsaw
POLAND
Kalisz
Piotrkow
● Pinsk

Saratov
Ekaterinenstadt (Marx)
Engels
VOLGA GERMAN REPUBLIC 1918-1941

● Zhitomir

AUSTRIA-HUNGARY

UKRAINE

Kishinev
Gildendorf
Odessa
● Lugansk

Volga

RUMANIA

KUBAN
Novorossiisk
TEREK

Caspian Sea

CRIMEA
Black   Sea

Tiflis
CAUCASIA
Baku

T U R K E Y

Russia obtained her first large German colony when Peter the Great annexed the Baltic lands in 1721. In 1762 Catherine the Great invited further German colonists to settle in Russia to stimulate agricultural development, offering them land, religious freedom and self-government. In the 1880's the industrial growth of Russian Poland led to a large influx of German industrial workers. German settlers continued to buy land in Southern Russia and on the Volga until 1914. There were over 1,771,000 Germans in Russia in 1897; 1,600,000 in 1959. The Volga Germans, deported by Stalin to Siberia, have disappeared

PERSIA

0   300
|____|____|
        Miles

THE EXPANSION OF CHINA 1720–1760

THE

RUSSIAN

EMPIRE

U r a l s

Okhotsk ⊙

Yakutsk ⊙

Tobolsk ⊙

Yeniseisk ⊙

Tomsk ⊙

Krasnoyarsk ⊙

Nerchinsk ⊙

Albazin ●

Omsk ⊙

Irkutsk ⊙

Lake Baikal

Amur

Harbin ●

Semipalatinsk ⊙

Ustkamenogorsk ⊙

Maimachin ■

M O N G O L S

Lake Balkhash

Kulja ●

Urumchi ●

Hami ●

Peking ○

DOMINIONS OF THE ZUNGAR KALMUKS

Nanking ○

Yarkand ●

Sian ○

Khotan ●

C H I N A

Chengtu ○

T I B E T

Lhasa ◉

Canton ○

H i m a l a y a s

Yunnan ○

⊙ Cities founded by the Russians before 1720

■ The Chinese Empire in 1720, ruled by the Manchu Dynasty

▨ Under Chinese control by 1720, providing the Manchus with a reservoir of military power

▨ Conquered by China between 1724 and 1764

▨ Conquered by China in 1780

0   500
Miles

40

RUSSIAN EXPANSION UNDER CATHERINE THE GREAT 1762-1796

The Provinces of Russia in 1750

Territory annexed by Russia 1762-1796, giving Russia an outlet on the Black Sea, and a common frontier with Prussia and Austria

FINLAND

White Sea

Archangel
ARCHANGEL

Helsingfors

ST. PETERSBURG

ESTONIA

LIVONIA

Baltic Sea

KURLAND

Novgorod
NOVGOROD

Pskov

Vologda

Viatka

Perm

KAZAN

Tver

MOSCOW

Moscow

Kazan

Ufa

NIZHNI NOVGOROD

UFA

Niemen

Vilna
LITHUANIA

Minsk

SMOLENSK

PRUSSIA

WHITE RUSSIA

Pinsk

Orel

Stavropol

Samara

Warsaw

BELGOROD

AUSTRIA

PODLESIA

Lutsk

KIEV

Kiev

VORONEZH

Belgorod

ASTRAKHAN

Dniester

Dnieper

PODOLIA

ZAPOROZHE

Jassy

Odessa

Taganrog

Astrakhan

Kutchuk
Kainardji

Sebastopol

CRIMEA

KUBAN

Caspian Sea

KABARDA

Tarki

THE OTTOMAN EMPIRE

Black Sea

Constantinople

Kars

0   200
Miles

PERSIA

41

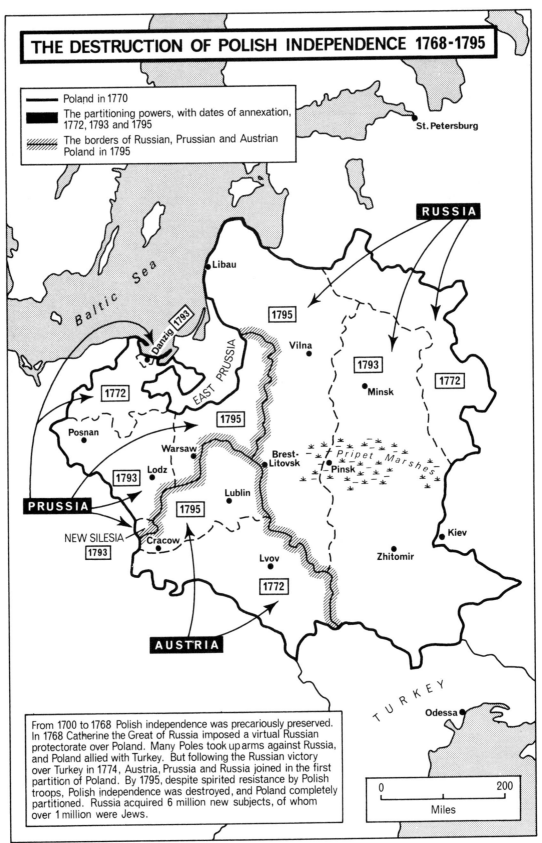

THE DESTRUCTION OF POLISH INDEPENDENCE 1768-1795

Poland in 1770

The partitioning powers, with dates of annexation, 1772, 1793 and 1795

The borders of Russian, Prussian and Austrian Poland in 1795

St. Petersburg

RUSSIA

Baltic Sea

Libau

1795

Danzig 1793

Vilna

EAST PRUSSIA

1793

1772

1795

Minsk

Posnan

Warsaw

Brest-Litovsk

Pripet Marshes

1793

Lodz

Pinsk

Lublin

PRUSSIA

1795

NEW SILESIA

Cracow

Kiev

1793

Lvov

Zhitomir

AUSTRIA

1772

TURKEY

Odessa

From 1700 to 1768 Polish independence was precariously preserved. In 1768 Catherine the Great of Russia imposed a virtual Russian protectorate over Poland. Many Poles took up arms against Russia, and Poland allied with Turkey. But following the Russian victory over Turkey in 1774, Austria, Prussia and Russia joined in the first partition of Poland. By 1795, despite spirited resistance by Polish troops, Polish independence was destroyed, and Poland completely partitioned. Russia acquired 6 million new subjects, of whom over 1 million were Jews.

0   200

Miles

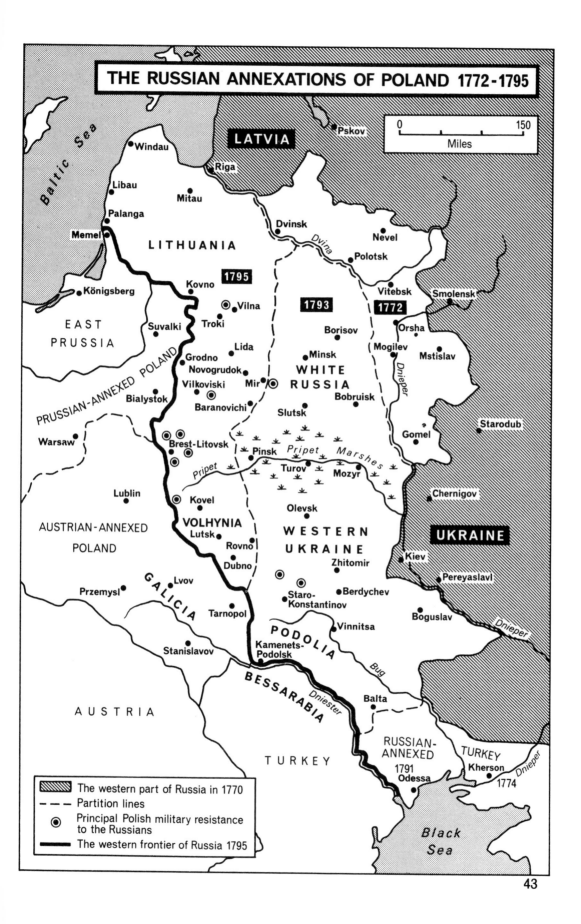

THE RUSSIAN ANNEXATIONS OF POLAND 1772-1795

Baltic Sea

LATVIA

Pskov

0   150

Miles

Windau

Riga

Libau

Mitau

Palanga

Dvinsk

Nevel

Memel

LITHUANIA

Dvina

Polotsk

Vitebsk

Smolensk

Königsberg

EAST
PRUSSIA

Kovno

1795

Vilna

Troki

Suvalki

Lida

Grodno

Novogrudok

Vilkoviski

Mir

Bialystok

Baranovichi

1793

Borisov

Minsk

WHITE
RUSSIA

Mogilev

1772

Orsha

Mstislav

Dnieper

Bobruisk

Slutsk

Warsaw

Brest-Litovsk

Pinsk

Pripet

Turov

Marshes

Mozyr

Gomel

Starodub

Lublin

Kovel

Pripet

Olevsk

VOLHYNIA

Lutsk

Rovno

WESTERN
UKRAINE

Dubno

Zhitomir

Chernigov

UKRAINE

Kiev

Lvov

Pereyaslavl

Przemysl

GALICIA

Tarnopol

Staro-
Konstantinov

Berdychev

Boguslav

Dnieper

Vinnitsa

Stanislavov

Kamenets-
Podolsk

PODOLIA

Bug

AUSTRIA

BESSARABIA

Dniester

Balta

TURKEY

RUSSIAN-
ANNEXED

1791
Odessa

TURKEY

Kherson

Dnieper

1774

Black
Sea

AUSTRIAN-ANNEXED

POLAND

PRUSSIAN-ANNEXED POLAND

The western part of Russia in 1770

Partition lines

Principal Polish military resistance
to the Russians

The western frontier of Russia 1795

43

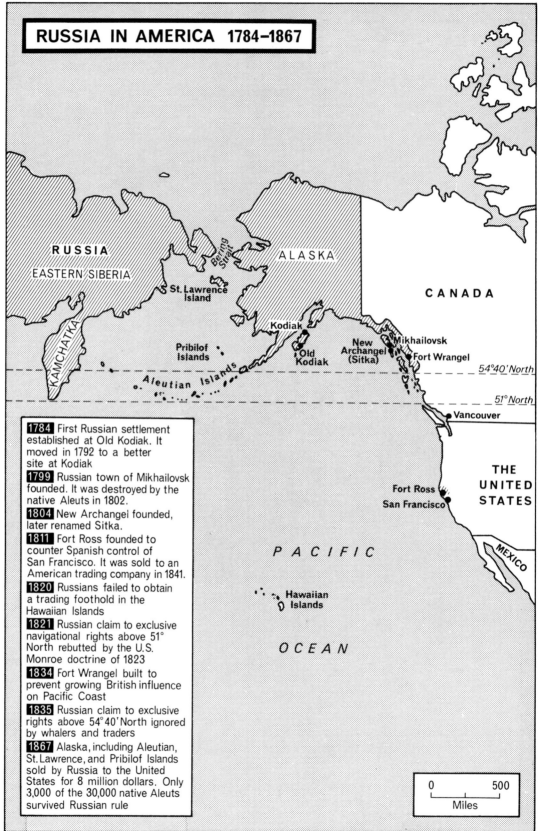

RUSSIA IN AMERICA 1784–1867

RUSSIA
EASTERN SIBERIA

KAMCHATKA

St. Lawrence Island

Bering Strait

ALASKA

CANADA

Kodiak

Pribilof Islands

Old Kodiak

New Archangel (Sitka)

Mikhailovsk

Fort Wrangel

Aleutian Islands

54°40′ North

51° North

Vancouver

Fort Ross
San Francisco

THE UNITED STATES

MEXICO

PACIFIC

Hawaiian Islands

OCEAN

1784 First Russian settlement established at Old Kodiak. It moved in 1792 to a better site at Kodiak

1799 Russian town of Mikhailovsk founded. It was destroyed by the native Aleuts in 1802.

1804 New Archangel founded, later renamed Sitka.

1811 Fort Ross founded to counter Spanish control of San Francisco. It was sold to an American trading company in 1841.

1820 Russians failed to obtain a trading foothold in the Hawaiian Islands

1821 Russian claim to exclusive navigational rights above 51° North rebutted by the U.S. Monroe doctrine of 1823

1834 Fort Wrangel built to prevent growing British influence on Pacific Coast

1835 Russian claim to exclusive rights above 54°40′ North ignored by whalers and traders

1867 Alaska, including Aleutian, St. Lawrence, and Pribilof Islands sold by Russia to the United States for 8 million dollars. Only 3,000 of the 30,000 native Aleuts survived Russian rule

0   500
Miles

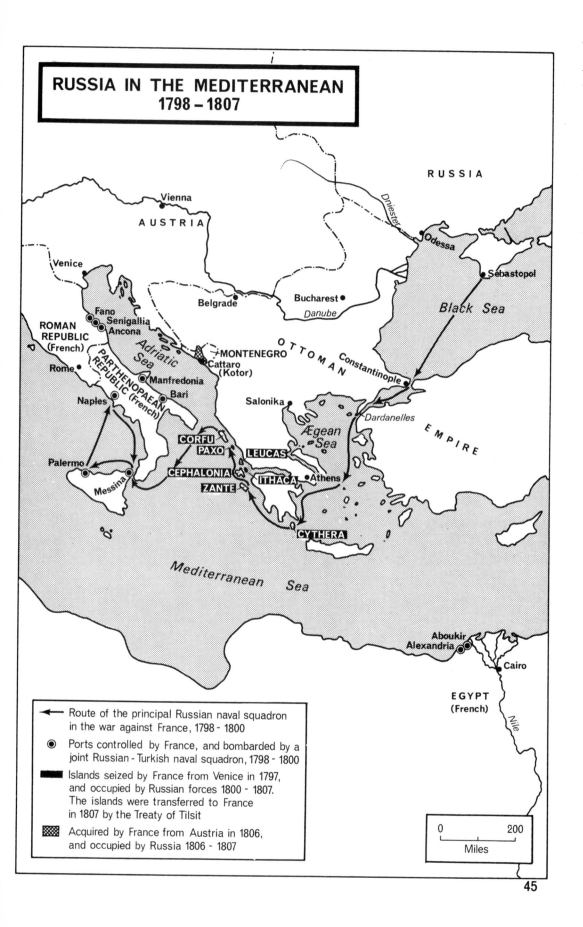

RUSSIA IN THE MEDITERRANEAN
1798 – 1807

RUSSIA

AUSTRIA

Vienna

Venice

Odessa

Sébastopol

Dniester

Belgrade

Bucharest

Danube

Black Sea

Fano
Senigallia
Ancona

ROMAN
REPUBLIC
(French)

Adriatic Sea

MONTENEGRO
Cattaro
(Kotor)

O T T O M A N

Constantinople

Rome

PARTHENOPAEAN
REPUBLIC
(French)

Manfredonia
Bari

Salonika

E M P I R E

Dardanelles

Naples

CORFU
PAXO

Ægean Sea

Palermo

CEPHALONIA

LEUCAS

Messina

ZANTE

ITHACA

Athens

Mediterranean Sea

CYTHERA

Aboukir
Alexandria

Cairo

EGYPT
(French)

Nile

Route of the principal Russian naval squadron
in the war against France, 1798 - 1800

⊙ Ports controlled by France, and bombarded by a
joint Russian - Turkish naval squadron, 1798 - 1800

Islands seized by France from Venice in 1797,
and occupied by Russian forces 1800 - 1807.
The islands were transferred to France
in 1807 by the Treaty of Tilsit

Acquired by France from Austria in 1806,
and occupied by Russia 1806 - 1807

0   200
Miles

RUSSIA AND TURKEY 1721-1829

*The Turks are falling like skittles, but, thank
God, our men stand fast, though headless*
RUSSIAN SOLDIERS' SAYING

Kiev

Dnieper

Khotin
1788

Uman
1738

Dniester

Bug

Prut

Kishinev
1739

BESSARABIA

Jassy
1806

Riabaya
Mogila
1770

Ochakov
1788

Perekop

Bendery
1770

1790

1789
1770, 1806

Fokshani

Kilia
1791

1788

Belgrade

Braila
1806

Ismail
1791, 1806

Bakhchisara
1736

Negotin
1810

Craiova
1807, 1828

Bucharest
1770, 1806,
1828

1828
Kustenje
1809

Vidin
1811, 1828

Danube

Rushchuk
1771
1811

Silistria
1810,
1774, 1828

Mangalia
1810, 1828

Nikopol
1829

Kutchuk
Kainardji

Turnovo
1810

1774
Shumla
1810

1829
Varna
1810

1791

TURKEY IN EUROPE

Black

Adrianople
1829

Midia
1829

Enos
1829

Corlu
1829

Bosphorus

Constantinople

The Straits

Dardanelles

Aegean Sea

TURKEY

THE BLACK SEA AND THE STRAITS

1739 Treaty of Belgrade: Russian ships not allowed
into the Sea of Azov or the Black Sea

1774 Treaty of Kutchuk Kainardji: Russian merchant
ships gained the right to navigate the Black
Sea and pass the Straits; but cargoes could
be requisitioned at will

1829 Treaty of Adrianople: Russia obtained the
right of unhindered passage of unarmed ships

0   100
Miles

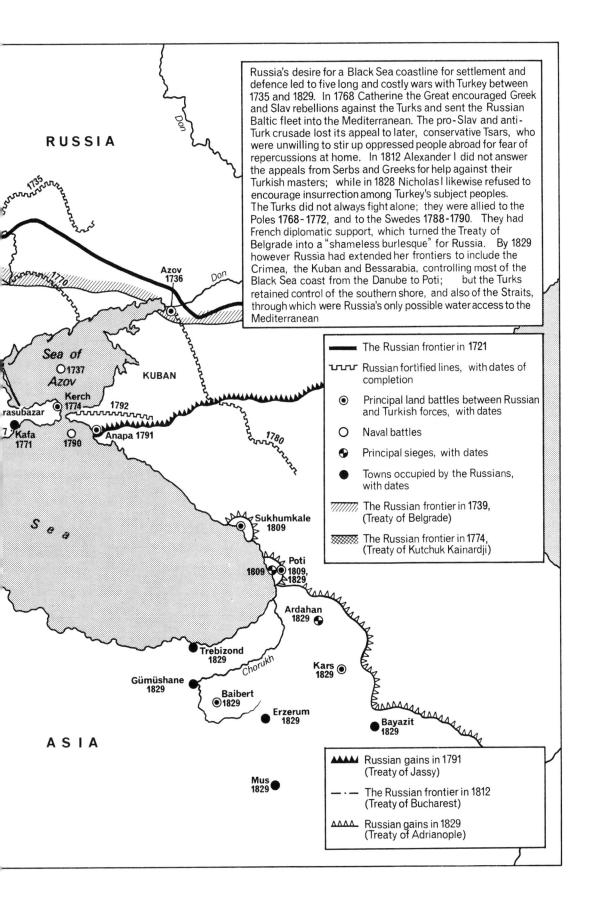

RUSSIA

Don

Russia's desire for a Black Sea coastline for settlement and defence led to five long and costly wars with Turkey between 1735 and 1829. In 1768 Catherine the Great encouraged Greek and Slav rebellions against the Turks and sent the Russian Baltic fleet into the Mediterranean. The pro-Slav and anti-Turk crusade lost its appeal to later, conservative Tsars, who were unwilling to stir up oppressed people abroad for fear of repercussions at home. In 1812 Alexander I did not answer the appeals from Serbs and Greeks for help against their Turkish masters; while in 1828 Nicholas I likewise refused to encourage insurrection among Turkey's subject peoples. The Turks did not always fight alone; they were allied to the Poles 1768-1772, and to the Swedes 1788-1790. They had French diplomatic support, which turned the Treaty of Belgrade into a "shameless burlesque" for Russia. By 1829 however Russia had extended her frontiers to include the Crimea, the Kuban and Bessarabia, controlling most of the Black Sea coast from the Danube to Poti; but the Turks retained control of the southern shore, and also of the Straits, through which were Russia's only possible water access to the Mediterranean

1735

Azov 1736

Don

Sea of Azov
○1737

KUBAN

Kerch 1774

1792

rasubazar

7 Kafa 1771

○1790

Anapa 1791

1780

———— The Russian frontier in 1721

ⅬⅬⅬⅬ Russian fortified lines, with dates of completion

◉ Principal land battles between Russian and Turkish forces, with dates

○ Naval battles

◐ Principal sieges, with dates

● Towns occupied by the Russians, with dates

▨▨ The Russian frontier in 1739, (Treaty of Belgrade)

▨▨ The Russian frontier in 1774, (Treaty of Kutchuk Kainardji)

S e a

Sukhumkale 1809

Poti
1809 ◉◐ 1809, 1829

Ardahan 1829 ◐

Trebizond 1829

Chorukh

Kars 1829 ◉

Gümüshane 1829

Baibert
◉1829

Erzerum 1829

Bayazit 1829

ASIA

Mus 1829 ●

▲▲▲▲ Russian gains in 1791 (Treaty of Jassy)

—·— The Russian frontier in 1812 (Treaty of Bucharest)

△△△△ Russian gains in 1829 (Treaty of Adrianople)

RUSSIA AND SWEDEN 1700-1809

0   300
Miles

From 1621 Sweden controlled the Baltic Sea and the Gulfs of Finland and Bothnia. In 1700 Peter the Great allied Russia with Poland and Denmark, in 1714 with Prussia and Hanover. His first conquest was Ingria, giving Russia a small but valued outlet on the Baltic. After several defeats, the Russians finally broke Sweden's dominance in 1721. Russia's annexation of Finland in 1809 further extended her control of the Baltic.

LAPLAND

S W E D E N

Gulf of Bothnia

Tornea

Uleaborg

Vasa

FINLAND

KARELIA

Kexholm

Nystad
Abo

Helsingfors

Vyborg

Noteborg
St Petersburg

ALAND IS.

Gulf of Finland

Narva

INGRIA

Ivangorod

Novgorod

Reval

DAGO

ESTLAND

Stockholm

Dorpat

Pskov

ÖSEL

LIVLAND

GOTLAND

Riga

Baltic Sea

DENMARK

Copenhagen

POLAND

Stralsund

BORNHOLM

SWEDISH POMERANIA

Stettin

HANOVER

PRUSSIA

▬▬▬	Sweden in 1700
■	Swedish territory conquered by Peter the Great during the Great Northern War 1700-1721, and annexed to Russia at the Treaty of Nystad 1721
▨	Conquered by Russia, 1743
▨	Swedish territory conquered by Alexander I and annexed to Russia in 1809

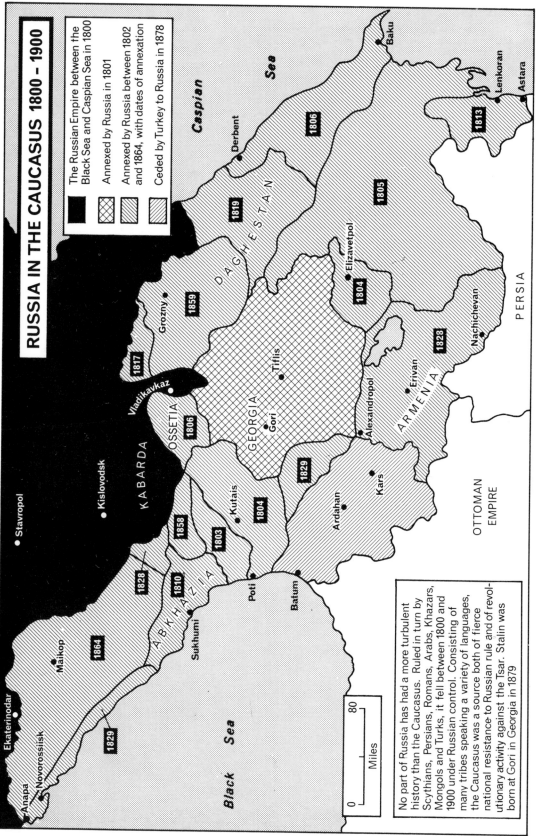

RUSSIA IN THE CAUCASUS 1800 - 1900

The Russian Empire between the Black Sea and Caspian Sea in 1800

Annexed by Russia in 1801

Annexed by Russia between 1802 and 1864, with dates of annexation

Ceded by Turkey to Russia in 1878

Caspian Sea

Baku

Lenkoran

Astara

1813

Derbent

1806

1805

Elizavetpol

1819

1804

D A G H E S T A N

Grozny

1859

Nachichevan

1817

Vladikavkaz

OSSETIA

1806

G E O R G I A

Tiflis

Gori

Alexandropol

A R M E N I A

Erivan

1828

K A B A R D A

Kislovodsk

Stavropol

1829

Kars

Ardahan

Kutais

1804

1803

1858

A B K H A Z I A

1828

1810

Sukhumi

Poti

Batum

OTTOMAN
EMPIRE

PERSIA

Ekaterinodar

Novorossiisk

Anapa

Maikop

1864

1829

Black Sea

0   80

Miles

No part of Russia has had a more turbulent
history than the Caucasus. Ruled in turn by
Scythians, Persians, Romans, Arabs, Khazars,
Mongols and Turks, it fell between 1800 and
1900 under Russian control. Consisting of
many tribes speaking a variety of languages,
the Caucasus was a source both of fierce
national resistance to Russian rule and of revolutionary activity against the Tsar. Stalin was
born at Gori in Georgia in 1879

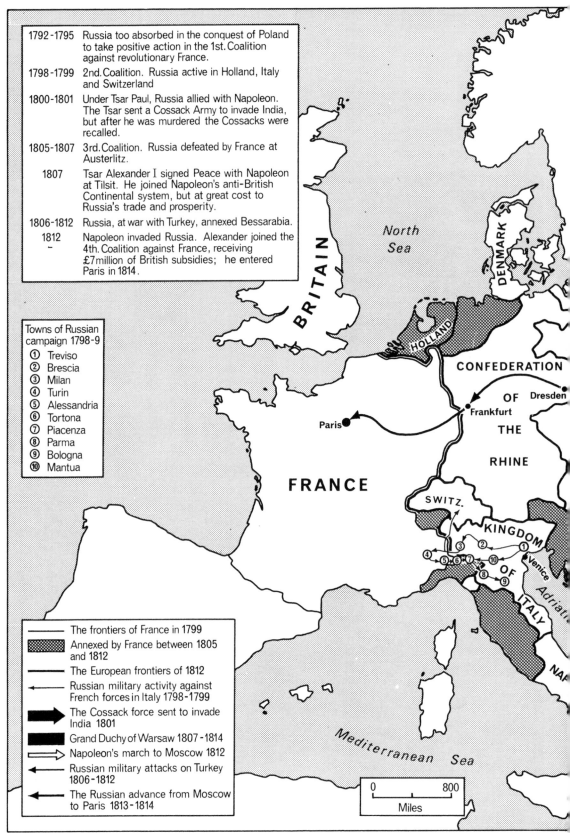

1792-1795   Russia too absorbed in the conquest of Poland to take positive action in the 1st. Coalition against revolutionary France.

1798-1799   2nd. Coalition. Russia active in Holland, Italy and Switzerland

1800-1801   Under Tsar Paul, Russia allied with Napoleon. The Tsar sent a Cossack Army to invade India, but after he was murdered the Cossacks were recalled.

1805-1807   3rd. Coalition. Russia defeated by France at Austerlitz.

1807   Tsar Alexander I signed Peace with Napoleon at Tilsit. He joined Napoleon's anti-British Continental system, but at great cost to Russia's trade and prosperity.

1806-1812   Russia, at war with Turkey, annexed Bessarabia.

1812 –   Napoleon invaded Russia. Alexander joined the 4th. Coalition against France, receiving £7 million of British subsidies; he entered Paris in 1814.

Towns of Russian campaign 1798-9
① Treviso
② Brescia
③ Milan
④ Turin
⑤ Alessandria
⑥ Tortona
⑦ Piacenza
⑧ Parma
⑨ Bologna
⑩ Mantua

North Sea

BRITAIN

DENMARK

HOLLAND

CONFEDERATION

OF

THE

RHINE

Dresden

Frankfurt

Paris

FRANCE

SWITZ.

KINGDOM

OF

ITALY

Venice

Adriatic

NAP

Mediterranean Sea

—— The frontiers of France in 1799

▦ Annexed by France between 1805 and 1812

—— The European frontiers of 1812

← Russian military activity against French forces in Italy 1798-1799

➡ The Cossack force sent to invade India 1801

■ Grand Duchy of Warsaw 1807-1814

⇨ Napoleon's march to Moscow 1812

← Russian military attacks on Turkey 1806-1812

← The Russian advance from Moscow to Paris 1813-1814

0   800
Miles

RUSSIA AND EUROPE 1789-1815

R U S S I A

Tver

Moscow

Borodino

Viazma

Riazan

Riga

Smolensk

Tula

Tilsit

Borisov

Baltic Sea

USSIA

Kalisz

GRAND
DUCHY
OF WARSAW

Napoleon championed Polish independence, and many Polish emigres joined him after 1795. In 1807 he established a Grand Duchy of Warsaw, entirely out of Prussian and Austrian Poland. The Russians planned to crush this new state, but to forestall them Napoleon marched to Moscow in 1812. 85.000 Poles served in his army. After his defeat most of the Grand Duchy was transferred to Russia, giving Russia a further 3 million Polish and 300,000 Jewish citizens.

Austerlitz

Vienna

AUSTRIA

Jassy

BESS-
ARABIA

Ismail

RUMANIANS

Bucharest

CROATS

Iasika

Black Sea

SERBS

Tirnovo

Shumla

Varna

BULGARS

TURKEY IN EUROPE

GREEKS

TURKEY IN ASIA

Balkan peoples under Turkish rule, whom Alexander planned to enlist in an anti-French crusade in return for helping them obtain independ-ence from Turkey. The plan failed.

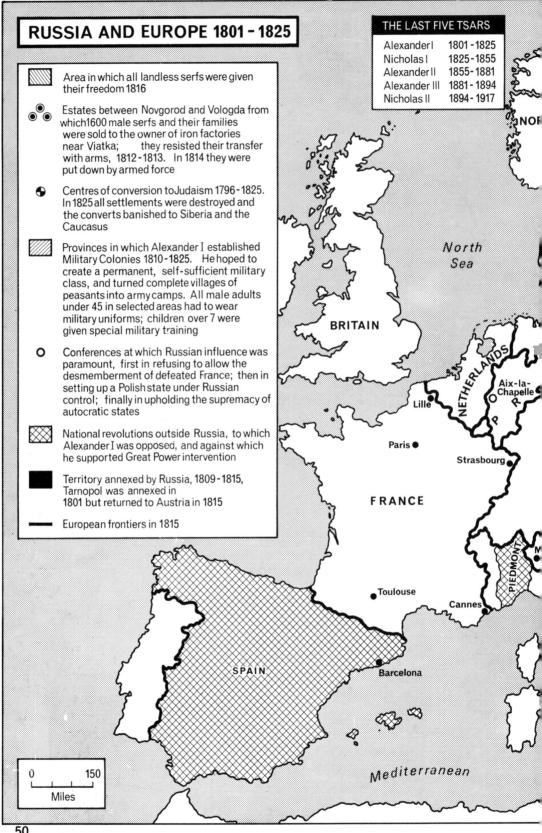

RUSSIA AND EUROPE 1801-1825

Area in which all landless serfs were given their freedom 1816

Estates between Novgorod and Vologda from which 1600 male serfs and their families were sold to the owner of iron factories near Viatka; they resisted their transfer with arms, 1812 - 1813. In 1814 they were put down by armed force

Centres of conversion to Judaism 1796 - 1825. In 1825 all settlements were destroyed and the converts banished to Siberia and the Caucasus

Provinces in which Alexander I established Military Colonies 1810 - 1825. He hoped to create a permanent, self-sufficient military class, and turned complete villages of peasants into army camps. All male adults under 45 in selected areas had to wear military uniforms; children over 7 were given special military training

Conferences at which Russian influence was paramount, first in refusing to allow the desmemberment of defeated France; then in setting up a Polish state under Russian control; finally in upholding the supremacy of autocratic states

National revolutions outside Russia, to which Alexander I was opposed, and against which he supported Great Power intervention

Territory annexed by Russia, 1809 - 1815, Tarnopol was annexed in 1801 but returned to Austria in 1815

European frontiers in 1815

NOR

North Sea

BRITAIN

NETHERLANDS

Aix-la-Chapelle

Lille

OROP

Paris

Strasbourg

FRANCE

PIEDMONT

M

Toulouse

Cannes

0   150
Miles

SPAIN

Barcelona

Mediterranean

Viatka

FINLAND

ALAND
ISLANDS

St.
Petersburg

Vologda

SWEDEN

Novgorod

Moscow

Baltic Sea

Tula

Saratov

R U S S I A

Mogilev

Bobrov

S I A

Pavlovsk

POLAND

Ekaterinoslav

Carlsbad

Lemberg

Troppau

Tarnopol

Prague

BESSARABIA

Nikolaev

Vienna

AUSTRIA-
HUNGARY

Laibach

Bucharest

Black Sea

Belgrade

T

U

Cattaro

R

NAPLES

Constantinople

K

E

Y

aples

GREECE

Athens

Sea

Like Catherine the Great on her accession,
Alexander I was looked to on his accession
(in 1801) as a potential source of liberal-
ization. In the war against Napoleon he acted
as the enemy of tyrants and friend of the
oppressed. But by 1820 he had become a
pillar of autocracy both in Russia and
abroad. Under Alexander, Russia's western
frontier reached its furthest western extent,
and from 1820 to 1917 it was unchanged

RUSSIA UNDER NICHOLAS I 1825 - 1855

Nicholas I, known as the Gendarme of Europe, was equally the gendarme of Russia. In 1827 he set up a special Corps of Gendarmes, as the main instrument of the political police. The country was divided into Gendarme Districts, each commanded by a General. There were an estimated total of at least 4,000 Gendarmes in 1837, when the Districts were reorganised; and at least 8,000 by 1855. A squadron was set up to patrol the Moscow-St. Petersburg railway in 1846

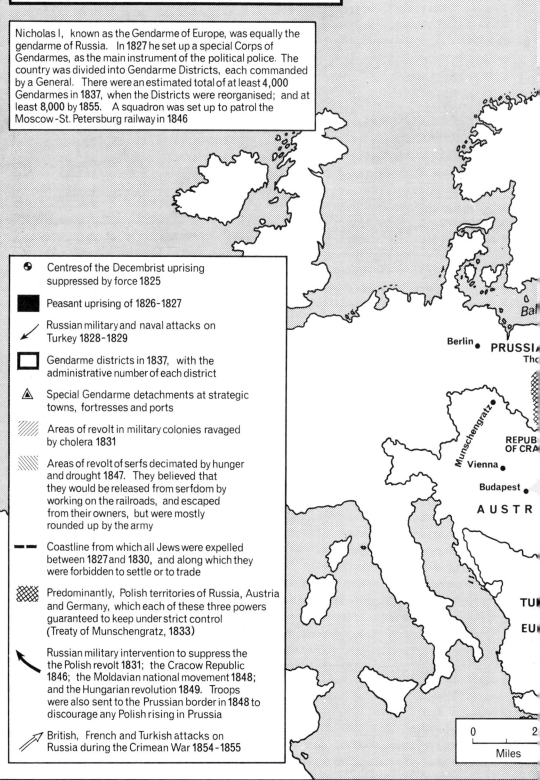

⊕ Centres of the Decembrist uprising suppressed by force 1825

▮ Peasant uprising of 1826-1827

↙ Russian military and naval attacks on Turkey 1828-1829

▭ Gendarme districts in 1837, with the administrative number of each district

▲ Special Gendarme detachments at strategic towns, fortresses and ports

▨ Areas of revolt in military colonies ravaged by cholera 1831

▧ Areas of revolt of serfs decimated by hunger and drought 1847. They believed that they would be released from serfdom by working on the railroads, and escaped from their owners, but were mostly rounded up by the army

▬ ▬ Coastline from which all Jews were expelled between 1827 and 1830, and along which they were forbidden to settle or to trade

▨ Predominantly, Polish territories of Russia, Austria and Germany, which each of these three powers guaranteed to keep under strict control (Treaty of Munschengratz, 1833)

↖ Russian military intervention to suppress the the Polish revolt 1831; the Cracow Republic 1846; the Moldavian national movement 1848; and the Hungarian revolution 1849. Troops were also sent to the Prussian border in 1848 to discourage any Polish rising in Prussia

↗ British, French and Turkish attacks on Russia during the Crimean War 1854-1855

Berlin • PRUSSIA
Thc

Munschengratz

REPUB
OF CRA

Vienna •

Budapest •

AUSTR

TU
EU

Bal

0   2
Miles

51

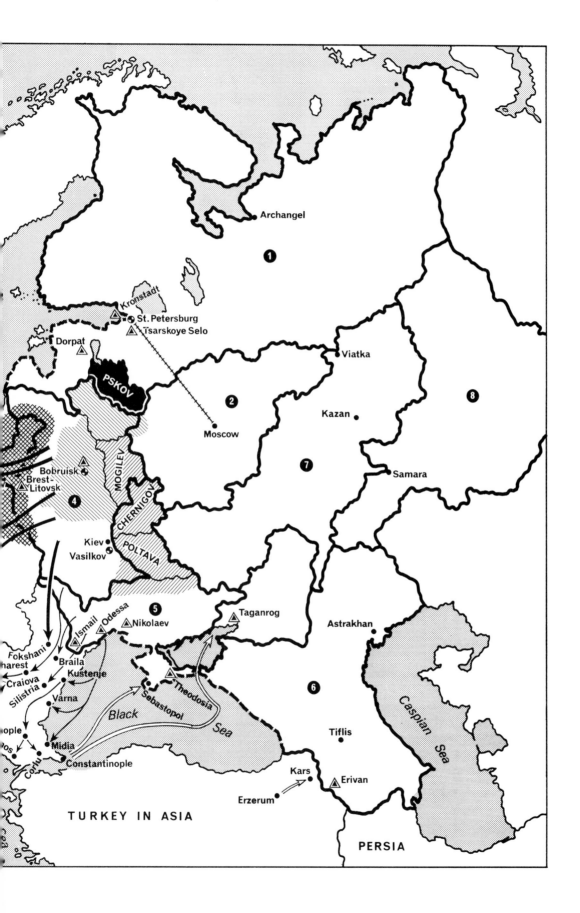

Archangel

①

Kronstadt
△ St. Petersburg
△ Tsarskoye Selo

Dorpat △

PSKOV

②

Viatka

Moscow

Kazan

⑧

MOGILEV

Bobruisk △
Brest-
Litovsk △

④

CHERNIGOV

POLTAVA

Kiev
Vasilkov

⑦

Samara

Ismail △ Odessa
△ Nikolaev

⑤

△ Taganrog

Astrakhan

Fokshani
harest
Craiova
Silistria
Varna

Braila
Kustenje

△

Theodosia

⑥

Sebastopol

Black

Sea

Tiflis

ople

Midia

Corfu

Constantinople

Kars

△ Erivan

Erzerum

Caspian

Sea

TURKEY IN ASIA

PERSIA

THE POLISH REVOLT IN 1831

After Napoleon's defeat in 1814, Russia set up its new Polish territory as a separate kingdom, CONGRESS POLAND, ruled directly by the Tsar. After 1814, Alexander I adopted a liberal, pro-Polish policy. But in 1825 his successor, Nicholas I, began to restrict Polish liberties. In 1830 the Poles rose in open war against Russian rule. They hoped for help from France, but it never came. The revolt was crushed by superior Russian force.

Palanga

Memel

Königsberg

Danzig

P R U S S I A

Masurian Lakes

0   50
Miles

Suvalki

Vilna

Grodno

Posen

Bialystok

R U S S I A

Kalisz

Lodz

Warsaw

Brest-Litovsk

Pripet Marshes

Pinsk

Piotrkow

Breslau

SILESIA

Czenstochowa

Kovel

Krasnik

REPUBLIC OF CRACOW

Cracow

Tarnow

GALICIA

Przemysl

Lvov

AUSTRIA

Tarnopol

☐ Congress Poland, ruled by the Russian Tsar 1815-1914

▨ Principal areas of Polish partisan activity in 1831 against the local Russian authorities

⊙ Battles between Russian and Polish troops in 1831

↗ Polish troop movements. All these ended in exile across the Prussian, Austrian and Cracovian borders

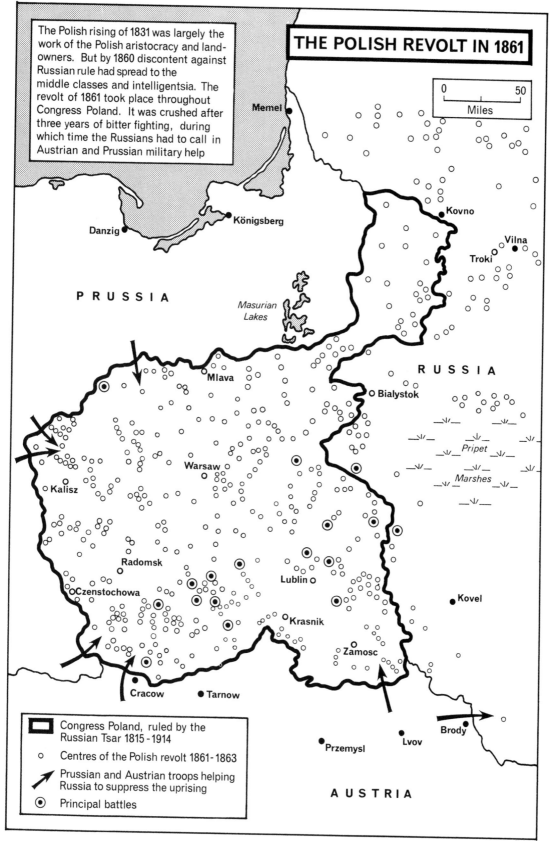

THE POLISH REVOLT IN 1861

The Polish rising of 1831 was largely the work of the Polish aristocracy and land-owners. But by 1860 discontent against Russian rule had spread to the middle classes and intelligentsia. The revolt of 1861 took place throughout Congress Poland. It was crushed after three years of bitter fighting, during which time the Russians had to call in Austrian and Prussian military help

0   50
Miles

Memel

Kovno

Vilna

Troki

Danzig

Königsberg

PRUSSIA

Masurian
Lakes

RUSSIA

Mlava

Bialystok

Pripet

Marshes

Warsaw

Kalisz

Radomsk

Lublin

Kovel

Czenstochowa

Krasnik

Zamosc

Cracow

Tarnow

Brody

Przemysl

Lvov

AUSTRIA

☐ Congress Poland, ruled by the Russian Tsar 1815-1914

○ Centres of the Polish revolt 1861-1863

➚ Prussian and Austrian troops helping Russia to suppress the uprising

⊙ Principal battles

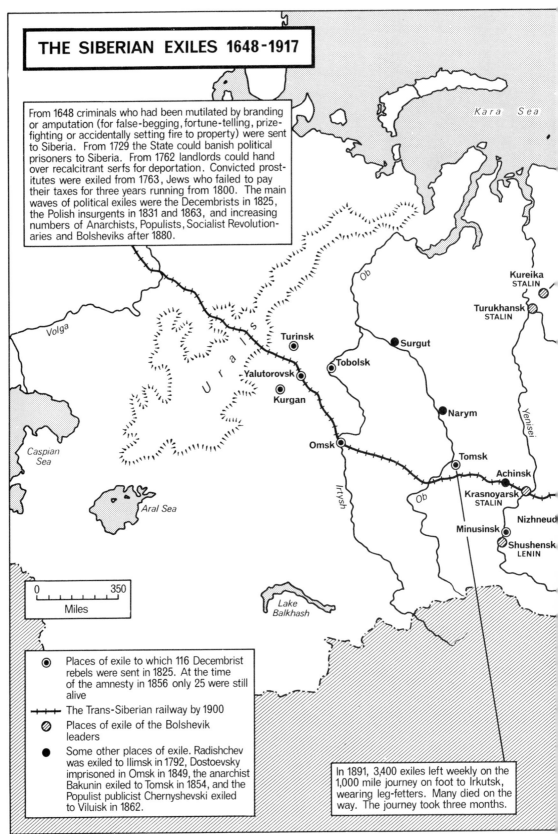

THE SIBERIAN EXILES 1648-1917

From 1648 criminals who had been mutilated by branding or amputation (for false-begging, fortune-telling, prize-fighting or accidentally setting fire to property) were sent to Siberia. From 1729 the State could banish political prisoners to Siberia. From 1762 landlords could hand over recalcitrant serfs for deportation. Convicted prostitutes were exiled from 1763, Jews who failed to pay their taxes for three years running from 1800. The main waves of political exiles were the Decembrists in 1825, the Polish insurgents in 1831 and 1863, and increasing numbers of Anarchists, Populists, Socialist Revolutionaries and Bolsheviks after 1880.

Kara Sea

Volga

U r a l s

Caspian Sea

Aral Sea

Ob

Kureika
STALIN

Turukhansk
STALIN

Turinsk

Surgut

Tobolsk

Yalutorovsk

Kurgan

Narym

Yenisei

Omsk

Tomsk

Achinsk

Krasnoyarsk
STALIN

Nizhneud

Minusinsk

Shushensk
LENIN

Irtysh

Ob

Lake Balkhash

```
0          350
|__|__|__|__|
    Miles
```

⊙ Places of exile to which 116 Decembrist rebels were sent in 1825. At the time of the amnesty in 1856 only 25 were still alive

┼┼┼ The Trans-Siberian railway by 1900

⊘ Places of exile of the Bolshevik leaders

● Some other places of exile. Radishchev was exiled to Ilimsk in 1792, Dostoevsky imprisoned in Omsk in 1849, the anarchist Bakunin exiled to Tomsk in 1854, and the Populist publicist Chernyshevski exiled to Viluisk in 1862.

In 1891, 3,400 exiles left weekly on the 1,000 mile journey on foot to Irkutsk, wearing leg-fetters. Many died on the way. The journey took three months.

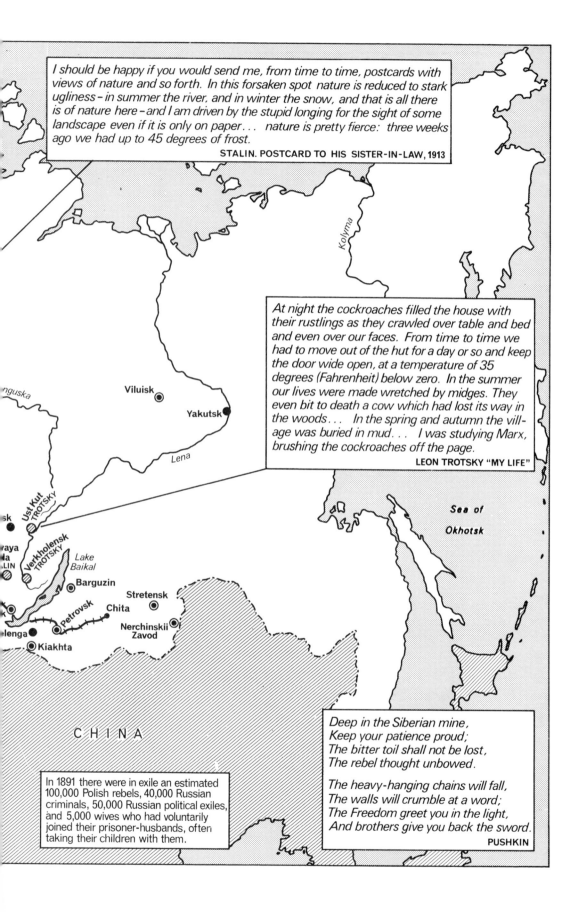

I should be happy if you would send me, from time to time, postcards with views of nature and so forth. In this forsaken spot nature is reduced to stark ugliness – in summer the river, and in winter the snow, and that is all there is of nature here – and I am driven by the stupid longing for the sight of some landscape even if it is only on paper... nature is pretty fierce: three weeks ago we had up to 45 degrees of frost.

STALIN. POSTCARD TO HIS SISTER-IN-LAW, 1913

At night the cockroaches filled the house with their rustlings as they crawled over table and bed and even over our faces. From time to time we had to move out of the hut for a day or so and keep the door wide open, at a temperature of 35 degrees (Fahrenheit) below zero. In the summer our lives were made wretched by midges. They even bit to death a cow which had lost its way in the woods... In the spring and autumn the village was buried in mud... I was studying Marx, brushing the cockroaches off the page.

LEON TROTSKY "MY LIFE"

Kolyma

Sea of

Okhotsk

nguska

Viluisk

Yakutsk

Lena

Ust Kut
TROTSKY

sk

vaya
la
LIN

Verkholensk
TROTSKY

Lake Baikal

Barguzin

Stretensk

Petrovsk

Chita

Nerchinskii
Zavod

lenga

Kiakhta

C H I N A

Deep in the Siberian mine,
Keep your patience proud;
The bitter toil shall not be lost,
The rebel thought unbowed.

The heavy-hanging chains will fall,
The walls will crumble at a word;
The Freedom greet you in the light,
And brothers give you back the sword.

PUSHKIN

In 1891 there were in exile an estimated 100,000 Polish rebels, 40,000 Russian criminals, 50,000 Russian political exiles, and 5,000 wives who had voluntarily joined their prisoner-husbands, often taking their children with them.

THE ANARCHISTS 1840-1906

"What is property? Property is theft" wrote the French philosopher Proudhon, the father of anarchism, in 1840. He urged the destruction of officialdom, bureaucracy money and state organisation in order to make all men equal and free. But he shunned violent revolt, fearing that revolution might bring new tyranny. The Russian, Bakunin, bent anarchism to violence. "The passion to destroy is at the same time a passion to create," he wrote in 1842. Bakunin believed that the Russian peasant would be the instrument of anarchic revolt, and encouraged terrorist acts. The murder of Tsar Alexander II at St. Petersburg in 1881 encouraged further assassinations, aimed at provoking revolution. The Russian anarchist, Prince Kropotkin, said after the execution of one of the 5 assassins: "By her death she was dealing an even more terrible blow, from which the autocracy will never recover."

St.Petersburg

Viatka

Baltic Sea

Riga

LITHUANIA

Kovno

Vilna

Minsk

Grodno

Bialystok

Warsaw

POLAND

Moscow

Tula

Orel

Nizhni Novgorod

Volga

Samara

Nezhin

Kiev

Kharkov

UKRAINE

Ekaterinoslav

Kishinev

Odessa

Volga

Sebastopol

Yalta

Black Sea

Caspian Sea

Batum

Tiflis

CAUCASIA

Baku

⊙   Anarchist groups meeting from the 1840's to 1880's

●   Revolutionary anarchist groups in existence from 1903 and "revolting" in 1905-1906

▨   The "Forest Brethren" carrying out terrorist activity in 1905-1906

0   300

Miles

RUSSIAN INDUSTRY BY 1860

0 — 200
Miles

Archangel

Urals

Vyborg
Schlüsselburg
Reval
St. Petersburg — 540,000
Narva
LEATHER

Viatka
Kama
Perm — GOLD
COAL
COPPER
LEATHER
Ufa
COPPER

WOOL
Dorpat
Pskov
Riga
Libau
Mitau — 77,000
WOOL
Dvinsk

Tver
Vladimir
Yegorevsk
Moscow — 460,000
LEATHER

Yaroslavl
LINEN
Volga
Nizhni Novgorod
Kazan — 63,000

COAL

Baltic Sea

Kovno
Vilna — 69,000
Grodno
Bialystok
Warsaw
Lodz
LINEN
LINEN

Kaluga
Tula
LEATHER
Orel

Riazan
LINEN

WOOL
Voronezh

Saratov — 84,000

Dniepier

LINEN

Chernigov

Kiev — 68,000
LINEN
Kharkov
Poltava
Donets

Volga

Kishinev — 94,000
64,000
Nikolaev
Odessa — 120,000

COAL
Don

Caspian Sea

TOBACCO
Caucasus
Baku
OIL

Black Sea

POPULATION
1811: 41,000,000
1863: 74,000,000

── The Russian frontier 1815-1914
● Principal cities, with their estimated population in 1860
╫ Railways built by 1860
┼ Railways under construction in 1860
◉ Factory development before 1860
◓ Towns with large factory growth from 1860
▬ Industries expanding rapidly from 1860
▦ Centres of the iron and steel production
▨ Sugar factories

PRINCIPAL IMPORTS: Cotton, machine tools, alcohol, dyes, fruit and nuts, wool, tea, olive and vegetable oil, silk, sugar, zinc, steel, iron, copper, horses. cattle, poultry, salt. Over 80% of all imports and exports went through the ports of St. Petersburg and Odessa

PRINCIPAL EXPORTS: Wheat, rye, cereals, flour, flax, hemp, wool, animal fat, lard, seeds, wood, wood products, paper

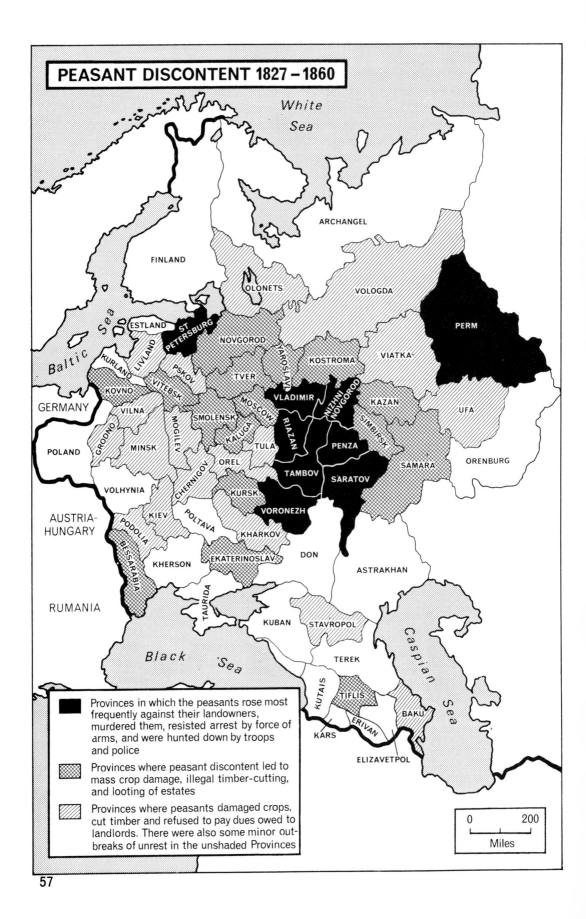

PEASANT DISCONTENT 1827–1860

White Sea

ARCHANGEL

FINLAND

Baltic Sea

OLONETS

VOLOGDA

PERM

ESTLAND

ST PETERSBURG

NOVGOROD

KOSTROMA

VIATKA

KURLAND

LIVLAND

PSKOV

YAROSLAVL

KAZAN

UFA

KOVNO

VITEBSK

TVER

VLADIMIR

NIZHNI NOVGOROD

SIMBIRSK

GERMANY

VILNA

SMOLENSK

MOSCOW

RIAZAN

ORENBURG

GRODNO

MOGILEV

KALUGA

PENZA

SAMARA

POLAND

MINSK

OREL

TULA

CHERNIGOV

KURSK

TAMBOV

SARATOV

VOLHYNIA

KIEV

AUSTRIA-HUNGARY

PODOLIA

POLTAVA

VORONEZH

BESSARABIA

KHARKOV

EKATERINOSLAV

DON

ASTRAKHAN

KHERSON

RUMANIA

TAURIDA

KUBAN

STAVROPOL

Black Sea

TEREK

Caspian Sea

KUTAIS

TIFLIS

BAKU

ERIVAN

KARS

ELIZAVETPOL

■ Provinces in which the peasants rose most frequently against their landowners, murdered them, resisted arrest by force of arms, and were hunted down by troops and police

▨ Provinces where peasant discontent led to mass crop damage, illegal timber-cutting, and looting of estates

▨ Provinces where peasants damaged crops, cut timber and refused to pay dues owed to landlords. There were also some minor outbreaks of unrest in the unshaded Provinces

0   200
Miles

SERFS IN 1860

White Sea
VOLOGDA
PERM
NOVGOROD
PSKOV
TVER
YAROSLAVL
KOSTROMA
KOVNO
VITEBSK
MOSCOW
VLADIMIR
NIZHNI NOVGOROD
VILNA
GRODNO
MOGILEV
SMOLENSK
KALUGA
RIAZAN
SIMBIRSK
MINSK
TULA
PENZA
OREL
TAMBOV
SARATOV
CHERNIGOV
VOLHYNIA
KURSK
KIEV
POLTAVA
VORONEZH
PODOLIA
KHARKOV
DON
KHERSON
EKATERINOSLAV
KUBAN
KUTAIS
TIFLIS

GERMANY

AUSTRIA-HUNGARY

RUMANIA

TURKEY

PERSIA

Baltic Sea

Black Sea

Caspian Sea

■ Provinces where over half of
the peasants were serfs

▨ Provinces where 36% to 55%
of the peasants were serfs

▤ Provinces where 16% to 35%
of the peasants were serfs

0   200
Miles

58

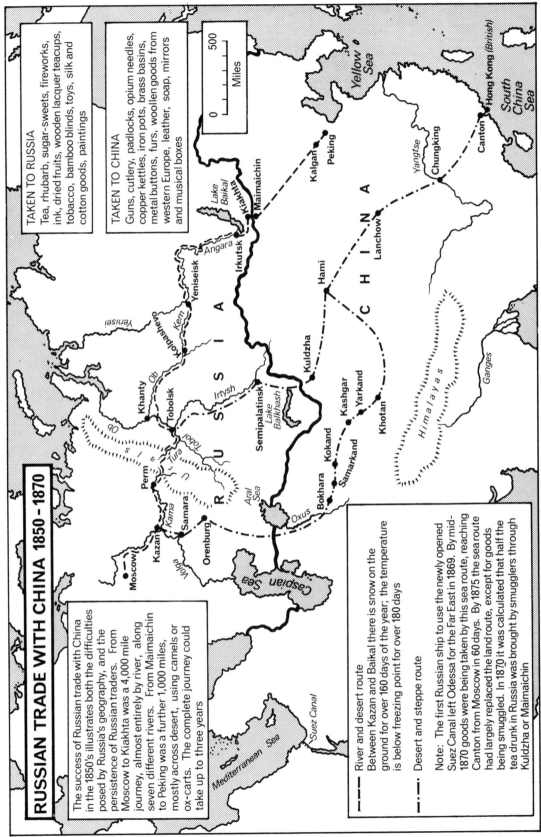

RUSSIAN TRADE WITH CHINA 1850 – 1870

The success of Russian trade with China in the 1850's illustrates both the difficulties posed by Russia's geography, and the persistence of Russian traders. From Moscow to Kiakhta was a 4,000 mile journey, almost entirely by river, along seven different rivers. From Maimaichin to Peking was a further 1,000 miles, mostly across desert, using camels or ox-carts. The complete journey could take up to three years

TAKEN TO RUSSIA

Tea, rhubarb, sugar-sweets, fireworks, ink, dried fruits, wooden lacquer teacups, tobacco, bamboo blinds, toys, silk and cotton goods, paintings

TAKEN TO CHINA

Guns, cutlery, padlocks, opium needles, copper kettles, iron pots, brass basins, metal buttons, furs, woollen goods from western Europe, leather, soap, mirrors and musical boxes

0   500
Miles

– – – River and desert route
Between Kazan and Baikal there is snow on the ground for over 160 days of the year; the temperature is below freezing point for over 180 days

–·– Desert and steppe route

Note: The first Russian ship to use the newly opened Suez Canal left Odessa for the Far East in 1869. By mid-1870 goods were being taken by this sea route, reaching Canton from Moscow in 60 days. By 1875 the sea route had largely replaced the land route, except for goods being smuggled. In 1870 it was calculated that half the tea drunk in Russia was brought by smugglers through Kuldzha or Maimaichin

59

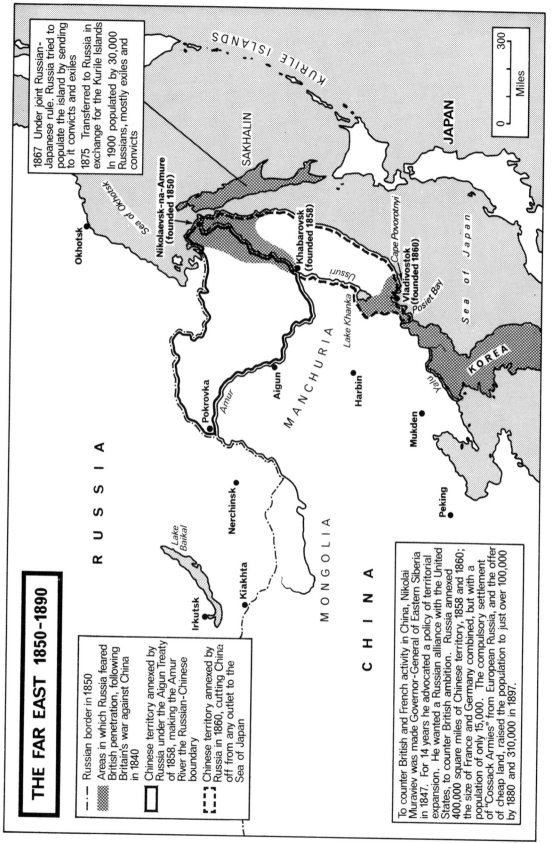

THE FAR EAST 1850-1890

Legend:

- — · — Russian border in 1850

▨ Areas in which Russia feared British penetration, following Britain's war against China in 1840

▭ Chinese territory annexed by Russia under the Aigun Treaty of 1858, making the Amur River the Russian-Chinese boundary

▯ Chinese territory annexed by Russia in 1860, cutting China off from any outlet to the Sea of Japan

RUSSIA

MONGOLIA

CHINA

MANCHURIA

KOREA

JAPAN

KURILE ISLANDS

SAKHALIN

Sea of Okhotsk

Sea of Japan

Lake Baikal

Lake Khanka

Amur

Ussuri

Yalu

Posiet Bay

Okhotsk

Irkutsk

Kiakhta

Nerchinsk

Pokrovka

Aigun

Harbin

Mukden

Peking

Nikolaevsk-na-Amure (founded 1850)

Khabarovsk (founded 1858)

Vladivostok (founded 1860)

Cape Povorotnyi

1867 Under joint Russian-Japanese rule. Russia tried to populate the island by sending to it convicts and exiles

1875 Transferred to Russia in exchange for the Kurile Islands In 1900 populated by 30,000 Russians, mostly exiles and convicts

To counter British and French activity in China, Nikolai Muraviev was made Governor-General of Eastern Siberia in 1847. For 14 years he advocated a policy of territorial expansion. He wanted a Russian alliance with the United States, to counter British ambition. Russia annexed 400,000 square miles of Chinese territory, 1858 and 1860; the size of France and Germany combined, but with a population of only 15,000. The compulsory settlement of "Cossack Armies" from European Russia, and the offer of cheap land, raised the population to just over 100,000 by 1880 and 310,000 in 1897.

Miles 0   300

60

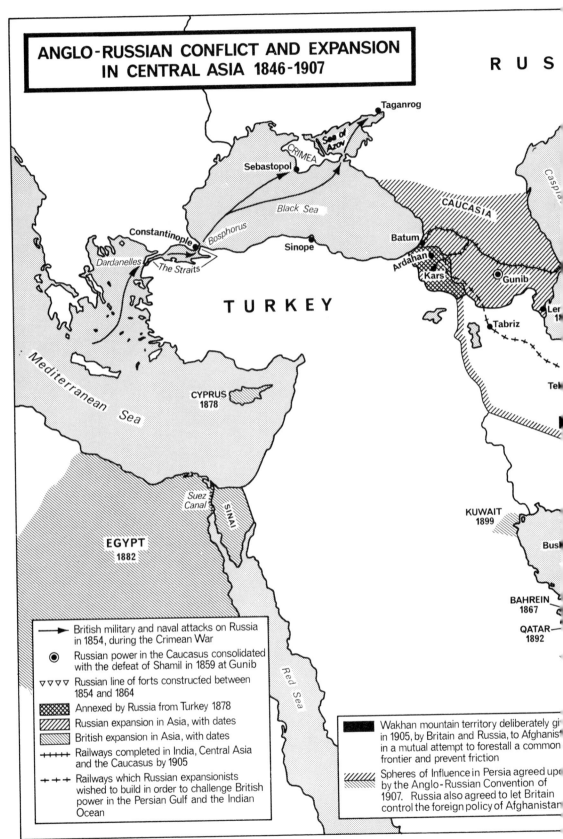

ANGLO-RUSSIAN CONFLICT AND EXPANSION IN CENTRAL ASIA 1846-1907

R U S

Taganrog

CRIMEA

Sea of Azov

Sebastopol

CAUCASIA

Caspia

Black Sea

Batum

Constantinople

Bosphorus

Sinope

Ardahan

Kars

Gunib

Ler
1

Dardanelles

The Straits

T U R K E Y

Tabriz

Mediterranean Sea

Te

CYPRUS
1878

Suez
Canal

SINAI

KUWAIT
1899

EGYPT
1882

Bus

Red Sea

BAHREIN
1867

QATAR
1892

→ British military and naval attacks on Russia in 1854, during the Crimean War

◉ Russian power in the Caucasus consolidated with the defeat of Shamil in 1859 at Gunib

▽▽▽▽ Russian line of forts constructed between 1854 and 1864

▨ Annexed by Russia from Turkey 1878

▨ Russian expansion in Asia, with dates

▨ British expansion in Asia, with dates

++++ Railways completed in India, Central Asia and the Caucasus by 1905

+ + + Railways which Russian expansionists wished to build in order to challenge British power in the Persian Gulf and the Indian Ocean

■ Wakhan mountain territory deliberately gi
in 1905, by Britain and Russia, to Afghanis
in a mutual attempt to forestall a common
frontier and prevent friction

▨ Spheres of Influence in Persia agreed upo
by the Anglo-Russian Convention of
1907. Russia also agreed to let Britain
control the foreign policy of Afghanistan

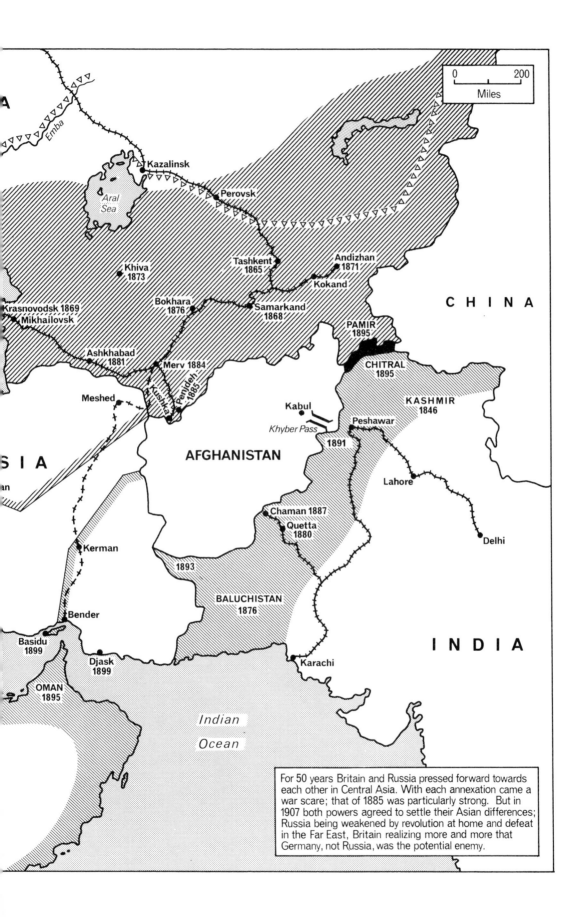

Emba

Kazalinsk

Aral
Sea

Perovsk

Khiva
1873

Tashkent
1865

Andizhan
1871

Kokand

CHINA

Krasnovodsk 1869
Mikhailovsk

Bokhara
1876

Samarkand
1868

PAMIR
1895

Ashkhabad
1881

Merv 1884

CHITRAL
1895

KASHMIR
1846

Meshed

Kushka

Penjdeh
1885

Kabul

Peshawar

Khyber Pass

1891

Lahore

SIA

AFGHANISTAN

an

Chaman 1887

Quetta
1880

Delhi

Kerman

1893

Bender

BALUCHISTAN
1876

INDIA

Basidu
1899

Djask
1899

Karachi

OMAN
1895

Indian

Ocean

For 50 years Britain and Russia pressed forward towards
each other in Central Asia. With each annexation came a
war scare; that of 1885 was particularly strong. But in
1907 both powers agreed to settle their Asian differences;
Russia being weakened by revolution at home and defeat
in the Far East, Britain realizing more and more that
Germany, not Russia, was the potential enemy.

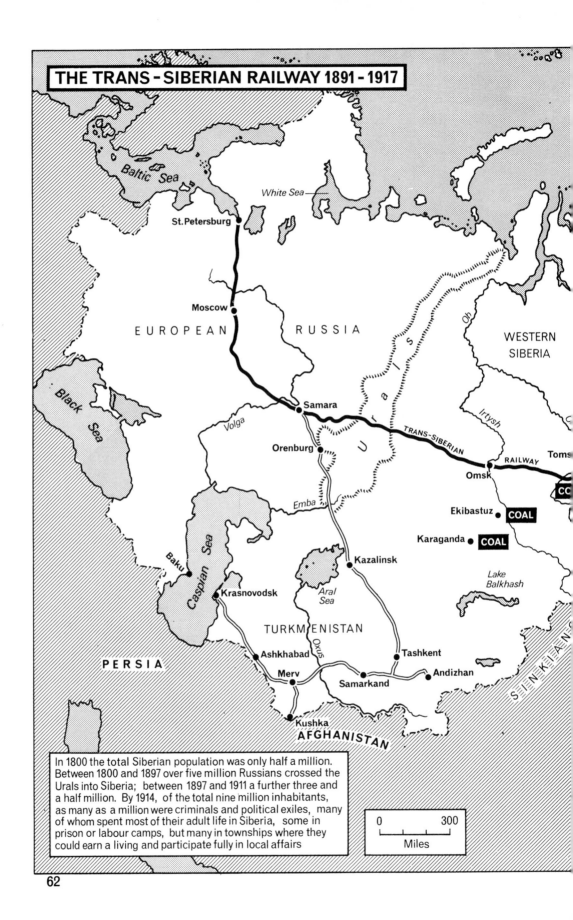

THE TRANS-SIBERIAN RAILWAY 1891-1917

Baltic Sea

White Sea

St. Petersburg

Moscow

EUROPEAN RUSSIA

WESTERN SIBERIA

Black Sea

Samara

Volga

Orenburg

TRANS-SIBERIAN

Irtysh

Ob

RAILWAY

Toms

Omsk

CO

Emba

Ekibastuz • COAL

Karaganda • COAL

Baku

Caspian Sea

Kazalinsk

Aral Sea

Lake Balkhash

Krasnovodsk

TURKMENISTAN

PERSIA

Ashkhabad

Merv

Samarkand

Tashkent

Andizhan

S I N K I A N G

Kushka

AFGHANISTAN

In 1800 the total Siberian population was only half a million.
Between 1800 and 1897 over five million Russians crossed the
Urals into Siberia; between 1897 and 1911 a further three and
a half million. By 1914, of the total nine million inhabitants,
as many as a million were criminals and political exiles, many
of whom spent most of their adult life in Siberia, some in
prison or labour camps, but many in townships where they
could earn a living and participate fully in local affairs

0   300
Miles

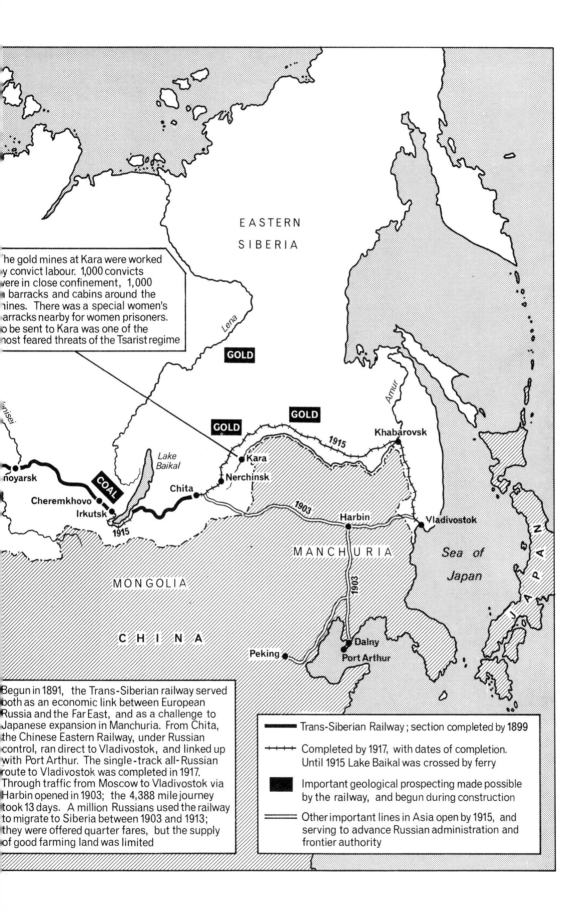

EASTERN
SIBERIA

The gold mines at Kara were worked
by convict labour. 1,000 convicts
were in close confinement, 1,000
in barracks and cabins around the
mines. There was a special women's
barracks nearby for women prisoners.
To be sent to Kara was one of the
most feared threats of the Tsarist regime

GOLD

GOLD

GOLD

Khabarovsk

1915

Kara

Nerchinsk

Lake
Baikal

noyarsk

COAL

Chita

1903

Cheremkhovo
Irkutsk

Harbin

Vladivostok

1915

MANCHURIA

Sea of
Japan

1903

MONGOLIA

CHINA

Dalny
Port Arthur

Peking

Begun in 1891, the Trans-Siberian railway served
both as an economic link between European
Russia and the Far East, and as a challenge to
Japanese expansion in Manchuria. From Chita,
the Chinese Eastern Railway, under Russian
control, ran direct to Vladivostok, and linked up
with Port Arthur. The single-track all-Russian
route to Vladivostok was completed in 1917.
Through traffic from Moscow to Vladivostok via
Harbin opened in 1903; the 4,388 mile journey
took 13 days. A million Russians used the railway
to migrate to Siberia between 1903 and 1913;
they were offered quarter fares, but the supply
of good farming land was limited

Trans-Siberian Railway; section completed by 1899

+++ Completed by 1917, with dates of completion.
Until 1915 Lake Baikal was crossed by ferry

Important geological prospecting made possible
by the railway, and begun during construction

Other important lines in Asia open by 1915, and
serving to advance Russian administration and
frontier authority

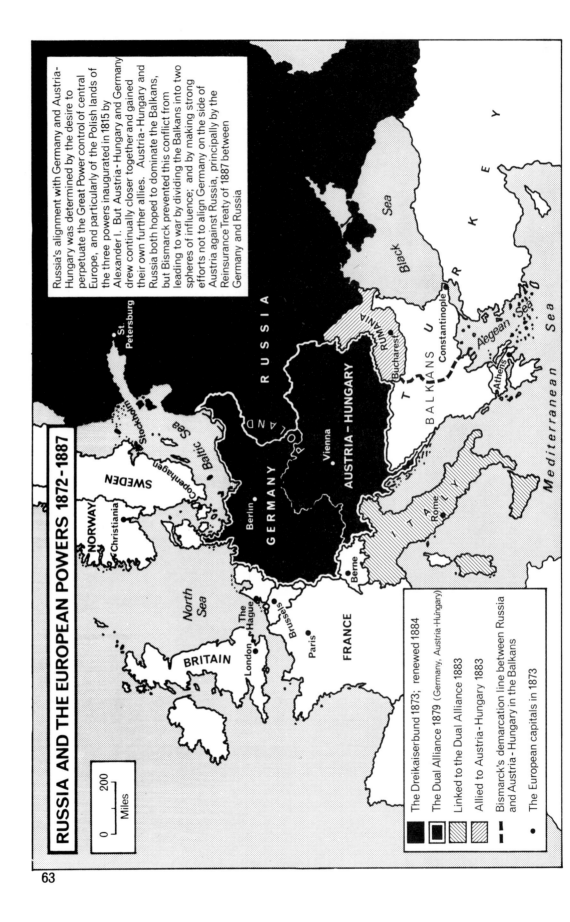

RUSSIA AND THE EUROPEAN POWERS 1872-1887

Russia's alignment with Germany and Austria-Hungary was determined by the desire to perpetuate the Great Power control of central Europe, and particularly of the Polish lands of the three powers inaugurated in 1815 by Alexander I. But Austria-Hungary and Germany drew continually closer together and gained their own further allies. Austria-Hungary and Russia both hoped to dominate the Balkans, but Bismarck prevented this conflict from leading to war by dividing the Balkans into two spheres of influence; and by making strong efforts not to align Germany on the side of Austria against Russia, principally by the Reinsurance Treaty of 1887 between Germany and Russia

SWEDEN

NORWAY

Christiania

St. Petersburg

Stockholm

Copenhagen

Baltic Sea

RUSSIA

POLAND

GERMANY

Berlin

Vienna

AUSTRIA-HUNGARY

RUMANIA

Bucharest

Black Sea

Constantinople

T U R K E Y

BALKANS

Aegean Sea

Athens

North Sea

The Hague

London

Brussels

Berne

I T A L Y

Rome

Mediterranean Sea

BRITAIN

Paris

FRANCE

0   200
Miles

The Dreikaiserbund 1873; renewed 1884

The Dual Alliance 1879 (Germany, Austria-Hungary)

Linked to the Dual Alliance 1883

Allied to Austria-Hungary 1883

Bismarck's demarcation line between Russia and Austria-Hungary in the Balkans

The European capitals in 1873

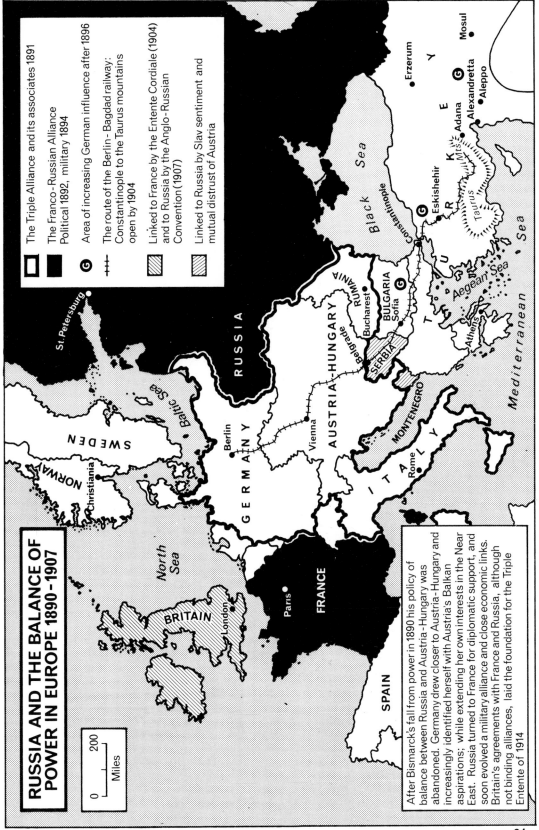

RUSSIA AND THE BALANCE OF POWER IN EUROPE 1890–1907

0   200
Miles

Legend

□ The Triple Alliance and its associates 1891

■ The Franco-Russian Alliance Political 1892, military 1894

Ⓖ Area of increasing German influence after 1896

┼┼┼ The route of the Berlin–Bagdad railway: Constantinople to the Taurus mountains open by 1904

▨ Linked to France by the Entente Cordiale (1904) and to Russia by the Anglo-Russian Convention (1907)

▨ Linked to Russia by Slav sentiment and mutual distrust of Austria

After Bismarck's fall from power in 1890 his policy of balance between Russia and Austria-Hungary was abandoned. Germany drew closer to Austria-Hungary and increasingly identified herself with Austria's Balkan aspirations; while extending her own interests in the Near East. Russia turned to France for diplomatic support, and soon evolved a military alliance and close economic links. Britain's agreements with France and Russia, although not binding alliances, laid the foundation for the Triple Entente of 1914

St. Petersburg

SWEDEN

NORWAY

Christiania

Baltic Sea

North Sea

BRITAIN

London

GERMANY

Berlin

Paris

FRANCE

SPAIN

RUSSIA

AUSTRIA-HUNGARY

Vienna

ITALY

Rome

RUMANIA

Belgrade

SERBIA

MONTENEGRO

BULGARIA

Bucharest

Sofia

Black Sea

Constantinople

TURKEY

Eskishehir

Taurus Mts.

Adana

Alexandretta

Aleppo

Mosul

Erzerum

Athens

Aegean Sea

Mediterranean Sea

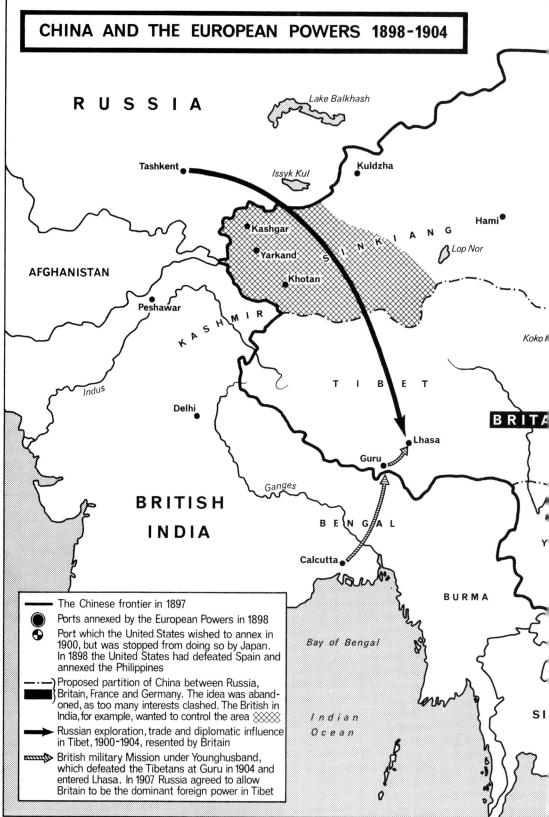

CHINA AND THE EUROPEAN POWERS 1898-1904

RUSSIA

Lake Balkhash

Tashkent

Issyk Kul

Kuldzha

Hami

Kashgar

SINKIANG

Yarkand

Lop Nor

AFGHANISTAN

Khotan

Peshawar

KASHMIR

Koko

Indus

TIBET

Delhi

BRITA

Lhasa

Guru

Ganges

BENGAL

BRITISH

INDIA

Calcutta

BURMA

The Chinese frontier in 1897

Ports annexed by the European Powers in 1898

Port which the United States wished to annex in 1900, but was stopped from doing so by Japan. In 1898 the United States had defeated Spain and annexed the Philippines

Proposed partition of China between Russia, Britain, France and Germany. The idea was abandoned, as too many interests clashed. The British in India, for example, wanted to control the area ⬦⬦⬦

Russian exploration, trade and diplomatic influence in Tibet, 1900-1904, resented by Britain

British military Mission under Younghusband, which defeated the Tibetans at Guru in 1904 and entered Lhasa. In 1907 Russia agreed to allow Britain to be the dominant foreign power in Tibet

Bay of Bengal

Indian Ocean

SI

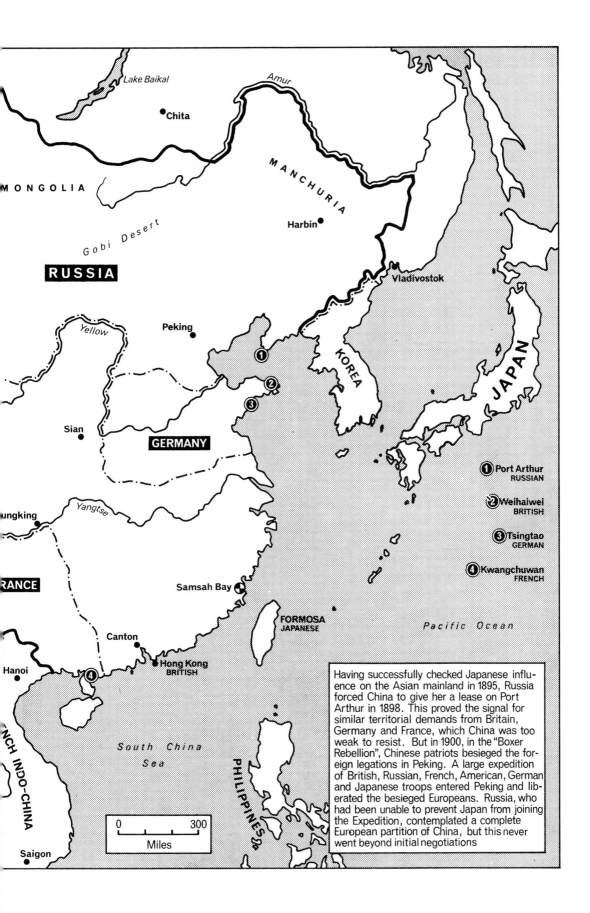

Lake Baikal

Amur

•Chita

M A N C H U R I A

MONGOLIA

Harbin•

Gobi Desert

RUSSIA

Vladivostok

Yellow

Peking

① KOREA

②

Sian •

③

GERMANY

JAPAN

① Port Arthur
RUSSIAN

② Weihaiwei
BRITISH

Yangtse

ungking

③ Tsingtao
GERMAN

④ Kwangchuwan
FRENCH

RANCE

Samsah Bay

FORMOSA
JAPANESE

Pacific Ocean

Canton •

Hanoi •

④

Hong Kong
BRITISH

South China
Sea

PHILIPPINES

Having successfully checked Japanese influence on the Asian mainland in 1895, Russia forced China to give her a lease on Port Arthur in 1898. This proved the signal for similar territorial demands from Britain, Germany and France, which China was too weak to resist. But in 1900, in the "Boxer Rebellion", Chinese patriots besieged the foreign legations in Peking. A large expedition of British, Russian, French, American, German and Japanese troops entered Peking and liberated the besieged Europeans. Russia, who had been unable to prevent Japan from joining the Expedition, contemplated a complete European partition of China, but this never went beyond initial negotiations

NCH INDO-CHINA

Saigon •

0   300

Miles

RUSSIA AND JAPAN IN THE FAR EAST 1860-1895

Kamchatka: part of Russia in 1650. Since 1750 used largely as a place of exile for criminals and political prisoners. Russian schoolboys were often threatened that slackers would be "sent to Kamchatka"–the furthest corner of the classroom. The peninsula has over 20 active volcanoes.

The struggle between Russia and Japan in the Far East was long and bitter. In 1860 Russia acquired an outlet on the Sea of Japan. The Japanese at once adopted a forward policy in China and Korea. When Japan defeated China in 1895 she expected to make wide territorial gains. But Russia, France, Britain and Germany combined to deprive Japan of the fruits of victory. This led to deep anti-Russian resentment throughout Japan. Throughout this period, European penetration in south China continued unabated.

SIBERIA

KAMCHATKA

Sea of Okhotsk

Petropavlovsk

RUSSIA

– Amur

EASTERN

Nikolaevsk

SAKHALIN

MANCHURIA

Khabarosvk

KURILE ISLANDS

Uruppu

Harbin

Sungari

Ussuri

Etorofu

Changchun

Kirin

Mukden

Vladivostok

Peking

Yalu

Sea of Japan

J A P A N

Pacific

Tientsin

Port Arthur

Wonsan

Weihaiwei

Seoul

Inchon

KOREA

Ocean

Tsingtao

Yellow Sea

Pusan

Yellow

Nanking

Hankow

Shanghai

0   500

Miles

Yangtse

Oshima

Territory annexed by Russia from China in 1858-1860

Okinawa

Islands annexed by Japan from China in 1874

Macao (Portuguese 1557)

Kowloon (British 1861)

RYUKYU ISLANDS

Islands annexed by Japan in return for Russian control of Sakhalin

⊙ **Korean ports open, as the result of Japanese pressure, to Japanese trade 1876-1878**

Hongkong (British 1841)

FORMOSA

Occupied by Japan during the war with China, 1894-95. Russia, France, Britain and Germany combined to prevent Japan keeping any of this territory

South China Sea

PHILIPPINES (Spanish 1521)

Only Chinese territory actually annexed by Japan after the war of 1894-1895

0   300
Miles

WAR DEAD,1904-05
Russian   120,000
Japanese   75,000

R U S S I A

Chita
Nerchinsk
Amur
Nikolaevsk

Argun

M A N C H U R I A

Hailar

Tsitsihar

Khabarovsk

Amur

SAKHALIN

Harbin

Sungari

C H I N A

Mukden

Vladivostok

Yalu

Sea of Japan

Peking

Port Arthur

Seoul

KOREA

J A P A N

Tokyo

Yellow Sea

Tsushima Strait

The Trans-Siberian Railway by 1895

Under increasing Russian control after 1895

Leased by Russia from China in 1898, together with the right to build a railway to Harbin; (completed by 1904)

The Chinese Eastern Railway, controlled by Russia after its completion in 1903

Russian economic penetration. Russia refused to allow Japan a sphere of influence in Korea

Japanese naval and military attacks 1904-1905

Annexed by Japan in 1905

After successfully halting Japanese expansion in 1895, the Russians adopted an active expansionist policy. For 10 years they pressed forward in Manchuria, and discussed the partition of China with the British Government in 1900. But Japan sought revenge for the humiliation of 1895, and in 1902 neutralized Britain by the Anglo-Japanese Alliance. In February 1904, under Russian provocation, Japan attacked Port Arthur. Russia was defeated on land and sea, and a peace treaty was signed in the United States in Sept.1905. The grave demoralization created by Russia's defeat led to a mass of revolutionary outbreaks in Russia, and to a serious weakening of the Tsarist mystique.

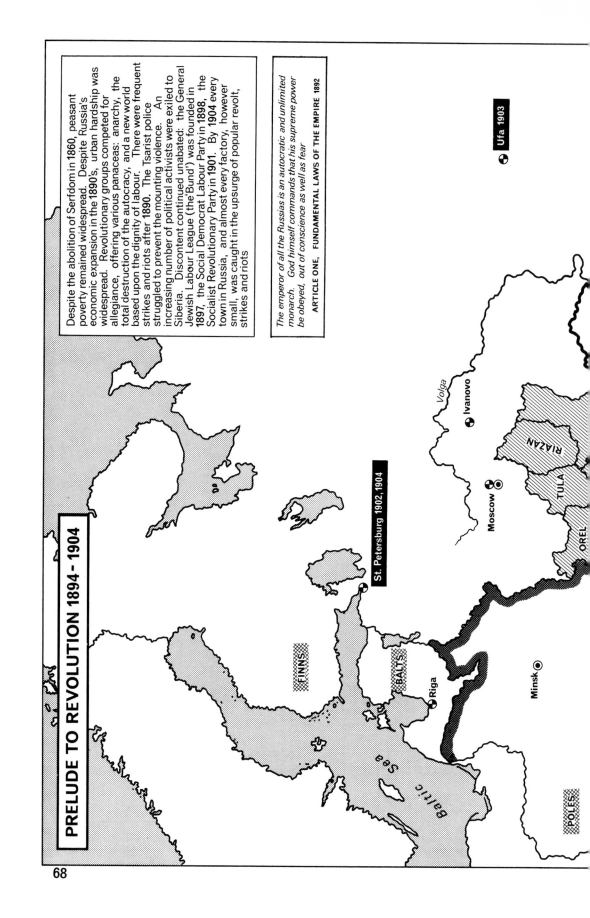

PRELUDE TO REVOLUTION 1894 - 1904

Despite the abolition of Serfdom in 1860, peasant poverty remained widespread. Despite Russia's economic expansion in the 1890's, urban hardship was widespread. Revolutionary groups competed for allegiance, offering various panaceas: anarchy, the total destruction of the autocracy, and a new world based upon the dignity of labour. There were frequent strikes and riots after 1890. The Tsarist police struggled to prevent the mounting violence. An increasing number of political activists were exiled to Siberia. Discontent continued unabated: the General Jewish Labour League (the 'Bund') was founded in 1897, the Social Democrat Labour Party in 1898, the Socialist Revolutionary Party in 1901. By 1904 every town in Russia, and almost every factory, however small, was caught in the upsurge of popular revolt, strikes and riots

The emperor of all the Russias is an autocratic and unlimited monarch. God himself commands that his supreme power be obeyed, out of conscience as well as fear

ARTICLE ONE, FUNDAMENTAL LAWS OF THE EMPIRE 1892

Ufa 1903

Volga

Ivanovo

RIAZAN

Moscow

TULA

OREL

St. Petersburg 1902, 1904

FINNS

BALTS

Riga

Minsk

Baltic Sea

POLES

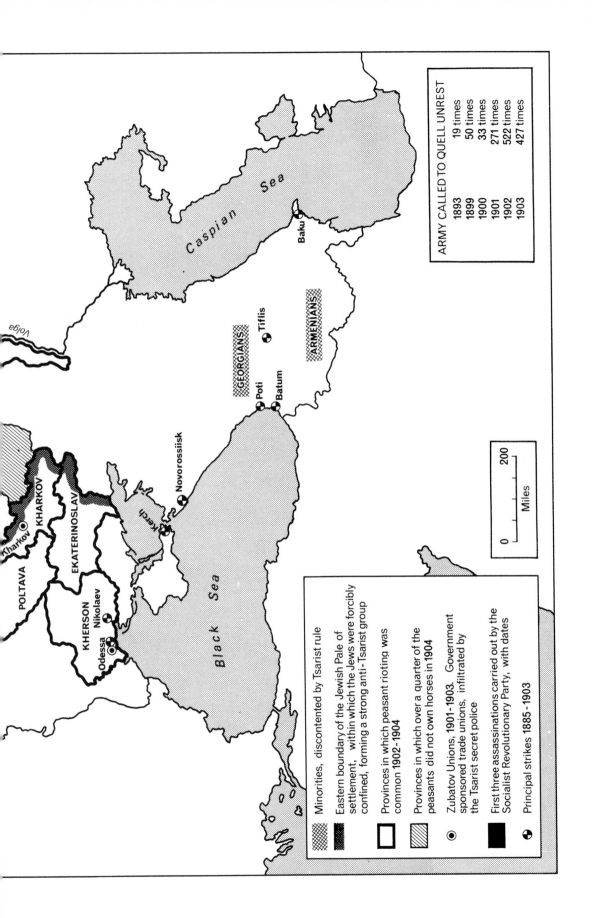

ARMY CALLED TO QUELL UNREST

1893	19 times
1899	50 times
1900	33 times
1901	271 times
1902	522 times
1903	427 times

Volga

Caspian Sea

Baku

GEORGIANS

Tiflis

ARMENIANS

Poti
Batum

Novorossiisk

Kerch

POLTAVA

Kharkov

KHARKOV

EKATERINOSLAV

KHERSON
Nikolaev

Odessa

Black Sea

0   200

Miles

Minorities, discontented by Tsarist rule

Eastern boundary of the Jewish Pale of settlement, within which the Jews were forcibly confined, forming a strong anti-Tsarist group

Provinces in which peasant rioting was common 1902-1904

Provinces in which over a quarter of the peasants did not own horses in 1904

Zubatov Unions, 1901-1903. Government sponsored trade unions, infiltrated by the Tsarist secret police

First three assassinations carried out by the Socialist Revolutionary Party, with dates

Principal strikes 1885-1903

THE JEWS AND THEIR ENEMIES 1648–1917

1903
1906 St. Petersburg
Tsarskoye Selo 1905

1891. 2,000 Jews depor
many of them in chains

Dusiata

Mogilev

Minsk   Starodub

Bialystok   Gomel

Sedlits   Konotop
                Nezhin
Lodz   Kiev
Czestochowa
            Zhitomir   Pereyaslavl   Sm

Berlin
1911   Elizavetgra
                                  Balta
Xanten   Anana
GERMANY   Nikolaevk
            Brest-   Kishinev
            Litovsk   Odessa

Tisza-
Eszlar

AUSTRIA - HUNGARY

RUMANIA

Baltic Sea

BULGARIA

Area in which the Ukrainian peasantry,
led by Bogdan Khmelnitski, massacred
over 100,000 Jews 1648-1656

The Pale of Settlement inside Russia, to
which Russian Jews were confined by law
1815-1917. Of Russia's 5 million Jews
in 1880, only 300,000 had managed to
live outside, mostly illegally

Principal mob attacks, or "pogroms",
against Jews, 1871-1906

Ritual murder charges, in Russia and
elsewhere, in which Jews were accused
of using the blood of Christian children
to mix with their Passover bread. These
charges led to harsh mob violence
against the Jews

Publishing centres before 1917 of the anti-
semitic forgery, "Protocols of Zion", which
claimed to be the Jewish plan for world
domination

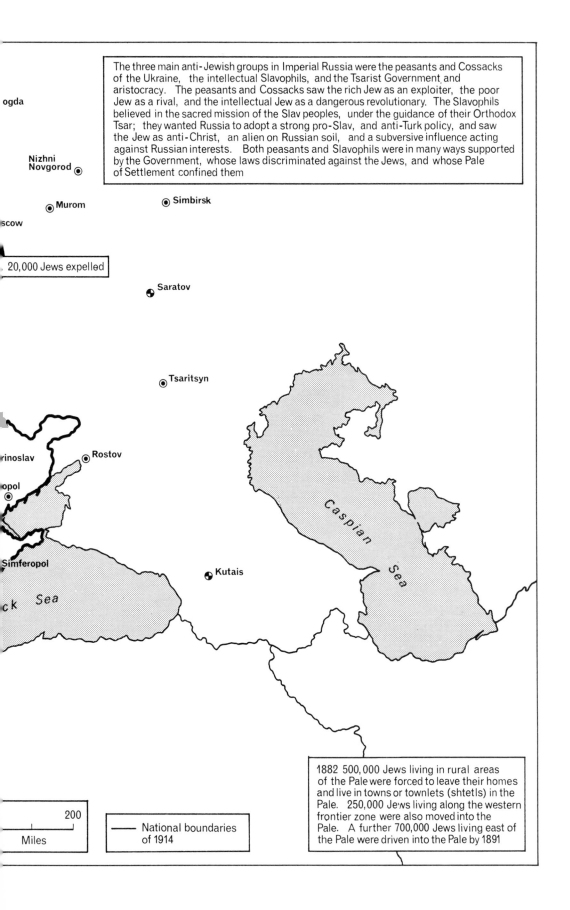

The three main anti-Jewish groups in Imperial Russia were the peasants and Cossacks of the Ukraine, the intellectual Slavophils, and the Tsarist Government and aristocracy. The peasants and Cossacks saw the rich Jew as an exploiter, the poor Jew as a rival, and the intellectual Jew as a dangerous revolutionary. The Slavophils believed in the sacred mission of the Slav peoples, under the guidance of their Orthodox Tsar; they wanted Russia to adopt a strong pro-Slav, and anti-Turk policy, and saw the Jew as anti-Christ, an alien on Russian soil, and a subversive influence acting against Russian interests. Both peasants and Slavophils were in many ways supported by the Government, whose laws discriminated against the Jews, and whose Pale of Settlement confined them

ogda

Nizhni
Novgorod ◉

◉ Simbirsk

◉ Murom

scow

20,000 Jews expelled

◉ Saratov

◉ Tsaritsyn

rinoslav

◉ Rostov

opol
◉

Simferopol

◉ Kutais

Caspian Sea

ck Sea

200

Miles

—— National boundaries
of 1914

1882 500,000 Jews living in rural areas
of the Pale were forced to leave their homes
and live in towns or townlets (shtetls) in the
Pale. 250,000 Jews living along the western
frontier zone were also moved into the
Pale. A further 700,000 Jews living east of
the Pale were driven into the Pale by 1891

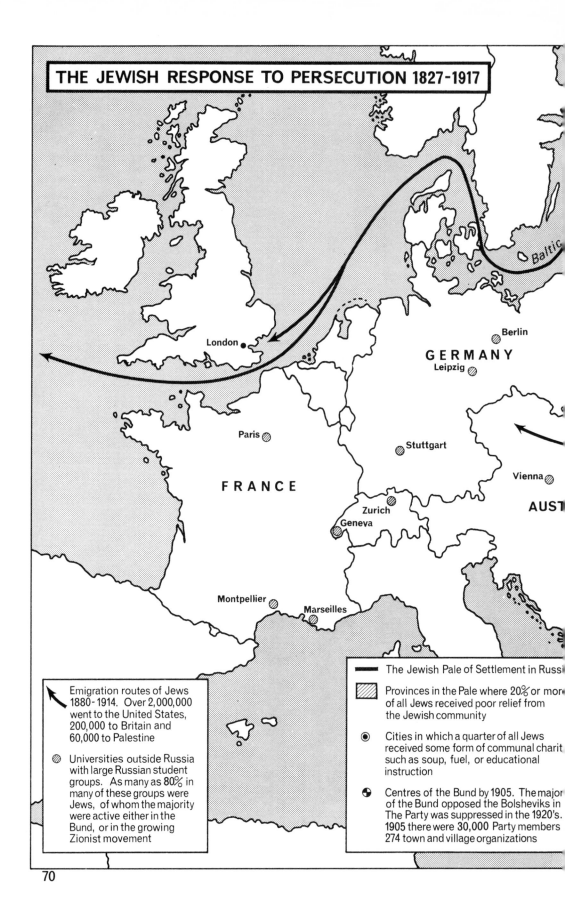

THE JEWISH RESPONSE TO PERSECUTION 1827-1917

Baltic

Berlin

GERMANY

Leipzig

London

Paris

Stuttgart

Vienna

FRANCE

AUST

Zurich

Geneva

Montpellier

Marseilles

The Jewish Pale of Settlement in Russi

Provinces in the Pale where 20% or mor
of all Jews received poor relief from
the Jewish community

Emigration routes of Jews
1880-1914. Over 2,000,000
went to the United States,
200,000 to Britain and
60,000 to Palestine

Cities in which a quarter of all Jews
received some form of communal charit
such as soup, fuel, or educational
instruction

Universities outside Russia
with large Russian student
groups. As many as 80% in
many of these groups were
Jews, of whom the majority
were active either in the
Bund, or in the growing
Zionist movement

Centres of the Bund by 1905. The major
of the Bund opposed the Bolsheviks in
The Party was suppressed in the 1920's.
1905 there were 30,000 Party members
274 town and village organizations

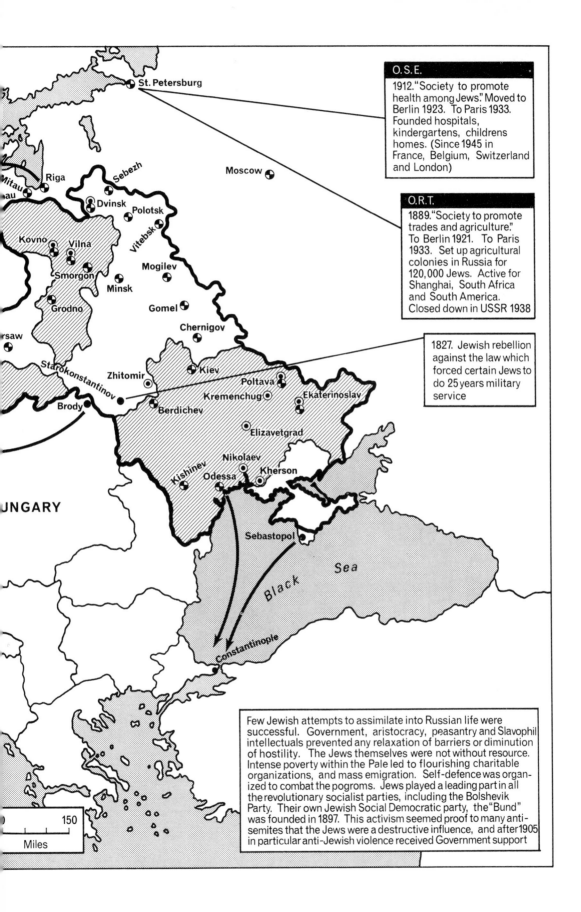

St. Petersburg

Moscow

O.S.E.

1912. "Society to promote health among Jews." Moved to Berlin 1923. To Paris 1933. Founded hospitals, kindergartens, childrens homes. (Since 1945 in France, Belgium, Switzerland and London)

Riga

Sebezh

Mitau
au

Dvinsk

Polotsk

O.R.T.

1889. "Society to promote trades and agriculture." To Berlin 1921. To Paris 1933. Set up agricultural colonies in Russia for 120,000 Jews. Active for Shanghai, South Africa and South America. Closed down in USSR 1938

Kovno

Vilna

Vitebsk

Mogilev

Smorgon

Minsk

Grodno

Gomel

Chernigov

1827. Jewish rebellion against the law which forced certain Jews to do 25 years military service

rsaw

Starokonstantinov

Zhitomir

Kiev

Poltava

Kremenchug

Ekaterinoslav

Brody

Berdichev

Elizavetgrad

Kishinev

Nikolaev

Odessa

Kherson

UNGARY

Sebastopol

Black Sea

Constantinople

Few Jewish attempts to assimilate into Russian life were successful. Government, aristocracy, peasantry and Slavophil intellectuals prevented any relaxation of barriers or diminution of hostility. The Jews themselves were not without resource. Intense poverty within the Pale led to flourishing charitable organizations, and mass emigration. Self-defence was organized to combat the pogroms. Jews played a leading part in all the revolutionary socialist parties, including the Bolshevik Party. Their own Jewish Social Democratic party, the "Bund" was founded in 1897. This activism seemed proof to many anti-semites that the Jews were a destructive influence, and after 1905 in particular anti-Jewish violence received Government support

150

Miles

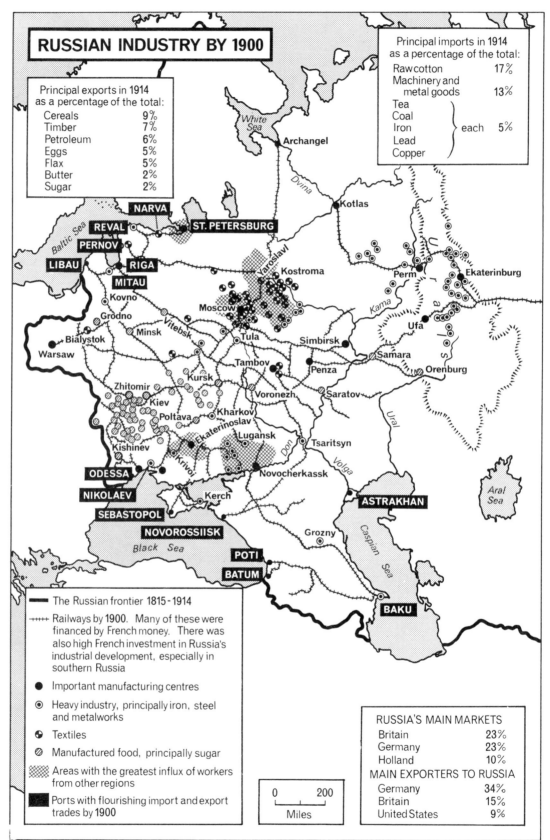

RUSSIAN INDUSTRY BY 1900

Principal exports in 1914
as a percentage of the total:

Cereals	9%
Timber	7%
Petroleum	6%
Eggs	5%
Flax	5%
Butter	2%
Sugar	2%

Principal imports in 1914
as a percentage of the total:

Raw cotton	17%
Machinery and metal goods	13%
Tea	
Coal	
Iron	each 5%
Lead	
Copper	

White Sea

Archangel

Dvina

Kotlas

NARVA

REVAL

PERNOV

ST. PETERSBURG

Baltic Sea

LIBAU

RIGA

MITAU

Kovno

Yaroslavl

Kostroma

Perm

Ekaterinburg

Grodno

Minsk

Vitebsk

Moscow

Kama

Ufa

Bialystok

Warsaw

Tula

Simbirsk

Samara

Orenburg

Kursk

Tambov

Penza

Zhitomir

Kiev

Poltava

Voronezh

Saratov

Kharkov

Kishinev

Krivoi

Ekaterinoslav

Lugansk

Don

Tsaritsyn

Volga

Ural

Aral Sea

ODESSA

NIKOLAEV

Kerch

Novocherkassk

SEBASTOPOL

ASTRAKHAN

NOVOROSSIISK

Black Sea

Grozny

Caspian Sea

POTI

BATUM

BAKU

—— The Russian frontier 1815-1914

++++ Railways by 1900. Many of these were
financed by French money. There was
also high French investment in Russia's
industrial development, especially in
southern Russia

● Important manufacturing centres

◉ Heavy industry, principally iron, steel
and metalworks

◕ Textiles

⊘ Manufactured food, principally sugar

▓ Areas with the greatest influx of workers
from other regions

▓ Ports with flourishing import and export
trades by 1900

0   200

Miles

RUSSIA'S MAIN MARKETS

Britain	23%
Germany	23%
Holland	10%

MAIN EXPORTERS TO RUSSIA

Germany	34%
Britain	15%
United States	9%

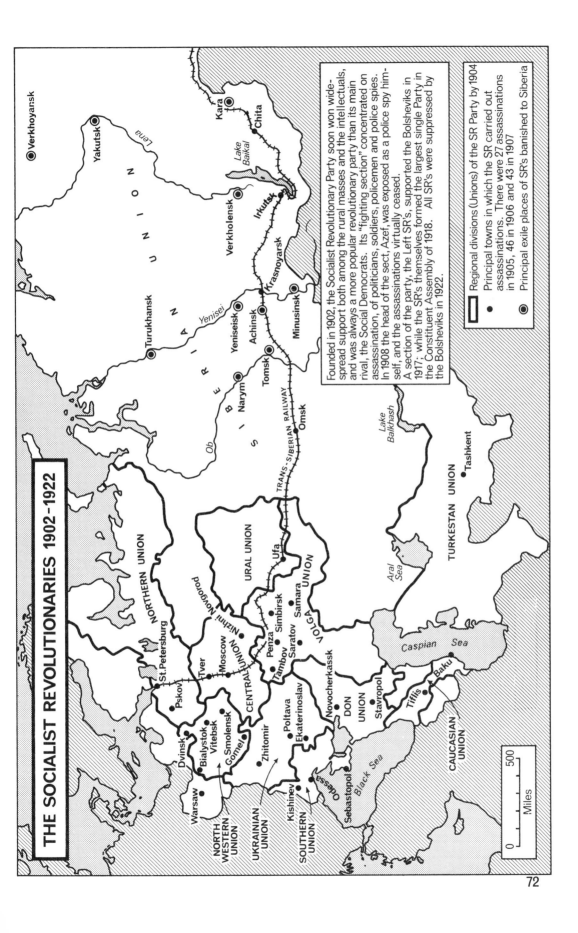

THE SOCIALIST REVOLUTIONARIES 1902–1922

Founded in 1902, the Socialist Revolutionary Party soon won widespread support both among the rural masses and the intellectuals, and was always a more popular revolutionary party than its main rival, the Social Democrats. Its "fighting section" concentrated on assassination, of politicians, soldiers, policemen and police spies. In 1908 the head of the sect, Azef, was exposed as a police spy himself, and the assassinations virtually ceased. A section of the party, the Left SR's, supported the Bolsheviks in 1917; while the SR's themselves formed the largest single Party in the Constituent Assembly of 1918. All SR's were suppressed by the Bolsheviks in 1922.

☐ Regional divisions (Unions) of the SR Party by 1904

• Principal towns in which the SR carried out assassinations. There were 27 assassinations in 1905, 46 in 1906 and 43 in 1907

◉ Principal exile places of SR's banished to Siberia

Verkhoyansk

Yakutsk

Lena

Kara

Chita

Lake Baikal

Verkholensk

Irkutsk

Krasnoyarsk

Minusinsk

Turukhansk

Yenisei

Yeniseisk

Achinsk

Narym

Tomsk

Omsk

TRANS-SIBERIAN RAILWAY

Ob

S I B E R I A

U N I O N

Lake Balkhash

Lake Balkhash

TURKESTAN UNION

Tashkent

Aral Sea

Caspian Sea

NORTHERN UNION

Nizhni Novgorod

URAL UNION

Ufa

VOLGA UNION

St. Petersburg

Tver

Moscow

CENTRAL UNION

Pskov

Penza

Tambov

Simbirsk

Saratov

Samara

Novocherkassk

DON UNION

Stavropol

Tiflis

Baku

CAUCASIAN UNION

Dvinsk

Bialystok

Vitebsk

Gomel

Smolensk

Zhitomir

Poltava

Ekaterinoslav

Warsaw

NORTH WESTERN UNION

UKRAINIAN UNION

Kishinev

SOUTHERN UNION

Odessa

Sebastopol

Black Sea

0   500

Miles

72

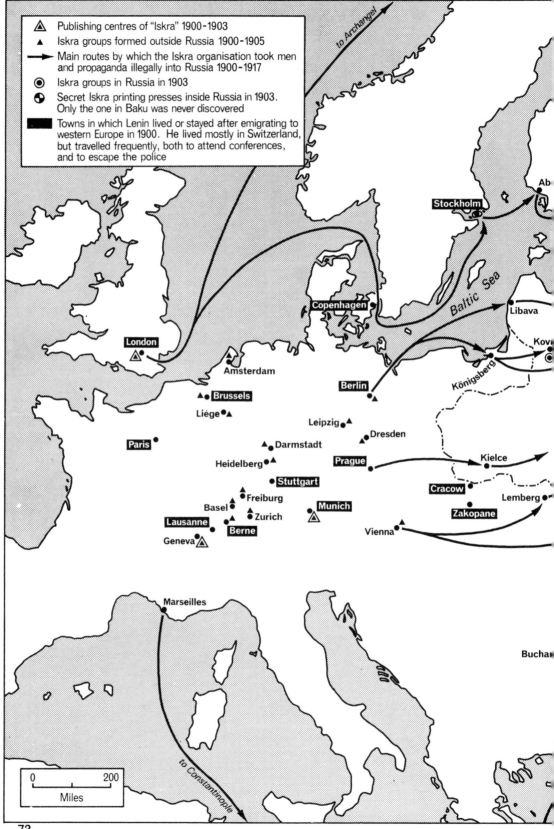

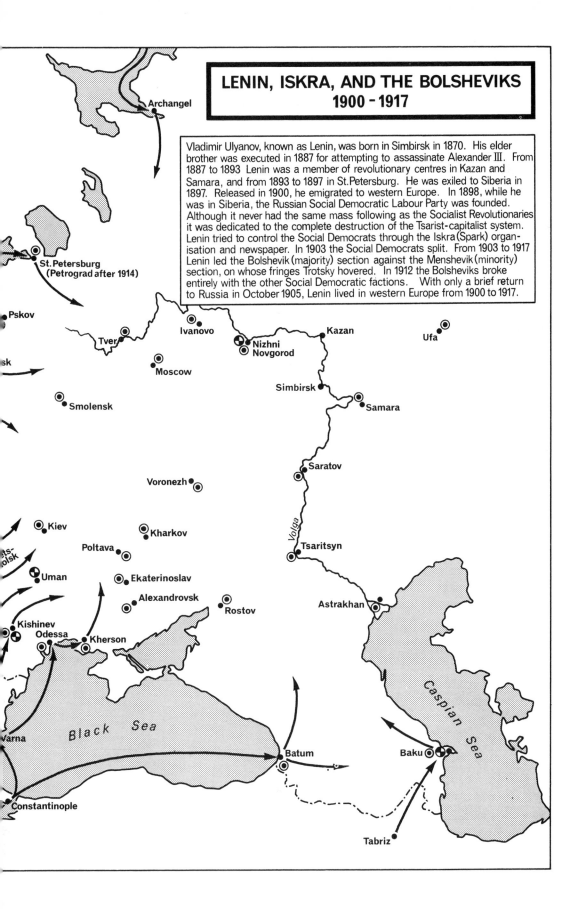

LENIN, ISKRA, AND THE BOLSHEVIKS 1900 - 1917

Vladimir Ulyanov, known as Lenin, was born in Simbirsk in 1870. His elder brother was executed in 1887 for attempting to assassinate Alexander III. From 1887 to 1893 Lenin was a member of revolutionary centres in Kazan and Samara, and from 1893 to 1897 in St.Petersburg. He was exiled to Siberia in 1897. Released in 1900, he emigrated to western Europe. In 1898, while he was in Siberia, the Russian Social Democratic Labour Party was founded. Although it never had the same mass following as the Socialist Revolutionaries it was dedicated to the complete destruction of the Tsarist-capitalist system. Lenin tried to control the Social Democrats through the Iskra (Spark) organisation and newspaper. In 1903 the Social Democrats split. From 1903 to 1917 Lenin led the Bolshevik (majority) section against the Menshevik (minority) section, on whose fringes Trotsky hovered. In 1912 the Bolsheviks broke entirely with the other Social Democratic factions. With only a brief return to Russia in October 1905, Lenin lived in western Europe from 1900 to 1917.

Archangel

St.Petersburg
(Petrograd after 1914)

Pskov

Tver

Ivanovo

Nizhni
Novgorod

Kazan

Ufa

Moscow

Smolensk

Simbirsk

Samara

Saratov

Voronezh

Volga

Kiev

Kharkov

Poltava

Tsaritsyn

Uman

Ekaterinoslav

Alexandrovsk

Rostov

Astrakhan

Kishinev
Odessa

Kherson

Black Sea

Caspian Sea

Varna

Batum

Baku

Constantinople

Tabriz

THE PROVINCES AND POPULATION OF EUROPEAN RUSSIA IN 1900

White Sea

NORWAY

ARCHANGEL

FINLAND

SWEDEN

VOLOGDA

OLONETS

Baltic Sea

ESTLAND

ST PETERSBURG

NOVGOROD

KOSTROMA

PERM

VIATKA

KURLAND

LIVLAND

PSKOV

YAROSLAVL

KOVNO

VITEBSK

TVER

GERMANY

VILNA

SMOLENSK

MOSCOW

VLADIMIR

NIZHNII NOVGOROD

KAZAN

UFA

GRODNO

MOGILEV

KALUGA

TULA

RIAZAN

PENZA

SIMBIRSK

POLISH PROVINCES

MINSK

OREL

ORENBURG

CHERNIGOV

TAMBOV

SARATOV

SAMARA

VOLHYNIA

KIEV

POLTAVA

KURSK

AUSTRIA-HUNGARY

PODOLIA

VORONEZH

BESSARABIA

KHARKOV

KHERSON

EKATERINOSLAV

DON

ASTRAKHAN

RUMANIA

TAURIDA

Caspian Sea

KUBAN

STAVROPOL

Black Sea

TEREK

TURKEY

TRANS-CAUCASIAN PROVINCES

PERSIA

The first official Russian census was held in 1897. The total population was just over 129 million - nearly as large as the combined populations of Britain, France, and Germany. Over 80% of all Russians were peasants. Finland was an autonomous Duchy, and, like Poland, was subdivided into Provinces

MAIN NATIONAL & ETHNIC GROUPS IN EUROPEAN RUSSIA IN 1900	
Russians	55 million
Ukrainians	22 million
Poles	8 million
White Russians	6 million
Jews	5 million
Balts	4 million
Caucasians	3 million
Germans	2 million

THE 1905 REVOLUTION IN THE COUNTRYSIDE

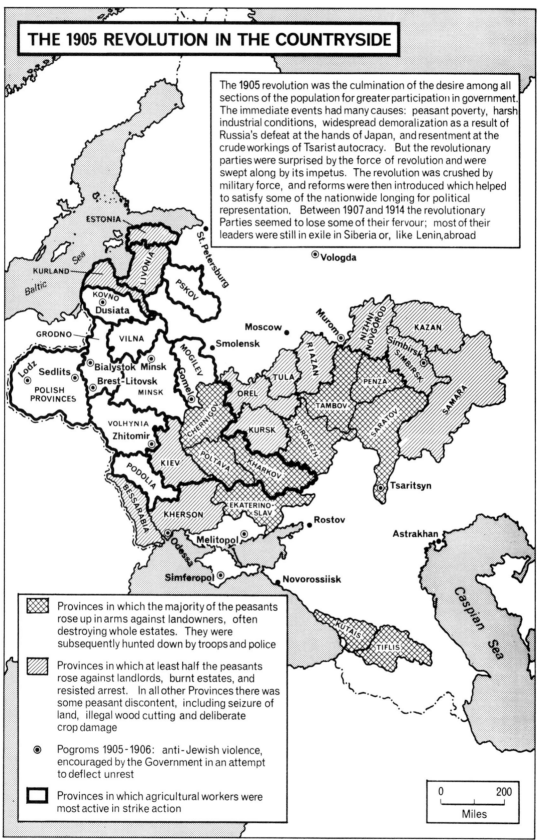

The 1905 revolution was the culmination of the desire among all sections of the population for greater participation in government. The immediate events had many causes: peasant poverty, harsh industrial conditions, widespread demoralization as a result of Russia's defeat at the hands of Japan, and resentment at the crude workings of Tsarist autocracy. But the revolutionary parties were surprised by the force of revolution and were swept along by its impetus. The revolution was crushed by military force, and reforms were then introduced which helped to satisfy some of the nationwide longing for political representation. Between 1907 and 1914 the revolutionary Parties seemed to lose some of their fervour; most of their leaders were still in exile in Siberia or, like Lenin, abroad

Vologda

ESTONIA
St Petersburg
KURLAND
LIVONIA
Baltic Sea
PSKOV
KOVNO
Dusiata
GRODNO
VILNA
Moscow
Smolensk
Murom
NIZHNI-NOVGOROD
KAZAN
SIMBIRSK
Lodz
Sedlits
Bialystok Minsk
MOGILEV
Gomel
RIAZAN
SIMBIRSK
POLISH
PROVINCES
Brest-Litovsk
MINSK
TULA
PENZA
SAMARA
OREL
TAMBOV
VOLHYNIA
Zhitomir
CHERNIGOV
KURSK
VORONEZH
SARATOV
KIEV
POLTAVA
KHARKOV
PODOLIA
Tsaritsyn
BESSARABIA
KHERSON
EKATERINO-SLAV
Rostov
Astrakhan
Odessa
Melitopol
Caspian Sea
Simferopol
Novorossiisk
KUTAIS
TIFLIS

Provinces in which the majority of the peasants rose up in arms against landowners, often destroying whole estates. They were subsequently hunted down by troops and police

Provinces in which at least half the peasants rose against landlords, burnt estates, and resisted arrest. In all other Provinces there was some peasant discontent, including seizure of land, illegal wood cutting and deliberate crop damage

Pogroms 1905-1906: anti-Jewish violence, encouraged by the Government in an attempt to deflect unrest

Provinces in which agricultural workers were most active in strike action

0   200
Miles

THE 1905 REVOLUTION IN THE TOWNS

BLOODY SUNDAY : ST. PETERSBURG

200,000 people gathered at the Winter Palace on 9 January 1905. Unarmed, they wished to appeal to Tsar Nicholas II for better working conditions and an end to the war with Japan. Their main plea was for elections based upon universal suffrage. It was a Sunday. Many carried ikons. But the Tsar had left the city, and troops fired on the crowd. As many as 500 people were killed, and over 3,000 wounded

Russian State Expenditure 1903 - 13
(in million roubles)

The war with Japan	3,016
Railways	886
Defence	455
Bad harvests	403
Redemption of loans before due date	199
Ports	24
Military expeditions (China and Persia)	20

- Principal strike centres, 1905 - 1906, encouraged by all the revolutionary Parties. By December 1905 every town in Russia had suffered from industrial unrest

- Revolutionary outbreaks in the Army and the Fleet; although these were widespread, the Army remained sufficiently loyal to the Tsar to crush the revolution by the end of 1906

- National groups who wanted a greater degree of autonomy and national recognition, and were particularly active in revolutionary activity At this time the Ukrainians, for example, were not allowed a single newspaper in their own language

- Uprisings in December 1905, suppressed by armed force

THE BATTLESHIP POTEMKIN

In the late summer of 1905 the crew of the Potemkin seized control of the ship, and for some months terrorized the Black Sea ports, even bombarding Odessa. They finally sought refuge in Rumania, where the ship was interned

BALTS

POLES

UKRAINIANS

GEORGIANS

ARMENIANS

Miles
0   200

Zlatoust
Ufa
Perm
Samara
Kazan
Saratov
Tsaritsyn
Astrakhan
Nizhnii Novgorod
Vologda
Yaroslavl
Tver
Moscow
Kolomna
Tula
Voronezh
Belgorod
St. Petersburg
Kronstadt
Narva
Helsingfors
Reval
Riga
Dvinsk
Libau
Vilna
Suvalki
Warsaw
Lodz
Lublin
Rovno
Kiev
Nikolaev
Odessa
Ekaterinoslav
Rostov
Sebastopol
Feodosia
Novorossisk
Sochi
Batum
Kars
Tiflis
Baku
Grozny
Krasnovodsk
Piatigorsk
Maikop
Mineralnye Vody
Stavropol
Armavir
Ekaterinodar
RUMANIA
Black Sea
Caspian Sea
Baltic Sea

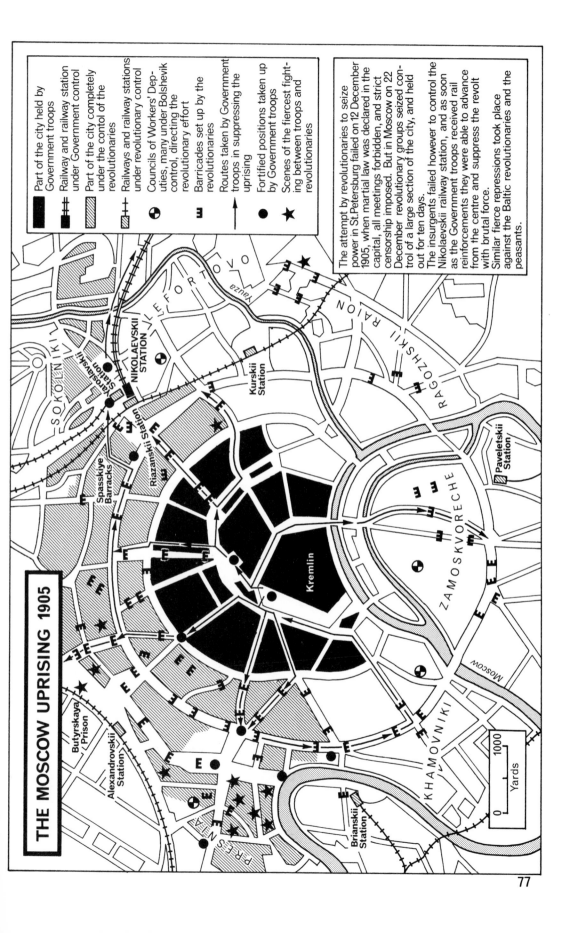

THE MOSCOW UPRISING 1905

Legend:

- Part of the city held by Government troops
- Railway and railway station under Government control
- Part of the city completely under the control of the revolutionaries
- Railways and railway stations under revolutionary control
- Councils of Workers' Deputies, many under Bolshevik control, directing the revolutionary effort
- Barricades set up by the revolutionaries
- Routes taken by Government troops in suppressing the uprising
- Fortified positions taken up by Government troops
- Scenes of the fiercest fighting between troops and revolutionaries

The attempt by revolutionaries to seize power in St.Petersburg failed on 12 December 1905, when martial law was declared in the capital, all meetings forbidden, and strict censorship imposed. But in Moscow on 22 December revolutionary groups seized control of a large section of the city, and held out for ten days.

The insurgents failed however to control the Nikolaevskii railway station, and as soon as the Government troops received rail reinforcements they were able to advance from the centre and suppress the revolt with brutal force.

Similar fierce repressions took place against the Baltic revolutionaries and the peasants.

Butyrskaya Prison

Alexandrovskii Station

SOKOLNIKI

LEFORTOVO

Yauza

Yaroslavskii Station

NIKOLAEVSKII STATION

Kurskii Station

Spasskiye Barracks

Riazanskii Station

RAGOZHSKII RAION

Kremlin

ZAMOSKVORECHE

PRESNIA

KHAMOVNIKI

Moscow

Brianskii Station

Paveletskii Station

0   1000
Yards

77

RUSSIA AND THE BALKANS 1876-1885

0   100
Miles

Russia wanted to drive the Turk from Europe and dominate the Balkans. Britain supported Russian protests against Turkish atrocities against the Bulgarians in 1875, which led Russia to attack Turkey. After defeating the Turks at Plevna in 1876 Russia tried to set up a large independent Bulgaria, but Britain and Austria-Hungary challenged Russia's aspirations, and under German mediation Russia agreed to the creation of a much smaller Bulgaria. Austria advanced her own Balkan interests by occupying the former Turkish province of Bosnia, which she formally annexed in 1908, and entering Novi Pazar.

RUSSIA

AUSTRIA-HUNGARY

BOSNIA

Sarajevo

Belgrade

SERBIA

NOVI PAZAR

Nish

Cattaro

MONTENEGRO

Skopje

MACEDONIA

Adriatic Sea

RUMANIA

Bucharest

Danube

Constanza

Plevna

BULGARIA

Silistria

Varna

Tirnovo

Sofia

Burgas

EAST RUMELIA

Black Sea

Midia

Adrianople

Constantinople

Kavalla

Rodosto

San Stephano

Dedeagatch

Chanak

Aegean Sea

TURKEY – IN – ASIA

GREECE

Athens

- – - – The boundary of Turkey-in-Europe 1876

Russian proposal for an independent "Big Bulgaria", agreed to by the Turks at the Treaty of San Stephano 1878

Bulgaria, autonomous, not independent, as allowed by Britain and Germany by the Treaty of Berlin 1878

Turkish territory added to Serbia, Rumania and Montenegro (who each gained their independence from Turkey) by the Treaty of Berlin 1878; and to Greece in 1881

Occupied by Austria-Hungary in 1878

Added to Bulgaria in 1885, when Bulgaria became fully independent of Turkey

RUSSIA, THE BALKANS, AND THE COMING OF WAR 1912-1914

0   500

Miles

BRITAIN

North Sea

St. Petersburg

Reval

Baltic Sea

Riga

BALTIC PROVINCES

Moscow

RUSSIA

Danzig

Berlin

Warsaw

Pripet Marshes

GERMANY

Breslau

POLISH PROVINCES

Kiev

VOLHYNIA

Paris

Lemberg

FRANCE

Vienna

Budapest

AUSTRIA - HUNGARY

BOSNIA

Sarajevo

Belgrade

RUMANIA

Black Sea

Adriatic Sea

SERBIA

BULGARIA

Constantinople

MONTENEGRO

ALBANIA

Skopje

Bosphorus

GREECE

Aegean Sea

Dardanelles

TURKEY

Russia's mid-century alignment with Germany was changed during the 1880's to a new alignment with France, while at the same time Austria and Germany drew closer together. In the two Balkan Wars of 1912 and 1913 Turkey was driven almost entirely from Europe, but Russia's position did not improve; for as a result of Turkey's defeat Austrian influence increased even further. In June 1914 a Bosnian Serb murdered the Austrian heir to the throne, Archduke Franz-Ferdinand, at Sarajevo. Austria invaded Serbia on 28 July 1914. Russia then declared war on Austria. Germany supported her ally Austria and declared war on Russia. France and Britain joined Russia against Germany and Austria. Turkey attacked Russia in October 1914

Countries in which Austrian and German influence worked against Russia. Greece had a pro-German King; Turkey a pro-German Minister of War and virtual dictator; Bulgaria and Rumania had both accepted alliance with the Central Powers

Area of Russia in which Germany hoped to expand as a result of war

Russia's only two Balkan Allies, both threatened by Austria. Austria had created the state of Albania in 1912 in order to cut Serbia off from the sea.

Countries in western Europe sympathetic to Russia. France had a military alliance with Russia dating from 1894. Britain a convention dating from 1907

GERMAN WAR AIMS
IN WESTERN RUSSIA
1914–1918

Reval

DAGÖ

ESTONIA

ÖSEL

LIVONIA

Baltic Sea

Riga

Libau

Mitau

Dvinsk

KURLAND

Kovno

WHITE
RUSSIA

Königsberg

Vilna

Danzig

Suwalki

Minsk

EAST
PRUSSIA

Bialystok

Berlin

Bromberg

Mlawa

Brest-
Litovsk

Pinsk

Posen

Warsaw

Kalisz

Lodz

Kovel

GERMANY

UKRAINE

POLAND

Breslau

Lublin

Komarov

Rovno

SILESIA

Kielce

GALICIA

Cracow

Lemberg

– – – Russia's western border in 1914

■ To be annexed by Germany as a
German-Polish frontier zone

▨ To be under German military
administration as a German-
Russian frontier zone

□ The "Tributary State" of Poland,
to be under German economic
and political supervision

▨ The Ukrainian People's Republic,
proclaimed on 16 July 1917. By
March 1918 the Ukrainian government
had fallen almost entirely under
German influence

AUSTRIA–HUNGARY

0   100

Miles

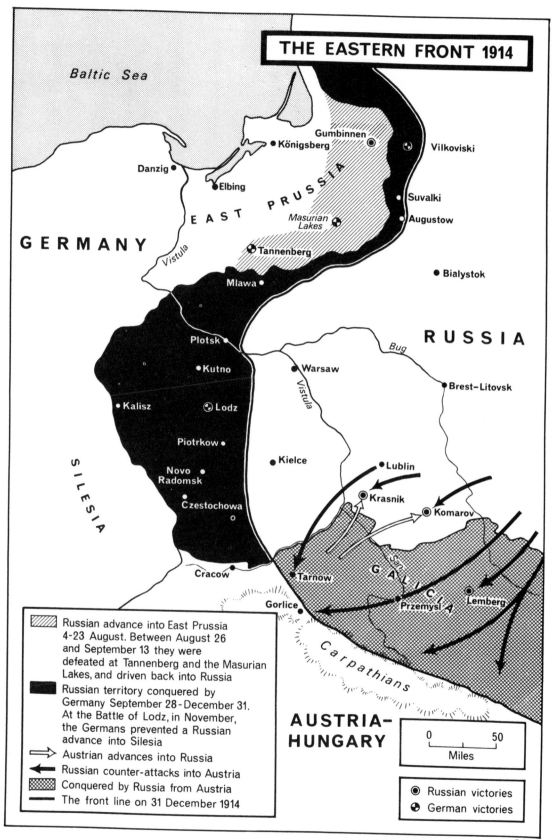

THE EASTERN FRONT 1914

Baltic Sea

GERMANY

EAST PRUSSIA

• Danzig

• Elbing

• Königsberg

Gumbinnen

• Vilkoviski

Masurian Lakes

• Suvalki

• Augustow

Tannenberg

• Mlawa

• Bialystok

RUSSIA

Vistula

• Plotsk

Bug

• Kutno

• Warsaw

• Brest-Litovsk

Vistula

• Kalisz

Lodz

• Piotrkow

• Kielce

SILESIA

Novo Radomsk •

• Lublin

• Czestochowa

Krasnik

Komarov

Cracow

Tarnow

GALICIA

Lemberg

Gorlice

Przemysl

Carpathians

AUSTRIA-HUNGARY

Russian advance into East Prussia 4-23 August. Between August 26 and September 13 they were defeated at Tannenberg and the Masurian Lakes, and driven back into Russia

Russian territory conquered by Germany September 28-December 31. At the Battle of Lodz, in November, the Germans prevented a Russian advance into Silesia

Austrian advances into Russia

Russian counter-attacks into Austria

Conquered by Russia from Austria

The front line on 31 December 1914

| 0 | | 50 |
Miles

Russian victories

German victories

81

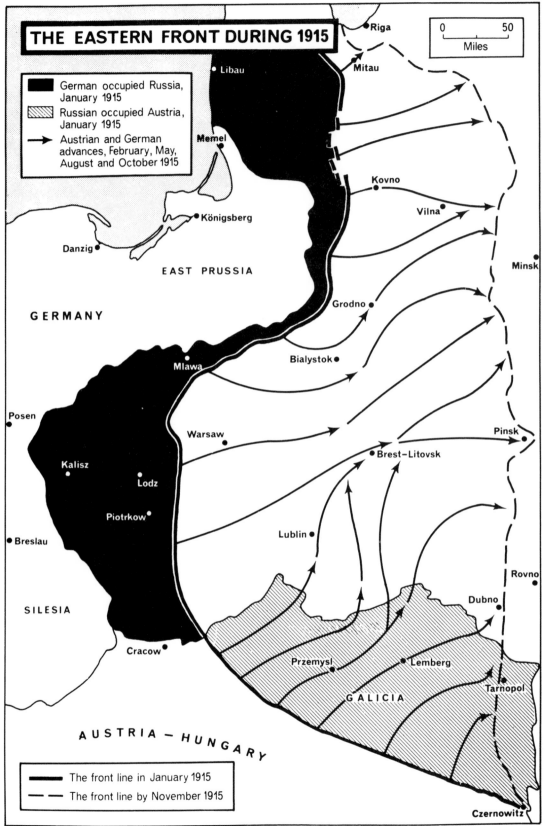

THE EASTERN FRONT DURING 1915

■ German occupied Russia,
January 1915

▨ Russian occupied Austria,
January 1915

→ Austrian and German
advances, February, May,
August and October 1915

0   50
Miles

Riga

Libau

Mitau

Memel

Kovno

Königsberg

Vilna

Danzig

Minsk

EAST PRUSSIA

GERMANY

Grodno

Mlawa

Bialystok

Posen

Warsaw

Pinsk

Kalisz

Lodz

Brest–Litovsk

Piotrkow

Breslau

Lublin

Rovno

SILESIA

Dubno

Cracow

Przemysl

Lemberg

Tarnopol

GALICIA

AUSTRIA – HUNGARY

Czernowitz

━━━ The front line in January 1915

╌╌╌ The front line by November 1915

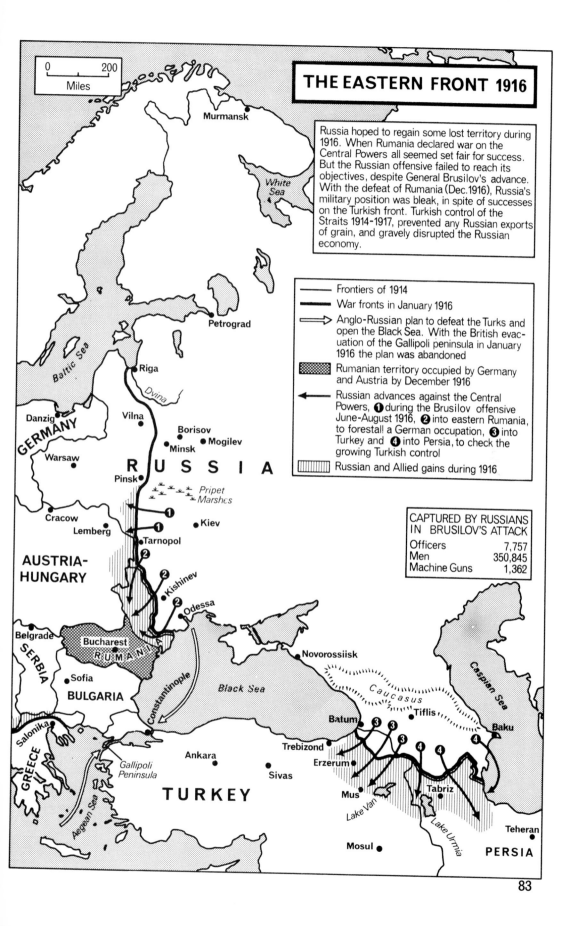

THE EASTERN FRONT 1916

Russia hoped to regain some lost territory during 1916. When Rumania declared war on the Central Powers all seemed set fair for success. But the Russian offensive failed to reach its objectives, despite General Brusilov's advance. With the defeat of Rumania (Dec.1916), Russia's military position was bleak, in spite of successes on the Turkish front. Turkish control of the Straits 1914-1917, prevented any Russian exports of grain, and gravely disrupted the Russian economy.

———	Frontiers of 1914
▬▬▬	War fronts in January 1916
⇨	Anglo-Russian plan to defeat the Turks and open the Black Sea. With the British evacuation of the Gallipoli peninsula in January 1916 the plan was abandoned
▨	Rumanian territory occupied by Germany and Austria by December 1916
←	Russian advances against the Central Powers, ❶during the Brusilov offensive June-August 1916, ❷into eastern Rumania, to forestall a German occupation, ❸into Turkey and ❹into Persia, to check the growing Turkish control
▥	Russian and Allied gains during 1916

CAPTURED BY RUSSIANS
IN BRUSILOV'S ATTACK

Officers	7,757
Men	350,845
Machine Guns	1,362

Murmansk

White Sea

Petrograd

Baltic Sea

Riga

Dvina

Danzig

GERMANY

Vilna

Borisov

Mogilev

Minsk

Warsaw

R U S S I A

Pinsk

Pripet Marshes

❶

Cracow

Lemberg

❶

Kiev

Tarnopol

AUSTRIA-
HUNGARY

❷

❷

Kishinev

❷

Odessa

Belgrade

Bucharest

R U M A N I A

SERBIA

Sofia

BULGARIA

Constantinople

Black Sea

Novorossiisk

Caucasus

Caspian Sea

Tiflis

Batum

Baku

❸

❸

❸

❹

❹

❹

Salonika

GREECE

Gallipoli
Peninsula

Ankara

Sivas

T U R K E Y

Trebizond

Erzerum

Mus

Lake Van

Tabriz

Lake Urmia

Teheran

Aegean Sea

Mosul

PERSIA

83

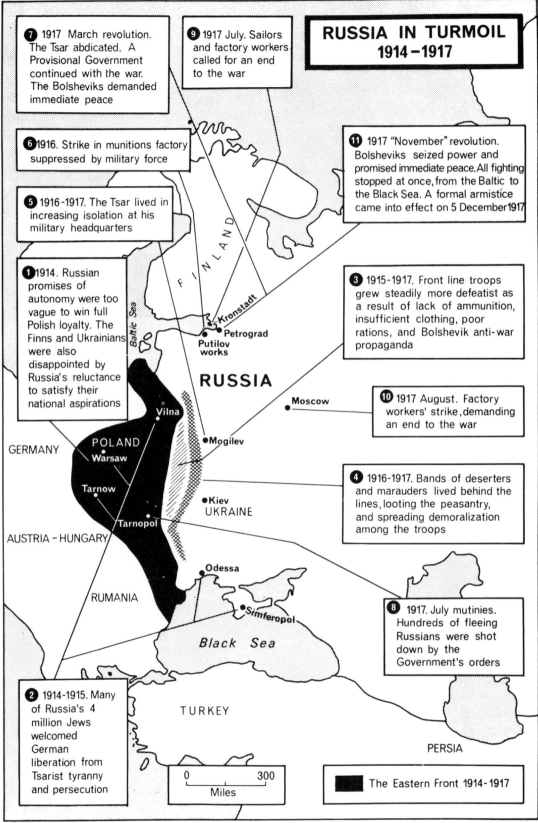

RUSSIA IN TURMOIL 1914 – 1917

7 1917 March revolution. The Tsar abdicated. A Provisional Government continued with the war. The Bolsheviks demanded immediate peace

9 1917 July. Sailors and factory workers called for an end to the war

6 1916. Strike in munitions factory suppressed by military force

11 1917 "November" revolution. Bolsheviks seized power and promised immediate peace. All fighting stopped at once, from the Baltic to the Black Sea. A formal armistice came into effect on 5 December 1917

5 1916-1917. The Tsar lived in increasing isolation at his military headquarters

1 1914. Russian promises of autonomy were too vague to win full Polish loyalty. The Finns and Ukrainians were also disappointed by Russia's reluctance to satisfy their national aspirations

3 1915-1917. Front line troops grew steadily more defeatist as a result of lack of ammunition, insufficient clothing, poor rations, and Bolshevik anti-war propaganda

10 1917 August. Factory workers' strike, demanding an end to the war

4 1916-1917. Bands of deserters and marauders lived behind the lines, looting the peasantry, and spreading demoralization among the troops

8 1917. July mutinies. Hundreds of fleeing Russians were shot down by the Government's orders

2 1914-1915. Many of Russia's 4 million Jews welcomed German liberation from Tsarist tyranny and persecution

FINLAND

Baltic Sea

Kronstadt

Petrograd

Putilov works

RUSSIA

Moscow

Vilna

POLAND

Warsaw

Mogilev

GERMANY

Tarnow

Kiev
UKRAINE

Tarnopol

AUSTRIA – HUNGARY

Odessa

RUMANIA

Simferopol

Black Sea

TURKEY

PERSIA

0   300
Miles

▬ The Eastern Front 1914-1917

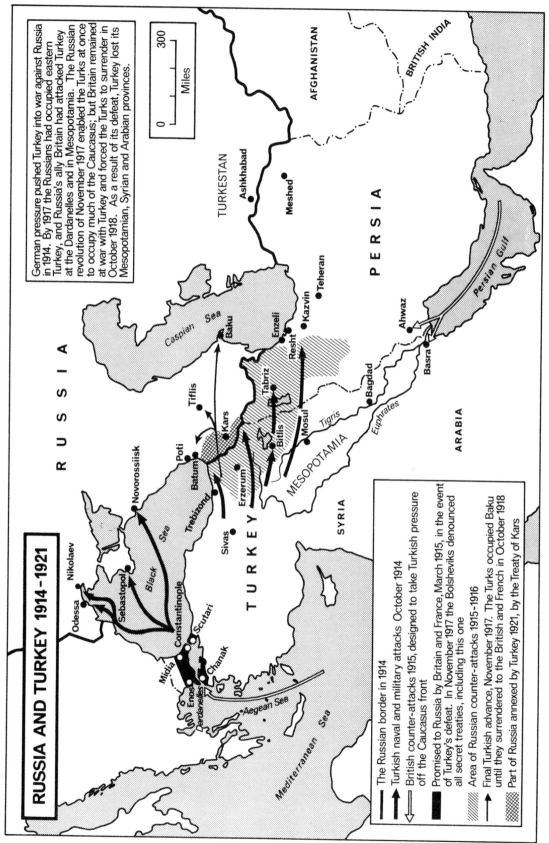

RUSSIA AND TURKEY 1914-1921

German pressure pushed Turkey into war against Russia in 1914. By 1917 the Russians had occupied eastern Turkey, and Russia's ally Britain had attacked Turkey at the Dardanelles and in Mesopotamia. The Russian revolution of November 1917 enabled the Turks at once to occupy much of the Caucasus; but Britain remained at war with Turkey and forced the Turks to surrender in October 1918. As a result of its defeat, Turkey lost its Mesopotamian, Syrian and Arabian provinces.

0   300

Miles

AFGHANISTAN

BRITISH INDIA

TURKESTAN

Ashkhabad

Meshed

P E R S I A

Teheran

Kazvin

Enzeli

Baku

Caspian Sea

Resht

Tabriz

Tiflis

R U S S I A

Kars

Bitlis

Mosul

Ahwaz

Persian Gulf

Basra

Bagdad

Tigris

Euphrates

MESOPOTAMIA

Erzerum

Battum

Poti

ARABIA

Novorossiisk

Trebizond

Sivas

SYRIA

Black Sea

Sebastopol

T U R K E Y

Nikolaev

Odessa

Constantinople

Scutari

Midia

Chanak

Enos

Dardanelles

Aegean Sea

Mediterranean Sea

The Russian border in 1914

Turkish naval and military attacks October 1914

British counter-attacks 1915, designed to take Turkish pressure off the Caucasus front

Promised to Russia by Britain and France, March 1915, in the event of Turkey's defeat. In November 1917 the Bolsheviks denounced all secret treaties, including this one

Area of Russian counter-attacks 1915-1916

Final Turkish advance, November 1917. The Turks occupied Baku until they surrendered to the British and French in October 1918

Part of Russia annexed by Turkey 1921, by the Treaty of Kars

85

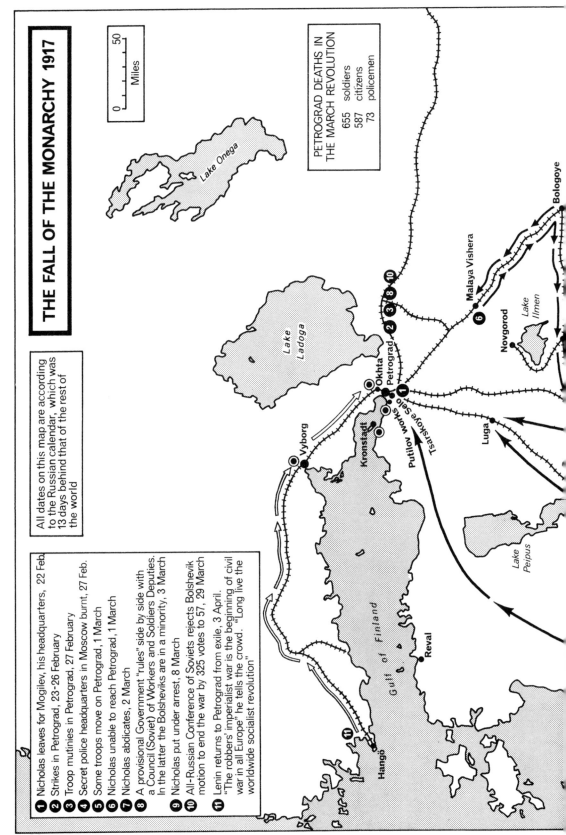

THE FALL OF THE MONARCHY 1917

0 50
Miles

Lake Onega

PETROGRAD DEATHS IN
THE MARCH REVOLUTION

655   soldiers
587   citizens
73   policemen

All dates on this map are according
to the Russian calendar, which was
13 days behind that of the rest of
the world

1. Nicholas leaves for Mogilev, his headquarters, 22 Feb.
2. Strikes in Petrograd, 23-26 February
3. Troop mutinies in Petrograd, 27 February
4. Secret police headquarters in Moscow burnt, 27 Feb.
5. Some troops move on Petrograd, 1 March
6. Nicholas unable to reach Petrograd, 1 March
7. Nicholas abdicates, 2 March
8. A provisional Government "rules" side by side with
   a Council (Soviet) of Workers and Soldiers Deputies.
   In the latter the Bolsheviks are in a minority, 3 March
9. Nicholas put under arrest, 8 March
10. All-Russian Conference of Soviets rejects Bolshevik
    motion to end the war by 325 votes to 57, 29 March
11. Lenin returns to Petrograd from exile, 3 April.
    "The robbers' imperialist war is the beginning of civil
    war in all Europe" he tells the crowd. "Long live the
    worldwide socialist revolution"

Lake Ladoga

Bologoye

Malaya Vishera

Lake Ilmen

Novgorod

Petrograd

Okhta

Tsarskoye Selo

Putilov works

Luga

Kronstadt

Vyborg

Lake Peipus

Gulf of Finland

Reval

Hangö

86

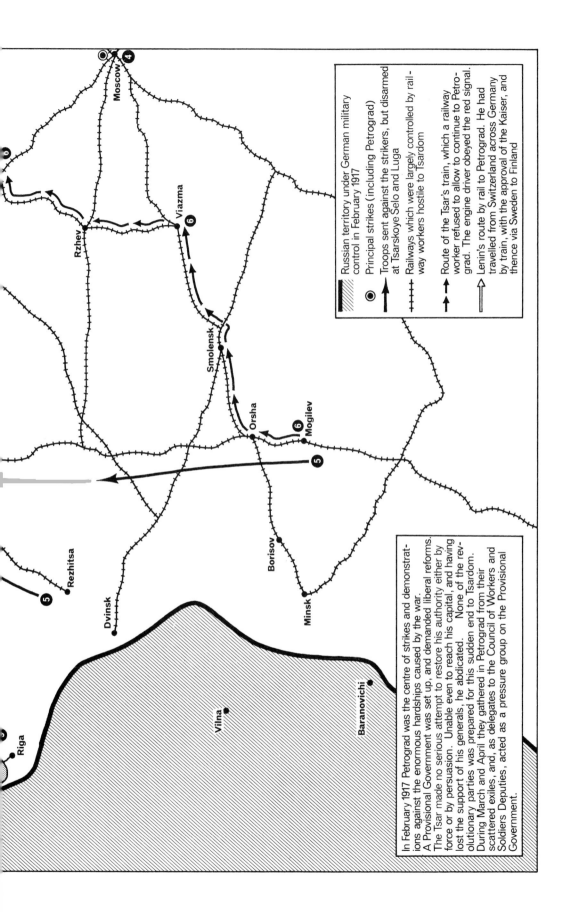

Russian territory under German military control in February 1917

⊙ Principal strikes (including Petrograd)

Troops sent against the strikers, but disarmed at Tsarskoye Selo and Luga

Railways which were largely controlled by railway workers hostile to Tsardom

Route of the Tsar's train, which a railway worker refused to allow to continue to Petrograd. The engine driver obeyed the red signal.

Lenin's route by rail to Petrograd. He had travelled from Switzerland across Germany by train, with the approval of the Kaiser, and thence via Sweden to Finland

In February 1917 Petrograd was the centre of strikes and demonstrations against the enormous hardships caused by the war. A Provisional Government was set up, and demanded liberal reforms. The Tsar made no serious attempt to restore his authority either by force or by persuasion. Unable even to reach his capital, and having lost the support of his generals, he abdicated. None of the revolutionary parties was prepared for this sudden end to Tsardom. During March and April they gathered in Petrograd from their scattered exiles, and, as delegates to the Council of Workers and Soldiers Deputies, acted as a pressure group on the Provisional Government.

Moscow

Rzhev

Viazma

Smolensk

Orsha

Mogilev

Borisov

Minsk

Rezhitsa

Dvinsk

Riga

Vilna

Baranovichi

LENIN'S RETURN TO RUSSIA 1917

Our tactics: absolute distrust; no support of new Government; Kerensky particularly suspect; to arm proletariat only guarantee; no rapprochement with other parties. This last is conditio sine qua non
**LENIN TO BOLSHEVIKS IN SWEDEN
TELEGRAM FROM BERN 26 MARCH 1917**

0   250
Miles

On 7 August 1914 Lenin was arrested in Cracow by the Austrians as an enemy alien and spy. He was released on 23 Aug., the Austrian Government having been persuaded that he was even more an enemy of Tsardom, and could "render great services" to Austria by fomenting anti-Tsarist troubles

Murmansk

Vyborg
Hangö
Petrograd

RUSSIA

Odessa

Stockholm

Trelleborg

Berlin

GERMANY

Cracow

Vienna

AUSTRIA-HUNGARY

Innsbruck

Berne
SWITZ

FRANCE

Paris

London

BRITAIN

Liverpool

Scapa Flow

North Sea

English Channel

SWEDEN

Baltic Sea

ITALY

BULGARIA

Black Sea

TURKEY

Aegean Sea

▰ The Central Powers and their conquests in February 1917

⇤— Lenin's route from Austria to Switzerland, 1914

•••▸••• Lenin's first proposed route back to Russia, which proved impossible for fear of arrest by the British

→ Lenin's actual route 9-16 April 1917

▨ Sea routes to Russia closed by Central Power minefields

When revolution broke out in Petrograd in February 1917, Lenin, the Bolshevik leader, was in Switzerland. Wartime was not conducive to travel, nor did his plan to go through Britain prove possible. Instead, the German Government, eager to see dissension and chaos in Russia, agreed with alacrity to his request to travel across "enemy" territory, and provided him with facilities. Thus Imperial Germany served as a hand-maiden to the Russian revolution of October 1917

THE LOCATION OF THE BOLSHEVIK LEADERS DURING THE FIRST REVOLUTION OF 1917

The only Bolshevik leaders, none of them very senior, who happened to be in Petrograd at the time of the February Revolution:
MOLOTOV, STEKLOV, SHLYAPNIKOV, LATSIS, and ZALUTSKI

Pacific Ocean

ALASKA

Bering Strait

Arctic Ocean

North Pole

GREENLAND

ORDZHONIKIDZE
Pokrovsk

Lena

SIBERIA

Chita

STALIN
Kureika

Turukhansk
SVERDLOV

Irkutsk

Yenisei

Achinsk
KAMENEV

New York
BUKHARIN
TROTSKY Ⓜ
VOLODARSKY Ⓜ

Ob

Narym
RYKOV

CHINA

Stockholm
KOLLONTAI
URITSKY Ⓜ

Atlantic Ocean

Stockholm

Petrograd

TRANS-SIBERIAN RAILWAY

Urals

SWEDEN

London
LITVINOV
CHICHERIN Ⓜ

London

Moscow
DZERZHINSKY

Paris
ANTONOV-OVSEENKO

Paris
FRANCE

TER-PETROSIAN
Kharkov

Jassy
RAKOVSKY

Vladikavkaz
KIROV

SWITZERLAND
LENIN
LUNACHARSKY Ⓜ
RADEK
ZINOVIEV

SWITZERLAND

Black Sea

PERSIA

Mediterranean Sea

New York

Halifax

U.S.A.

CANADA

///// Territory controlled by Germany and her allies in March 1917

⊙ Centre of the First Russian Revolution, and scene of all subsequent struggles for power during 1917

▬ The location of the Bolshevik leaders at the time of the March Revolution. The majority were in exile or out of Russia. They all made haste to return to Petrograd.

Ⓜ = Mensheviks and others who became Bolsheviks on their return to Petrograd

Most of the Social Democratic leaders of both the Bolshevik and Menshevik factions were abroad or in exile when revolution broke out in Russia in 1917. Those who were in Siberia reached Petrograd early in March, following the spontaneous amnesty of all political prisoners. Also returning in March were those living in Sweden. Next to return, in April, were the "specials" from Switzerland, led by Lenin. Finally, in May, came the "regulars" who had been in Switzerland, or elsewhere abroad.

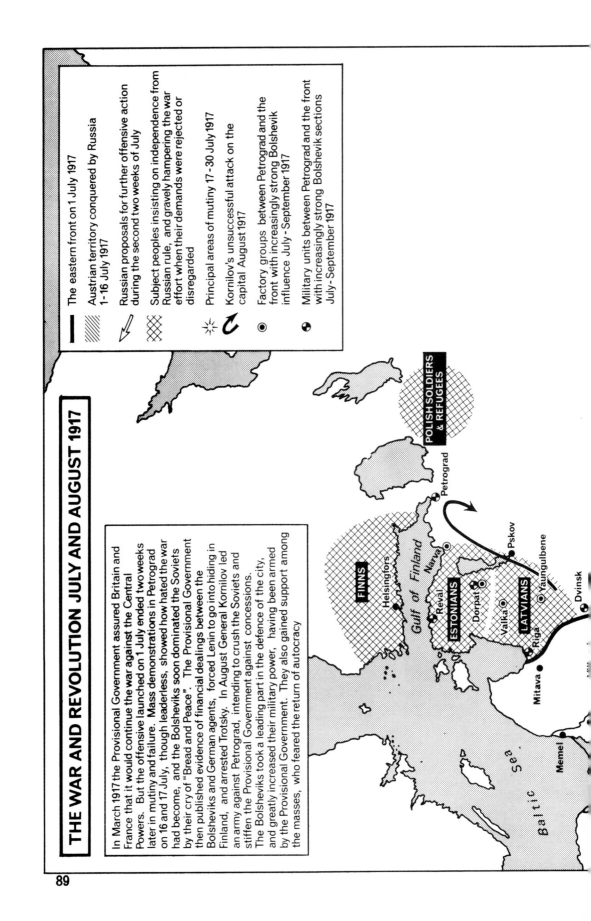

THE WAR AND REVOLUTION JULY AND AUGUST 1917

In March 1917 the Provisional Government assured Britain and France that it would continue the war against the Central Powers. But the offensive launched on 1 July ended two weeks later in mutiny and failure. Mass demonstrations in Petrograd on 16 and 17 July, though leaderless, showed how hated the war had become, and the Bolsheviks soon dominated the Soviets by their cry of "Bread and Peace". The Provisional Government then published evidence of financial dealings between the Bolsheviks and German agents, forced Lenin to go into hiding in Finland, and arrested Trotsky. In August General Kornilov led an army against Petrograd, intending to crush the Soviets and stiffen the Provisional Government against concessions. The Bolsheviks took a leading part in the defence of the city, and greatly increased their military power, having been armed by the Provisional Government. They also gained support among the masses, who feared the return of autocracy

	The eastern front on 1 July 1917
	Austrian territory conquered by Russia 1-16 July 1917
	Russian proposals for further offensive action during the second two weeks of July
	Subject peoples insisting on independence from Russian rule, and gravely hampering the war effort when their demands were rejected or disregarded
	Principal areas of mutiny 17 - 30 July 1917
	Kornilov's unsuccessful attack on the capital August 1917
	Factory groups between Petrograd and the front with increasingly strong Bolshevik influence July - September 1917
	Military units between Petrograd and the front with increasingly strong Bolshevik sections July - September 1917

POLISH SOLDIERS & REFUGEES

Petrograd

FINNS

Helsingfors

Gulf of Finland

Narva

Reval

ESTONIANS

Pskov

Dorpat

Valka

Yaungulbene

LATVIANS

Riga

Dvinsk

Mitava

Memel

Baltic Sea

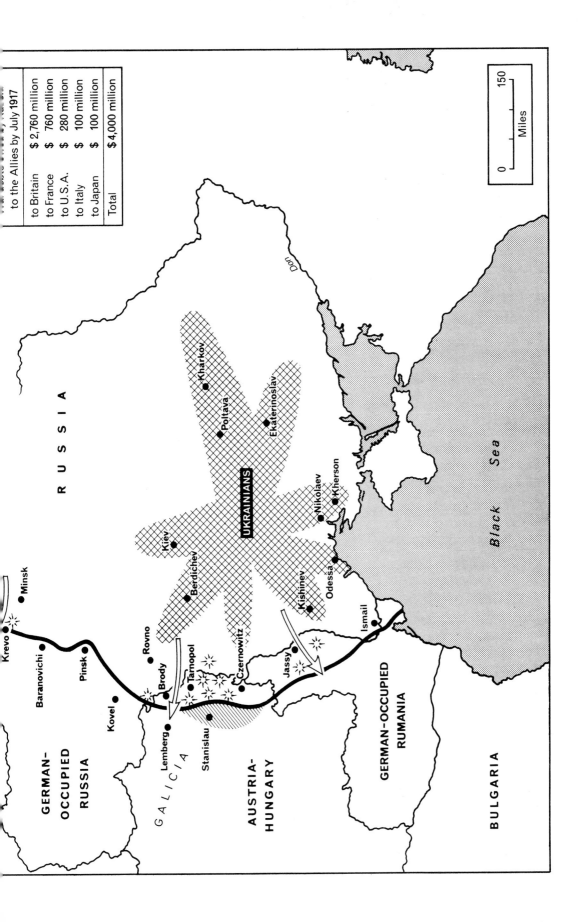

Russian War debts, owed to the Allies by July 1917	
to Britain	$ 2,760 million
to France	$ 760 million
to U.S.A.	$ 280 million
to Italy	$ 100 million
to Japan	$ 100 million
Total	$4,000 million

RUSSIA

GERMAN-OCCUPIED RUSSIA

Minsk

Krevo

Baranovichi

Pinsk

Kovel

Rovno

Brody

Lemberg

Tarnopol

G A L I C I A

Stanislau

Czernowitz

AUSTRIA-HUNGARY

Jassy

Kishinev

Ismail

GERMAN-OCCUPIED RUMANIA

BULGARIA

UKRAINIANS

Kiev

Berdichev

Odessa

Nikolaev

Kherson

Poltava

Kharkov

Ekaterinoslav

Don

Black Sea

0   150

Miles

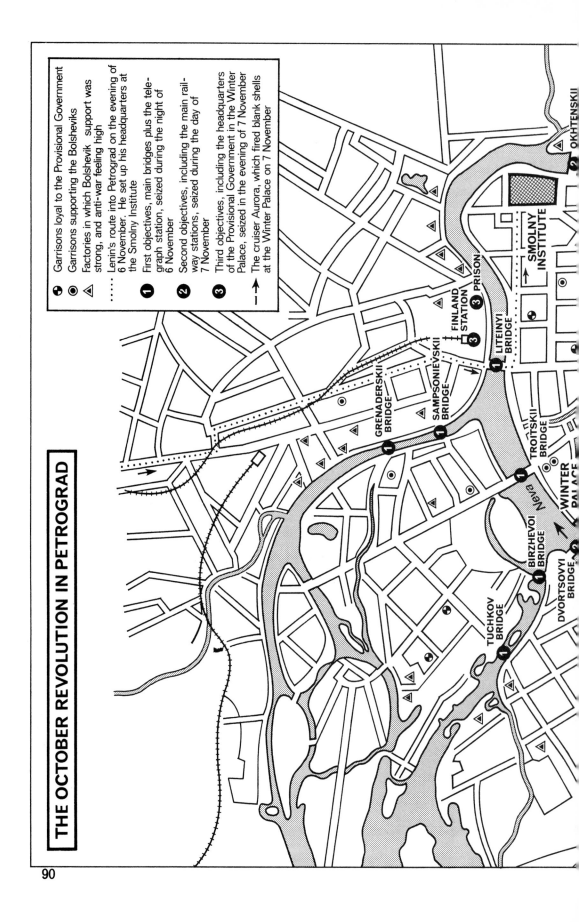

THE OCTOBER REVOLUTION IN PETROGRAD

Garrisons loyal to the Provisional Government

Garrisons supporting the Bolsheviks

Factories in which Bolshevik support was strong, and anti-war feeling high

Lenin's route into Petrograd on the evening of 6 November. He set up his headquarters at the Smolny Institute

1 First objectives, main bridges plus the telegraph station, seized during the night of 6 November

2 Second objectives, including the main railway stations, seized during the day of 7 November

3 Third objectives, including the headquarters of the Provisional Government in the Winter Palace, seized in the evening of 7 November

The cruiser Aurora, which fired blank shells at the Winter Palace on 7 November

OKHTENSKII

SMOLNY INSTITUTE

FINLAND STATION

PRISON

LITEINYI BRIDGE

GRENADERSKII BRIDGE

SAMPSONIEVSKII BRIDGE

TROITSKII BRIDGE

Neva

WINTER PALACE

BIRZHEVOI BRIDGE

TUCHKOV BRIDGE

DVORTSOVYI BRIDGE

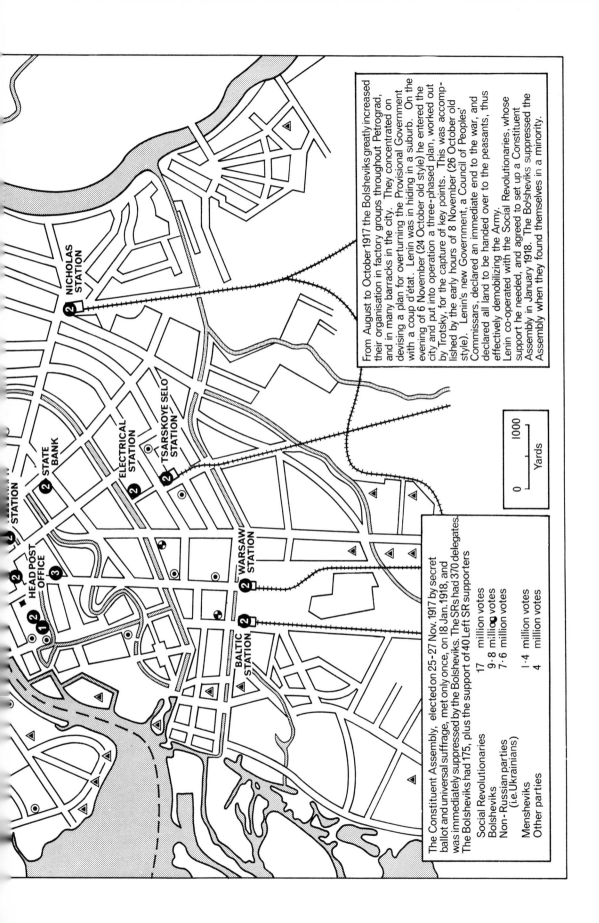

From August to October 1917 the Bolsheviks greatly increased their organisation in factory groups throughout Petrograd, and in many barracks in the city. They concentrated on devising a plan for overturning the Provisional Government with a coup d'état. Lenin was in hiding in a suburb. On the evening of 6 November (24 October old style) he entered the city and put into operation a three-phased plan, worked out by Trotsky, for the capture of key points. This was accomplished by the early hours of 8 November (26 October old style). Lenin's new Government, a Council of Peoples' Commissars, declared an immediate end to the war, and declared all land to be handed over to the peasants, thus effectively demobilizing the Army.
Lenin co-operated with the Social Revolutionaries, whose support he needed, and agreed to set up a Constituent Assembly in January 1918. The Bolsheviks suppressed the Assembly when they found themselves in a minority.

NICHOLAS STATION

STATE BANK

ELECTRICAL STATION

TSARSKOYE SELO STATION

HEAD POST OFFICE

WARSAW STATION

BALTIC STATION

0   1000

Yards

The Constituent Assembly, elected on 25-27 Nov. 1917 by secret ballot and universal suffrage, met only once, on 18 Jan. 1918, and was immediately suppressed by the Bolsheviks. The SRs had 370 delegates. The Bolsheviks had 175, plus the support of 40 Left SR supporters

Social Revolutionaries	17	million votes
Bolsheviks	9·8	million votes
Non-Russian parties (i.e. Ukrainians)	7·6	million votes
Mensheviks	1·4	million votes
Other parties	4	million votes

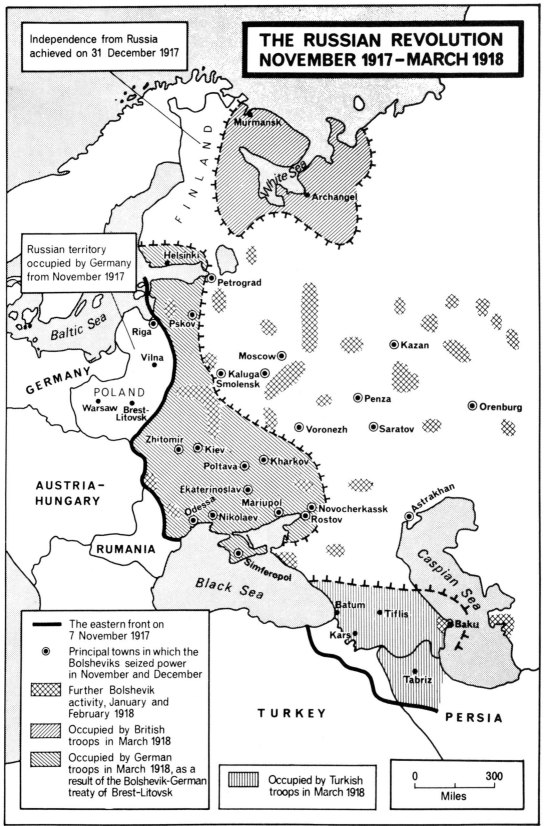

Independence from Russia
achieved on 31 December 1917

THE RUSSIAN REVOLUTION
NOVEMBER 1917 – MARCH 1918

Murmansk

White Sea

Archangel

Russian territory
occupied by Germany
from November 1917

FINLAND

Helsinki

Petrograd

Baltic Sea

Riga

Pskov

Moscow ◉

Kazan ◉

Vilna

Kaluga ◉
Smolensk

GERMANY

POLAND

Penza ◉

Orenburg ◉

Warsaw
Brest-
Litovsk

Voronezh ◉

Saratov ◉

Zhitomir

Kiev ◉

Poltava ◉

Kharkov ◉

AUSTRIA-
HUNGARY

Ekaterinoslav ◉

Astrakhan ◉

Odessa ◉
Nikolaev

Mariupol

Novocherkassk ◉
Rostov

Caspian Sea

RUMANIA

Simferopol

Black Sea

Batum

Tiflis

Baku

Kars

The eastern front on
7 November 1917

Principal towns in which the
Bolsheviks seized power
in November and December

Tabriz

Further Bolshevik
activity, January and
February 1918

TURKEY

PERSIA

Occupied by British
troops in March 1918

Occupied by German
troops in March 1918, as a
result of the Bolshevik-German
treaty of Brest-Litovsk

Occupied by Turkish
troops in March 1918

0   300
Miles

91

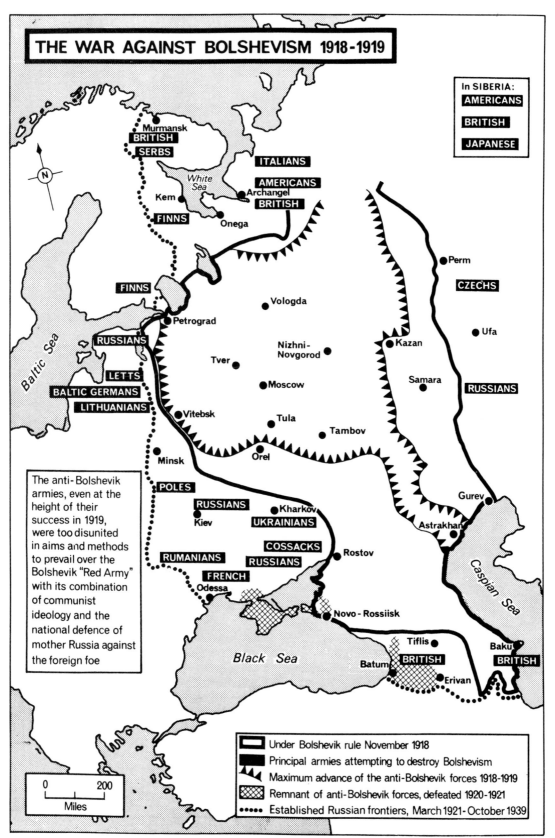

THE WAR AGAINST BOLSHEVISM 1918-1919

In SIBERIA:
AMERICANS
BRITISH
JAPANESE

Murmansk
BRITISH
SERBS

ITALIANS

White Sea

AMERICANS
Kem
Archangel
BRITISH

FINNS
Onega

Perm

CZECHS

FINNS

Vologda

Ufa

Petrograd

RUSSIANS

Nizhni-Novgorod
Kazan

Tver

Samara

LETTS
BALTIC GERMANS
LITHUANIANS

Moscow

RUSSIANS

Baltic Sea

Vitebsk

Tula

Tambov

Minsk

Orel

POLES

Gurev

RUSSIANS
Kiev

Kharkov

Astrakhan

UKRAINIANS

The anti-Bolshevik armies, even at the height of their success in 1919, were too disunited in aims and methods to prevail over the Bolshevik "Red Army" with its combination of communist ideology and the national defence of mother Russia against the foreign foe

COSSACKS

RUMANIANS
RUSSIANS

Rostov

FRENCH
Odessa

Caspian Sea

Novo-Rossiisk

Tiflis

Baku
BRITISH

Black Sea

Batum
BRITISH

Erivan

0   200
Miles

☐ Under Bolshevik rule November 1918

◤ Principal armies attempting to destroy Bolshevism

◤◤ Maximum advance of the anti-Bolshevik forces 1918-1919

▨ Remnant of anti-Bolshevik forces, defeated 1920-1921

•••• Established Russian frontiers, March 1921-October 1939

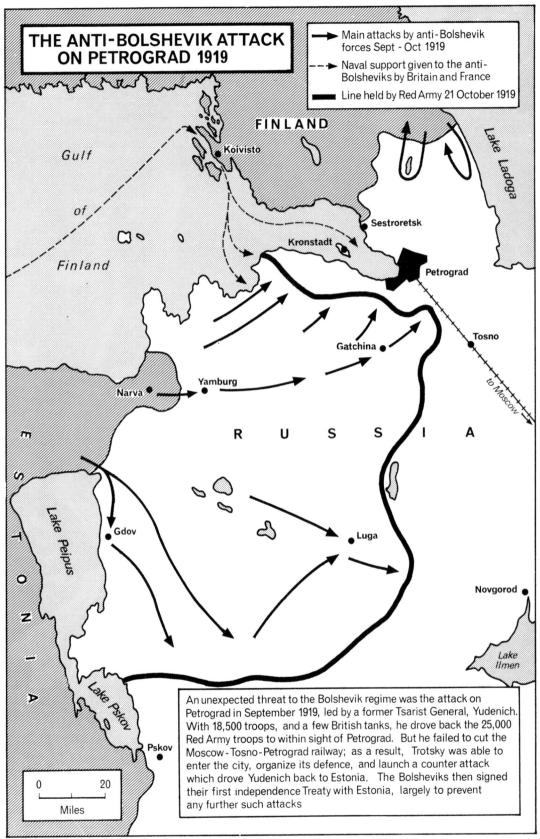

THE ANTI-BOLSHEVIK ATTACK ON PETROGRAD 1919

→ Main attacks by anti-Bolshevik forces Sept - Oct 1919

--→ Naval support given to the anti-Bolsheviks by Britain and France

━ Line held by Red Army 21 October 1919

FINLAND

Gulf

of

Finland

Koivisto

Lake Ladoga

Sestroretsk

Kronstadt

Petrograd

Tosno

Gatchina

to Moscow

Yamburg

Narva

R U S S I A

E
S
T
O
N
I
A

Lake Peipus

Gdov

Luga

Novgorod

Lake Pskov

Lake Ilmen

Pskov

0   20

Miles

An unexpected threat to the Bolshevik regime was the attack on Petrograd in September 1919, led by a former Tsarist General, Yudenich. With 18,500 troops, and a few British tanks, he drove back the 25,000 Red Army troops to within sight of Petrograd. But he failed to cut the Moscow-Tosno-Petrograd railway; as a result, Trotsky was able to enter the city, organize its defence, and launch a counter attack which drove Yudenich back to Estonia. The Bolsheviks then signed their first independence Treaty with Estonia, largely to prevent any further such attacks

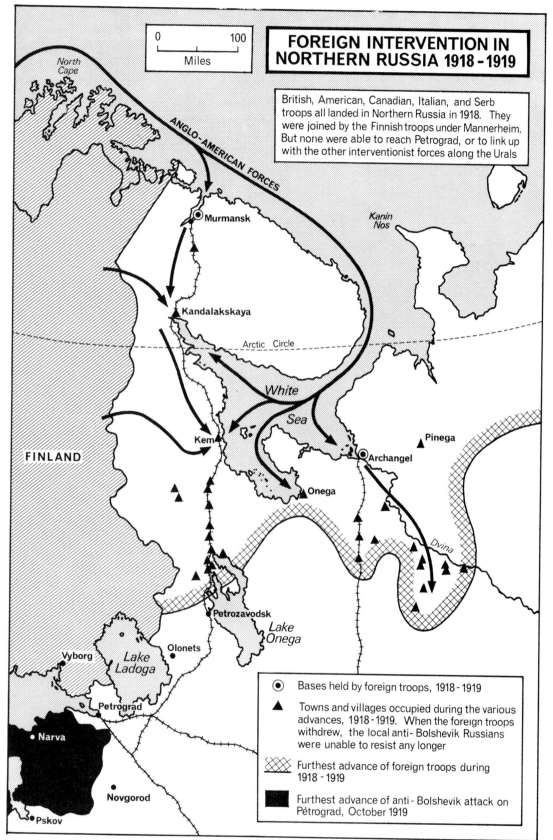

FOREIGN INTERVENTION IN NORTHERN RUSSIA 1918-1919

0   100
Miles

British, American, Canadian, Italian, and Serb troops all landed in Northern Russia in 1918. They were joined by the Finnish troops under Mannerheim. But none were able to reach Petrograd, or to link up with the other interventionist forces along the Urals

North Cape

ANGLO-AMERICAN FORCES

Murmansk

Kanin Nos

Kandalakskaya

Arctic Circle

White

Kem

Sea

FINLAND

Pinega

Archangel

Onega

Dvina

Petrozavodsk

Lake Onega

Olonets

Vyborg

Lake Ladoga

Petrograd

Narva

Novgorod

Pskov

⊙   Bases held by foreign troops, 1918-1919

▲   Towns and villages occupied during the various advances, 1918-1919. When the foreign troops withdrew, the local anti-Bolshevik Russians were unable to resist any longer

▨   Furthest advance of foreign troops during 1918-1919

■   Furthest advance of anti-Bolshevik attack on Petrograd, October 1919

94

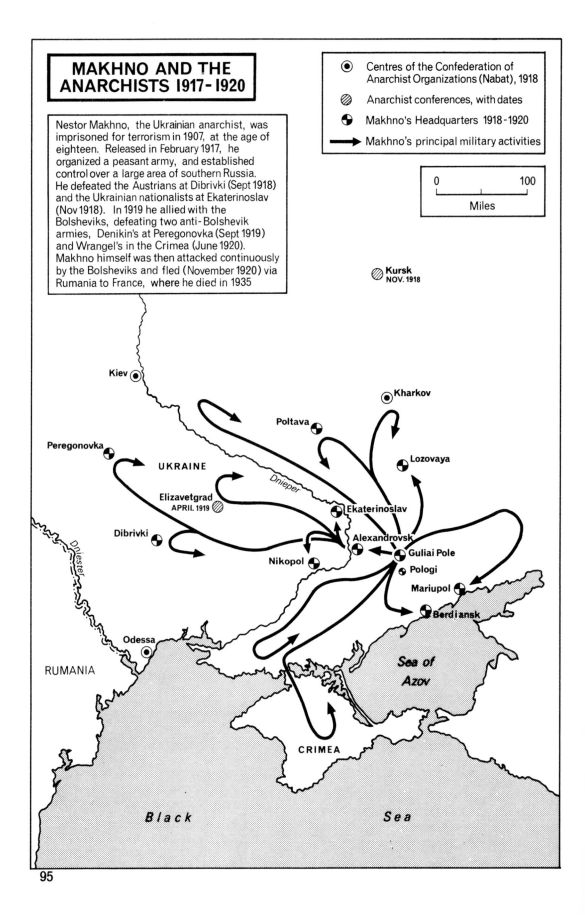

MAKHNO AND THE ANARCHISTS 1917-1920

Nestor Makhno, the Ukrainian anarchist, was imprisoned for terrorism in 1907, at the age of eighteen. Released in February 1917, he organized a peasant army, and established control over a large area of southern Russia. He defeated the Austrians at Dibrivki (Sept 1918) and the Ukrainian nationalists at Ekaterinoslav (Nov 1918). In 1919 he allied with the Bolsheviks, defeating two anti-Bolshevik armies, Denikin's at Peregonovka (Sept 1919) and Wrangel's in the Crimea (June 1920). Makhno himself was then attacked continuously by the Bolsheviks and fled (November 1920) via Rumania to France, where he died in 1935

◉ Centres of the Confederation of Anarchist Organizations (Nabat), 1918

▨ Anarchist conferences, with dates

◕ Makhno's Headquarters 1918-1920

→ Makhno's principal military activities

0   100
Miles

Kursk
NOV. 1918

Kiev ◉

Kharkov ◉

Poltava ◕

Peregonovka ◕

UKRAINE

Lozovaya ◕

Dnieper

Elizavetgrad
APRIL 1919 ▨

Dibrivki ◕

Ekaterinoslav ◕

Dniester

Alexandrovsk ◕

Guliai Pole ◕

Nikopol ◕

Pologi ◉

Mariupol ◕

Berdiansk ◕

Odessa ◉

RUMANIA

Sea of Azov

CRIMEA

Black   *Sea*

THE RUSSO-POLISH WAR 1920

Poland's established frontiers, June 1920

The eastern extent of Polish conquests, April, May and June 1920

Russian attacks following the Polish occupation of Kiev in June 1920

Polish lines of defence, August 1920

The 'Miracle of the Vistula'. Russian armies were defeated; they retreated to Russia

Seized by Poland from Lithuania, October 1920

Annexed by Poland from Russia, Treaty of Riga, March 1921

Poland's eastern frontier from 1921 to 1939

ESTONIA

LATVIA

Baltic Sea

DANZIG

LITHUANIA

Vilna

RUSSIA

Minsk

EAST PRUSSIA

Grodno

GERMANY

Vistula

Bialystok

Plotsk

Warsaw

Pinsk

Poznan

Radom

Lublin

POLAND

Kholm

Kiev

GERMANY

Vistula

Lvov

Cracow

Kamenets Podolsk

CZECHOSLOVAKIA

0   100
Miles

HUNGARY

RUMANIA

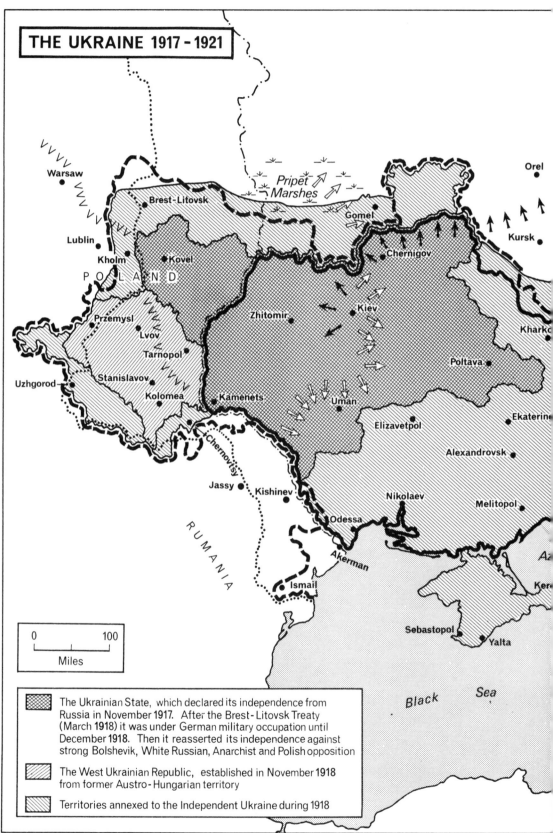

THE UKRAINE 1917-1921

Warsaw

Brest-Litovsk

Pripet Marshes

Orel

Gomel

Kursk

Lublin

Kholm · Kovel

Chernigov

P O L A N D

Przemysl

Zhitomir

Kiev

Kharko

Lvov

Tarnopol

Poltava

Uzhgorod

Stanislavov

Kolomea · Kamenets

Uman

Ekaterine

Elizavetpol

Chernovtsy

Alexandrovsk

Jassy · Kishinev

Nikolaev

Melitopol

Odessa

Akerman

Az

Ismail

Ker

R U M A N I A

Sebastopol

Yalta

0	100

Miles

Black Sea

The Ukrainian State, which declared its independence from Russia in November 1917. After the Brest-Litovsk Treaty (March 1918) it was under German military occupation until December 1918. Then it reasserted its independence against strong Bolshevik, White Russian, Anarchist and Polish opposition

The West Ukrainian Republic, established in November 1918 from former Austro-Hungarian territory

Territories annexed to the Independent Ukraine during 1918

Territory claimed by the Ukrainian nationalists as part of the"ethnographic" Ukraine

Boundary of the Ukrainian Soviet Socialist Republic 1921

Western boundary of the Soviet Union 1921-1939

Western boundary of the Soviet Union since 1945

Furthest northern advance of Denikin's anti-Bolshevik armies, November 1919. Denikin's Great Russian policies failed to gain him much Ukrainian support

Furthest eastern advance of the Polish Army in June 1920

Furthest western advance of the Red Army by August 1920

Voronezh

Buturlinovka

Lugansk

Taganrog

Rostov

iupol

Astrakhan

Ekaterinodar

Stavropol

Armavir

Novorossiisk

Mineralnye
Vody

Mozdok

Tuapse

Sochi

Caucasus

Caspian

Sea

Batum

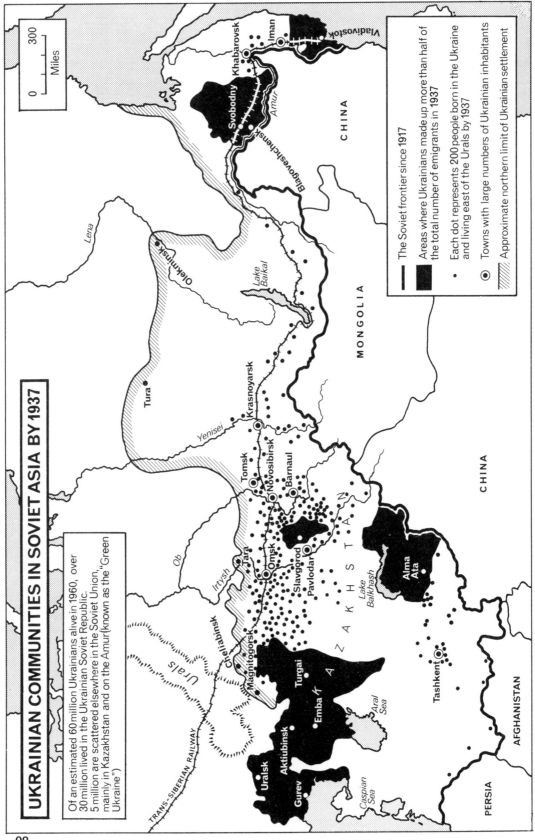

UKRAINIAN COMMUNITIES IN SOVIET ASIA BY 1937

Of an estimated 60 million Ukrainians alive in 1960, over 30 million lived in the Ukrainian Soviet Republic. 5 million are scattered elsewhere in the Soviet Union, mainly in Kazakhstan and on the Amur (known as the "Green Ukraine")

— The Soviet frontier since 1917

■ Areas where Ukrainians made up more than half of the total number of emigrants in 1937

• Each dot represents 200 people born in the Ukraine and living east of the Urals by 1937

⊙ Towns with large numbers of Ukrainian inhabitants

░ Approximate northern limit of Ukrainian settlement

300
Miles
0

Vladivostok
Iman
Khabarovsk
Svobodny
Amur
Blagoveshchensk
CHINA
MONGOLIA
Lena
Olekminsk
Lake Baikal
Tura
Krasnoyarsk
Yenisei
Tomsk
Novosibirsk
Barnaul
Ob
Irtysh
Tara
Omsk
Slavgrod
Pavlodar
Lake Balkhash
K A Z A K H S T A N
Alma Ata
CHINA
Cheliabinsk
Magnitogorsk
Urals
Turgai
Emba R
Aral Sea
Tashkent
Uralsk
Aktiubinsk
Gurev
Caspian Sea
PERSIA
AFGHANISTAN
TRANS-SIBERIAN RAILWAY

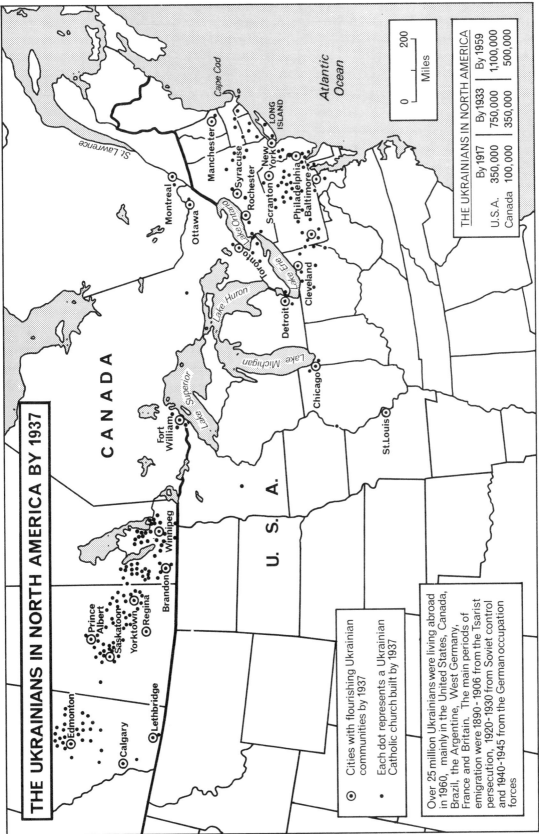

THE UKRAINIANS IN NORTH AMERICA BY 1937

CANADA

U. S. A.

Atlantic Ocean

St. Lawrence

Edmonton
Calgary
Lethbridge
Prince Albert
Saskatoon
Yorktown
Regina
Brandon
Winnipeg
Fort William

Lake Superior
Lake Michigan
Lake Huron
Lake Erie
Lake Ontario

St. Louis
Chicago
Detroit
Cleveland
Toronto
Ottawa
Montreal
Scranton
Rochester
Syracuse
Philadelphia
Baltimore
New York
Manchester
Cape Cod
LONG ISLAND

```
0        200
|————————|
   Miles
```

THE UKRAINIANS IN NORTH AMERICA

	By 1917	By 1933	By 1959
U.S.A.	350,000	750,000	1,100,000
Canada	100,000	350,000	500,000

◉ Cities with flourishing Ukrainian communities by 1937

• Each dot represents a Ukrainian Catholic church built by 1937

Over 25 million Ukrainians were living abroad in 1960, mainly in the United States, Canada, Brazil, the Argentine, West Germany, France and Britain. The main periods of emigration were 1890 - 1906 from the Tsarist persecution, 1920-1930 from Soviet control and 1940-1945 from the German occupation forces

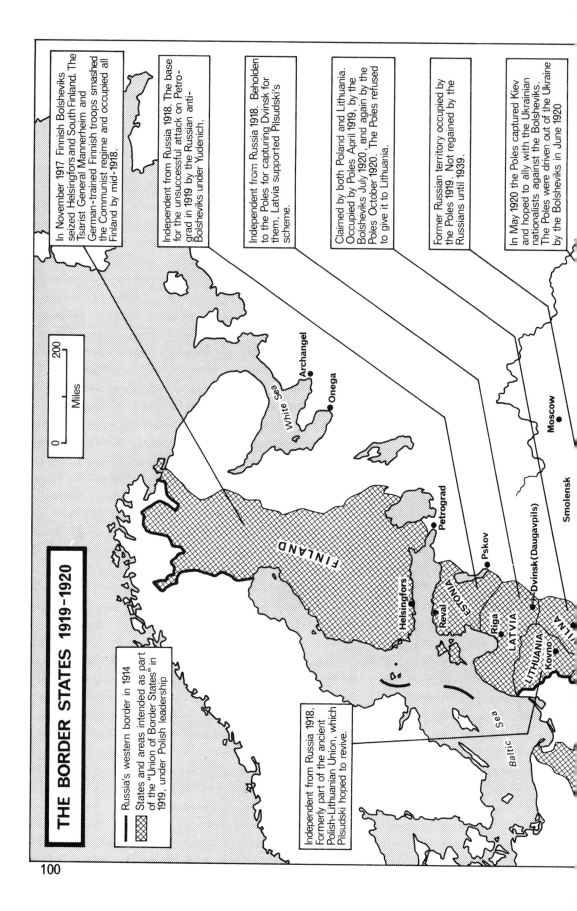

THE BORDER STATES 1919–1920

In November 1917 Finnish Bolsheviks seized Helsingfors and South Finland. The Tsarist General Mannerheim and German-trained Finnish troops smashed the Communist regime and occupied all Finland by mid-1918.

Independent from Russia 1918. The base for the unsuccessful attack on Petrograd in 1919 by the Russian anti-Bolsheviks under Yudenich.

Independent from Russia 1918. Beholden to the Poles for capturing Dvinsk for them. Latvia supported Pilsudski's scheme.

Claimed by both Poland and Lithuania. Occupied by Poles April 1919, by the Bolsheviks July 1920, and again by the Poles October 1920. The Poles refused to give it to Lithuania.

Former Russian territory occupied by the Poles 1919. Not regained by the Russians until 1939.

In May 1920 the Poles captured Kiev and hoped to ally with the Ukrainian nationalists against the Bolsheviks. The Poles were driven out of the Ukraine by the Bolsheviks in June 1920

Independent from Russia 1918. Formerly part of the ancient Polish-Lithuanian Union, which Pilsudski hoped to revive.

Russia's western border in 1914

States and areas intended as part of the "Union of Border States" in 1919, under Polish leadership

0 200
Miles

Archangel
Onega
White Sea
Moscow
Smolensk
Petrograd
Pskov
FINLAND
Helsingfors
Reval
ESTONIA
Riga
LATVIA
Dvinsk (Daugavpils)
LITHUANIA
Kovno
Baltic Sea

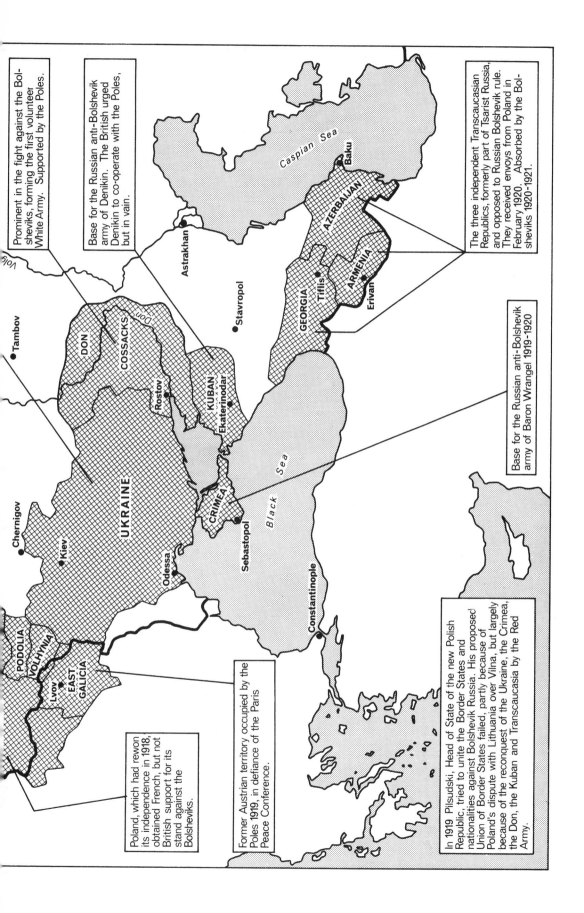

Prominent in the fight against the Bolsheviks, forming the first volunteer White Army. Supported by the Poles.

Base for the Russian anti-Bolshevik army of Denikin. The British urged Denikin to co-operate with the Poles, but in vain.

The three independent Transcaucasian Republics, formerly part of Tsarist Russia, and opposed to Russian Bolshevik rule. They received envoys from Poland in February 1920. Absorbed by the Bolsheviks 1920-1921.

Base for the Russian anti-Bolshevik army of Baron Wrangel 1919-1920

Poland, which had rewon its independence in 1918, obtained French, but not British support for its stand against the Bolsheviks.

Former Austrian territory occupied by the Poles 1919, in defiance of the Paris Peace Conference.

In 1919 Pilsudski, Head of State of the new Polish Republic, tried to unite the Border States and nationalities against Bolshevik Russia. His proposed Union of Border States failed, partly because of Poland's dispute with Lithuania over Vilna, but largely because of the reconquest of the Ukraine, the Crimea, the Don, the Kuban and Transcaucasia by the Red Army.

Caspian Sea

Baku

AZERBAIJAN

ARMENIA

GEORGIA

Tiflis

Erivan

Astrakhan

Stavropol

Tambov

DON

COSSACKS

Don

Rostov

KUBAN

Ekaterinodar

UKRAINE

Volga

Chernigov

Kiev

Odessa

CRIMEA

Sebastopol

Black Sea

Constantinople

PODOLIA

VOLHYNIA

Lvov

EAST GALICIA

SOVIET DIPLOMACY 1920-1940

North Sea

NORWAY

FINLAND

Leningrad

BRITAIN

London

Baltic Sea

ESTONIA

LATVIA

Smo

FLYI
SCHO

10,000 VEHICLES
4,500 TONS MUNITIONS

200 TANKS
3,300 MACHINE GUNS

1,000 OFFICERS & MEN

Bay of Biscay

FRANCE

Paris

GERMANY

Berlin

Warsaw

POLAND

CZECHO-
SLOVAKIA

AUSTRIA

RUMANIA

San Sebastian

Madrid

Barcelona

SPAIN

ITALY

1,000 OFFICERS & MEN

1,300 TRUCKS

1,300 RIFLES & GUNS
242 AEROPLANES

Mediterranean Sea

0 400
Miles

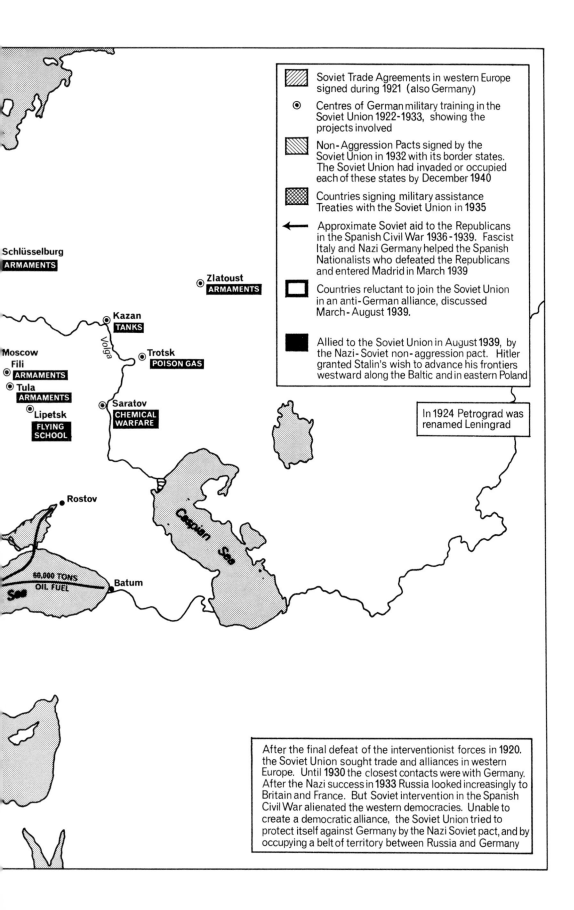

Soviet Trade Agreements in western Europe signed during 1921 (also Germany)

⊙ Centres of German military training in the Soviet Union 1922-1933, showing the projects involved

Non-Aggression Pacts signed by the Soviet Union in 1932 with its border states. The Soviet Union had invaded or occupied each of these states by December 1940

Countries signing military assistance Treaties with the Soviet Union in 1935

← Approximate Soviet aid to the Republicans in the Spanish Civil War 1936-1939. Fascist Italy and Nazi Germany helped the Spanish Nationalists who defeated the Republicans and entered Madrid in March 1939

Countries reluctant to join the Soviet Union in an anti-German alliance, discussed March-August 1939.

Allied to the Soviet Union in August 1939, by the Nazi-Soviet non-aggression pact. Hitler granted Stalin's wish to advance his frontiers westward along the Baltic and in eastern Poland

In 1924 Petrograd was renamed Leningrad

Schlüsselburg
ARMAMENTS

⊙ **Zlatoust**
ARMAMENTS

⊙ **Kazan**
TANKS

Volga

Moscow
Fili
⊙ ARMAMENTS
⊙ **Tula**
ARMAMENTS
⊙ **Lipetsk**
FLYING SCHOOL

⊙ **Trotsk**
POISON GAS

⊙ **Saratov**
CHEMICAL WARFARE

Caspian Sea

● **Rostov**

60,000 TONS OIL FUEL

Sea **Batum**

After the final defeat of the interventionist forces in 1920. the Soviet Union sought trade and alliances in western Europe. Until 1930 the closest contacts were with Germany. After the Nazi success in 1933 Russia looked increasingly to Britain and France. But Soviet intervention in the Spanish Civil War alienated the western democracies. Unable to create a democratic alliance, the Soviet Union tried to protect itself against Germany by the Nazi Soviet pact, and by occupying a belt of territory between Russia and Germany

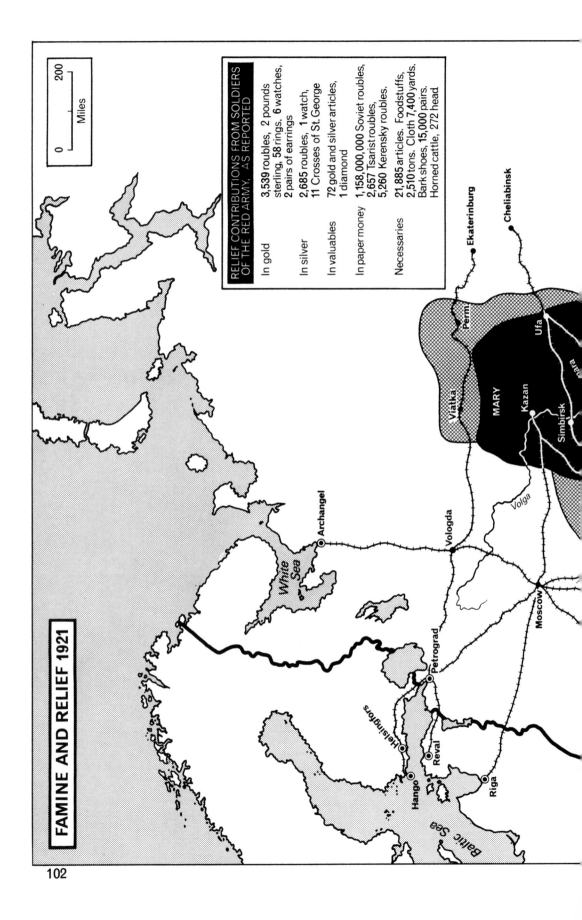

FAMINE AND RELIEF 1921

RELIEF CONTRIBUTIONS FROM SOLDIERS
OF THE RED ARMY, AS REPORTED

In gold
3,539 roubles, 2 pounds
sterling, 58 rings, 6 watches,
2 pairs of earrings

In silver
2,685 roubles, 1 watch,
11 Crosses of St. George

In valuables
72 gold and silver articles,
1 diamond

In paper money
1,158,000,000 Soviet roubles,
2,657 Tsarist roubles,
5,260 Kerensky roubles.

Necessaries
21,885 articles. Foodstuffs,
2,510 tons. Cloth 7,400 yards.
Bark shoes, 15,000 pairs.
Horned cattle, 272 head

0   200
Miles

Ekaterinburg

Cheliabinsk

Perm

Viatka

Ufa

MARY

Kazan

Simbirsk

Volga

Vologda

White
Sea

Archangel

Moscow

Petrograd

Helsingfors

Reval

Hango

Riga

Baltic Sea

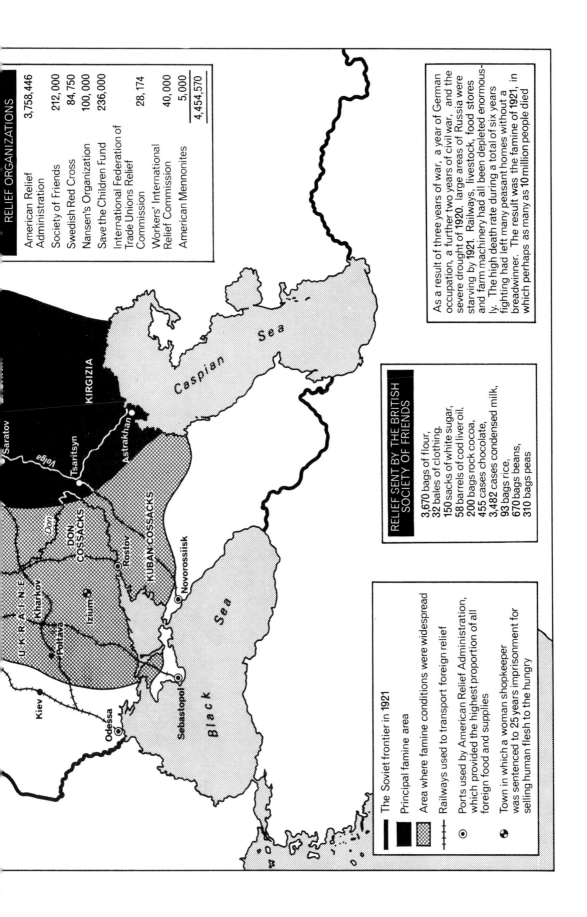

RELIEF ORGANIZATIONS

American Relief Administration	3,758,446
Society of Friends	212,000
Swedish Red Cross	84,750
Nansen's Organization	100,000
Save the Children Fund	236,000
International Federation of Trade Unions Relief Commission	28,174
Workers' International Relief Commission	40,000
American Mennonites	5,000
	4,454,570

As a result of three years of war, a year of German occupation, a further two years of civil war, and the severe drought of 1920, large areas of Russia were starving by 1921. Railways, livestock, food stores and farm machinery had all been depleted enormously. The high death rate during a total of six years fighting had left many peasant homes without a breadwinner. The result was the famine of 1921, in which perhaps as many as 10 million people died

RELIEF SENT BY THE BRITISH SOCIETY OF FRIENDS

3,670 bags of flour,
32 bales of clothing,
150 sacks of white sugar,
58 barrels of cod liver oil,
200 bags rock cocoa,
455 cases chocolate,
3,482 cases condensed milk,
93 bags rice,
670 bags beans,
310 bags peas

The Soviet frontier in 1921

Principal famine area

Area where famine conditions were widespread

Railways used to transport foreign relief

⊙ Ports used by American Relief Administration, which provided the highest proportion of all foreign food and supplies

⊕ Town in which a woman shopkeeper was sentenced to 25 years imprisonment for selling human flesh to the hungry

Saratov

Volga

Tsaritsyn

Astrakhan

KIRGIZIA

Caspian Sea

Don

DON COSSACKS

Rostov

KUBAN COSSACKS

Novorossiisk

UKRAINE

Kharkov

Izium

Poltava

Kiev

Odessa

Sebastopol

Black Sea

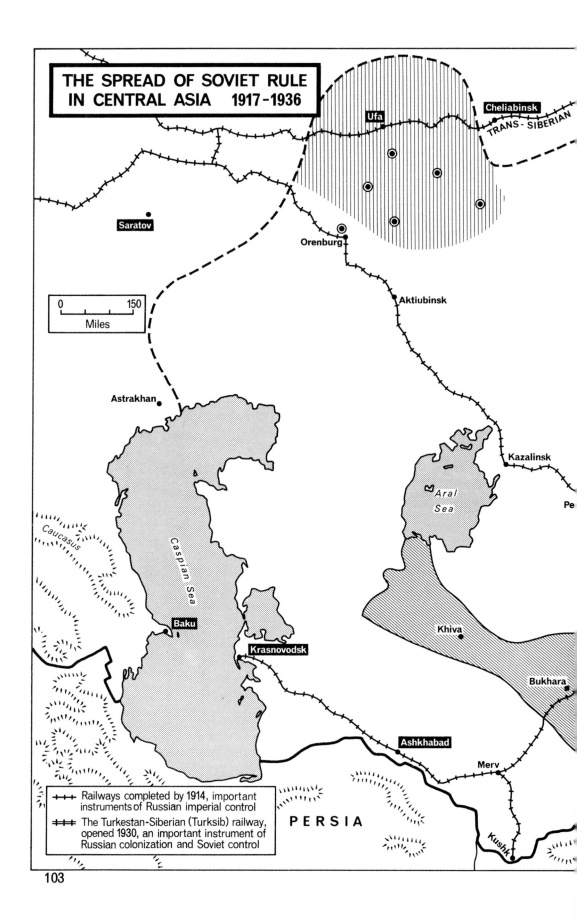

THE SPREAD OF SOVIET RULE
IN CENTRAL ASIA   1917-1936

Cheliabinsk

Ufa

TRANS - SIBERIAN

Saratov

Orenburg

Aktiubinsk

0   150
Miles

Astrakhan

Kazalinsk

*Aral
Sea*

Pe

Caucasus

Caspian Sea

Khiva

Baku

Krasnovodsk

Bukhara

Ashkhabad

Merv

Railways completed by 1914, important
instruments of Russian imperial control

The Turkestan-Siberian (Turksib) railway,
opened 1930, an important instrument of
Russian colonization and Soviet control

P E R S I A

Kushk

103

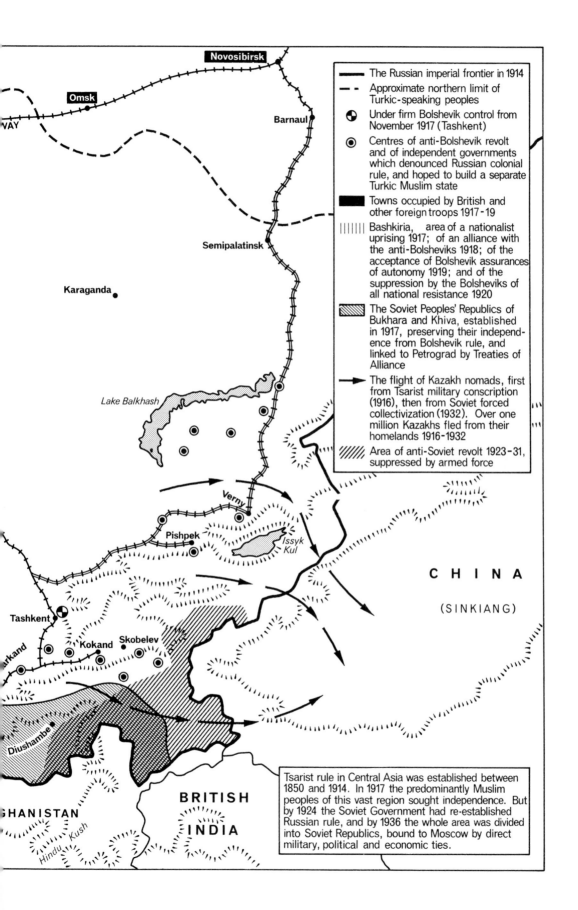

Novosibirsk

Omsk

Barnaul

WAY

Semipalatinsk

Karaganda

Lake Balkhash

Verny

Pishpek

Issyk Kul

CHINA

(SINKIANG)

Tashkent

Kokand Skobelev

arkand

Diushambe

HANISTAN

BRITISH

INDIA

Hindu Kush

▬▬▬	The Russian imperial frontier in 1914
▬ ▬ ▬	Approximate northern limit of Turkic-speaking peoples
◐	Under firm Bolshevik control from November 1917 (Tashkent)
◉	Centres of anti-Bolshevik revolt and of independent governments which denounced Russian colonial rule, and hoped to build a separate Turkic Muslim state
■	Towns occupied by British and other foreign troops 1917-19
‖‖‖	Bashkiria, area of a nationalist uprising 1917; of an alliance with the anti-Bolsheviks 1918; of the acceptance of Bolshevik assurances of autonomy 1919; and of the suppression by the Bolsheviks of all national resistance 1920
▧	The Soviet Peoples' Republics of Bukhara and Khiva, established in 1917, preserving their independence from Bolshevik rule, and linked to Petrograd by Treaties of Alliance
→	The flight of Kazakh nomads, first from Tsarist military conscription (1916), then from Soviet forced collectivization (1932). Over one million Kazakhs fled from their homelands 1916-1932
▨	Area of anti-Soviet revolt 1923-31, suppressed by armed force

Tsarist rule in Central Asia was established between 1850 and 1914. In 1917 the predominantly Muslim peoples of this vast region sought independence. But by 1924 the Soviet Government had re-established Russian rule, and by 1936 the whole area was divided into Soviet Republics, bound to Moscow by direct military, political and economic ties.

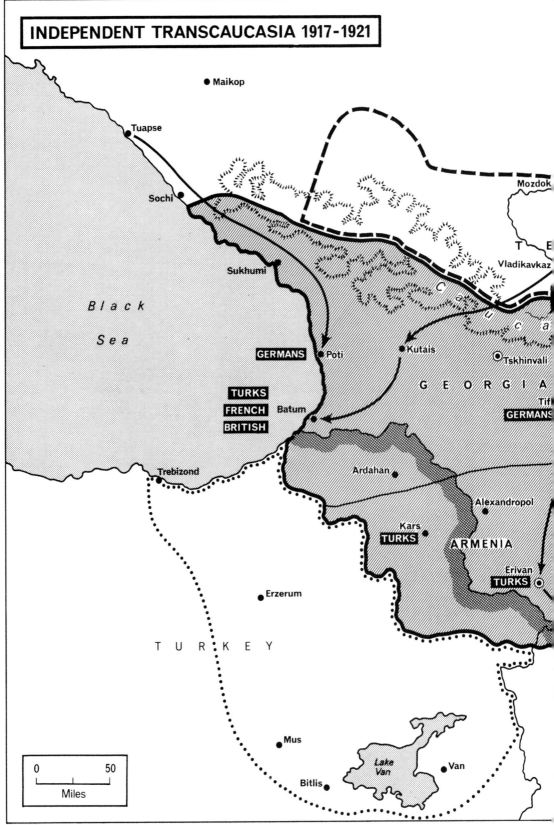

INDEPENDENT TRANSCAUCASIA 1917-1921

Maikop

Tuapse

Sochi

Sukhumi

Black

Sea

Mozdok

Vladikavkaz

T   E

C a u c a

Poti

GERMANS

Kutais

Tskhinvali

G E O R G I A

TURKS

FRENCH

BRITISH

Batum

Tif

GERMANS

Trebizond

Ardahan

Alexandropol

Kars

TURKS

A R M E N I A

Erivan

TURKS

Erzerum

T U R K E Y

Mus

Lake

Van

Van

Bitlis

0   50

Miles

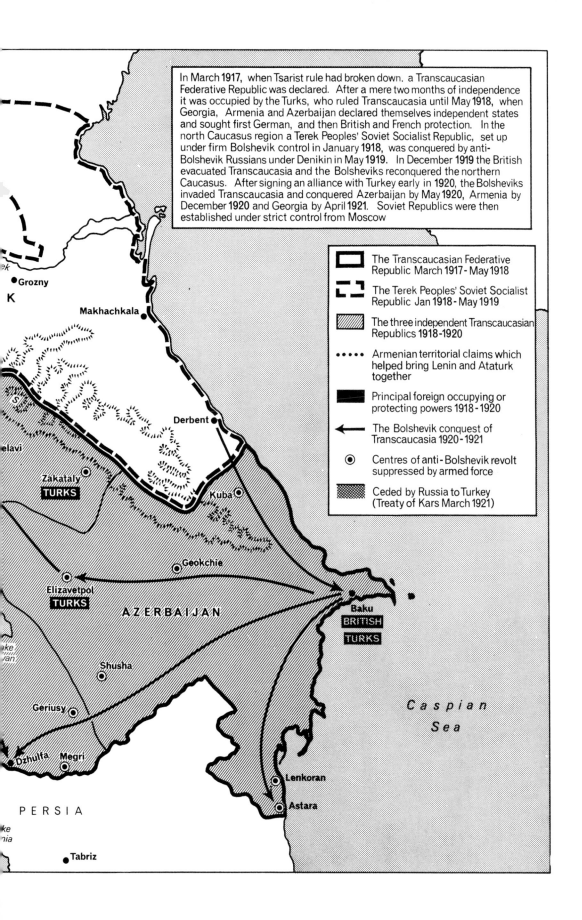

In March 1917, when Tsarist rule had broken down. a Transcaucasian Federative Republic was declared. After a mere two months of independence it was occupied by the Turks, who ruled Transcaucasia until May 1918, when Georgia, Armenia and Azerbaijan declared themselves independent states and sought first German, and then British and French protection. In the north Caucasus region a Terek Peoples' Soviet Socialist Republic, set up under firm Bolshevik control in January 1918, was conquered by anti-Bolshevik Russians under Denikin in May 1919. In December 1919 the British evacuated Transcaucasia and the Bolsheviks reconquered the northern Caucasus. After signing an alliance with Turkey early in 1920, the Bolsheviks invaded Transcaucasia and conquered Azerbaijan by May 1920, Armenia by December 1920 and Georgia by April 1921. Soviet Republics were then established under strict control from Moscow

The Transcaucasian Federative Republic March 1917 - May 1918

The Terek Peoples' Soviet Socialist Republic Jan 1918 - May 1919

The three independent Transcaucasian Republics 1918-1920

Armenian territorial claims which helped bring Lenin and Ataturk together

Principal foreign occupying or protecting powers 1918-1920

The Bolshevik conquest of Transcaucasia 1920-1921

Centres of anti-Bolshevik revolt suppressed by armed force

Ceded by Russia to Turkey (Treaty of Kars March 1921)

Grozny

K

Makhachkala

Derbent

elavi

Zakataly
TURKS

Kuba

Geokchie

Elizavetpol
TURKS

AZERBAIJAN

Baku
BRITISH
TURKS

Shusha

Caspian Sea

Geriusy

Dzhulfa Megri

Lenkoran

Astara

PERSIA

ke
nia

Tabriz

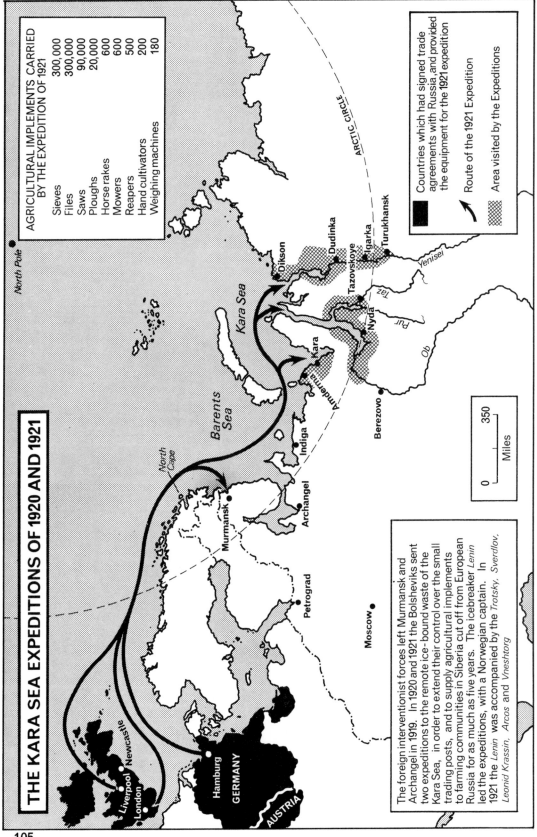

THE KARA SEA EXPEDITIONS OF 1920 AND 1921

AGRICULTURAL IMPLEMENTS CARRIED BY THE EXPEDITION OF 1921	
Sieves	300,000
Files	300,000
Saws	90,000
Ploughs	20,000
Horse rakes	600
Mowers	600
Reapers	500
Hand cultivators	200
Weighing machines	180

Countries which had signed trade agreements with Russia, and provided the equipment for the 1921 expedition

Route of the 1921 Expedition

Area visited by the Expeditions

ARCTIC CIRCLE

North Pole

Barents Sea

Kara Sea

North Cape

Dikson

Dudinka

Igarka

Tazovskoye

Turukhansk

Yenisei

Taz

Pur

Ob

Nyda

Kara

Amderma

Indiga

Berezovo

Archangel

Murmansk

Petrograd

Moscow

GERMANY

AUSTRIA

Hamburg

Liverpool *Newcastle*

London

0	350
Miles	

The foreign interventionist forces left Murmansk and Archangel in 1919. In 1920 and 1921 the Bolsheviks sent two expeditions to the remote ice-bound waste of the Kara Sea, in order to extend their control over the small trading posts, and to supply agricultural implements to farming communities in Siberia cut off from European Russia for as much as five years. The icebreaker *Lenin* led the expeditions, with a Norwegian captain. In 1921 the *Lenin* was accompanied by the *Trotsky, Sverdlov, Leonid Krassin, Arcos* and *Vneshtorg*

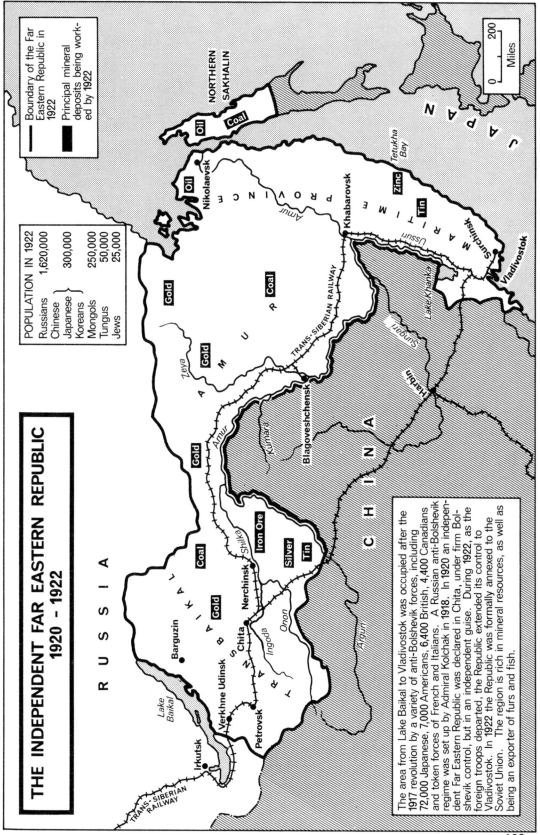

THE INDEPENDENT FAR EASTERN REPUBLIC
1920 - 1922

Boundary of the Far Eastern Republic in 1922

Principal mineral deposits being worked by 1922

POPULATION IN 1922	
Russians	1,620,000
Chinese	300,000
Japanese	
Koreans	250,000
Mongols	50,000
Tungus	25,000
Jews	

RUSSIA

Lake Baikal

Irkutsk

TRANS-SIBERIAN RAILWAY

Barguzin

Verkhne Udinsk

Petrovsk

Chita

Nerchinsk

Gold

Coal

Gold

Silver

Tin

Iron Ore

Shilka

Ingoda

Onon

Argun

Gold

Gold

Zeya

Amur

Gold

Coal

Blagoveshchensk

Kumara

TRANS-SIBERIAN RAILWAY

AMUR

CHINA

Harbin

Sungari

Oil

Nikolaevsk

Oil

Coal

NORTHERN SAKHALIN

Amur

MARITIME PROVINCE

Khabarovsk

Ussuri

Lake Khanka

Zinc

Tin

Tetukha Bay

Suchinsk

Vladivostok

JAPAN

200

0

Miles

The area from Lake Baikal to Vladivostok was occupied after the 1917 revolution by a variety of anti-Bolshevik forces, including 72,000 Japanese, 7,000 Americans, 6,400 British, 4,400 Canadians and token forces of French and Italians. A Russian anti-Bolshevik regime was set up by Admiral Kolchak in 1918. In 1920 an independent Far Eastern Republic was declared in Chita, under firm Bolshevik control, but in an independent guise. During 1922, as the foreign troops departed, the Republic extended its control to Vladivostok. In 1922 the Republic was formally annexed to the Soviet Union. The region is rich in mineral resources, as well as being an exporter of furs and fish.

106

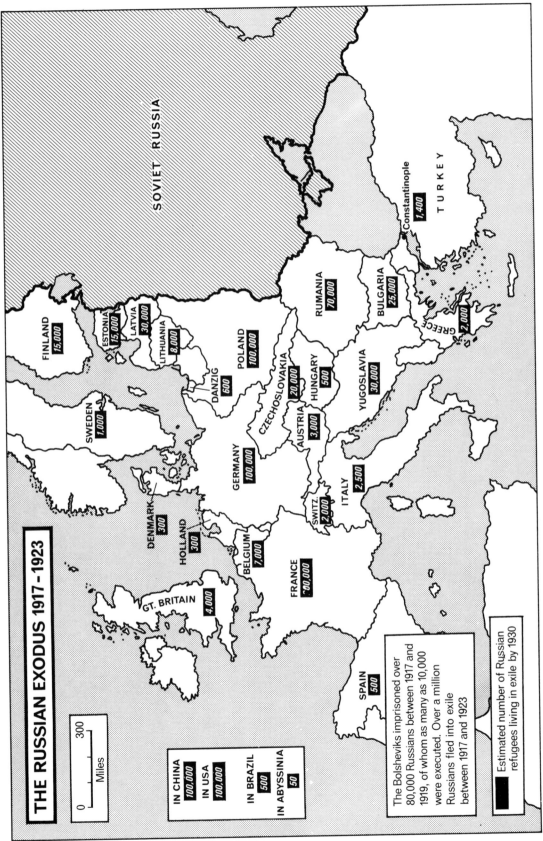

THE RUSSIAN EXODUS 1917–1923

SOVIET RUSSIA

TURKEY

Constantinople *1,400*

FINLAND *15,000*

ESTONIA *15,000*

LATVIA *30,000*

LITHUANIA *8,000*

SWEDEN *1,000*

POLAND *100,000*

DANZIG *600*

RUMANIA *70,000*

BULGARIA *25,000*

GREECE *2,000*

CZECHOSLOVAKIA *20,000*

AUSTRIA *3,000*

HUNGARY *500*

YUGOSLAVIA *30,000*

GERMANY *100,000*

ITALY *2,500*

SWITZ. *2,000*

DENMARK *300*

HOLLAND *300*

BELGIUM *7,000*

FRANCE *400,000*

GT. BRITAIN *4,000*

SPAIN *500*

Scale

Miles

0 — 300

IN CHINA *100,000*
IN USA *100,000*
IN BRAZIL *500*
IN ABYSSINIA *50*

The Bolsheviks imprisoned over 80,000 Russians between 1917 and 1919, of whom as many as 10,000 were executed. Over a million Russians fled into exile between 1917 and 1923

█ Estimated number of Russian refugees living in exile by 1930

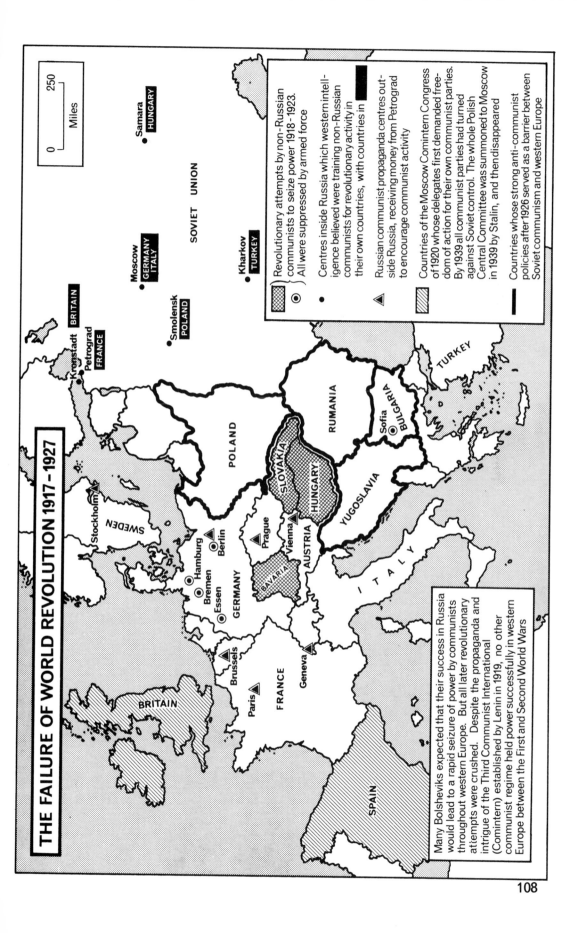

THE FAILURE OF WORLD REVOLUTION 1917–1927

Revolutionary attempts by non-Russian communists to seize power 1918–1923. All were suppressed by armed force

Centres inside Russia which western intelligence believed were training non-Russian communists for revolutionary activity in their own countries, with countries in

Russian communist propaganda centres outside Russia, receiving money from Petrograd to encourage communist activity

Countries of the Moscow Comintern Congress of 1920 whose delegates first demanded freedom of action for their own communist parties. By 1939 all communist parties had turned against Soviet control. The whole Polish Central Committee was summoned to Moscow in 1939 by Stalin, and then disappeared

Countries whose strong anti-communist policies after 1926 served as a barrier between Soviet communism and western Europe

Many Bolsheviks expected that their success in Russia would lead to a rapid seizure of power by communists throughout western Europe. But all later revolutionary attempts were crushed. Despite the propaganda and intrigue of the Third Communist International (Comintern) established by Lenin in 1919, no other communist regime held power successfully in western Europe between the First and Second World Wars

SOVIET UNION

Samara **HUNGARY**

Moscow **GERMANY ITALY**

Kharkov **TURKEY**

Smolensk **POLAND**

Petrograd **FRANCE**

Kronstadt **BRITAIN**

0 250 Miles

POLAND

RUMANIA

Sofia ⊙ **BULGARIA**

SLOVAKIA

HUNGARY

YUGOSLAVIA

TURKEY

Stockholm

SWEDEN

Prague ◬

Vienna ⊙ ◬

AUSTRIA

Hamburg ⊙

Bremen ⊙

Berlin ◬

Essen ⊙

BAVARIA

GERMANY

I T A L Y

Brussels ◬

Paris ◬

FRANCE

Geneva ◬

BRITAIN

SPAIN

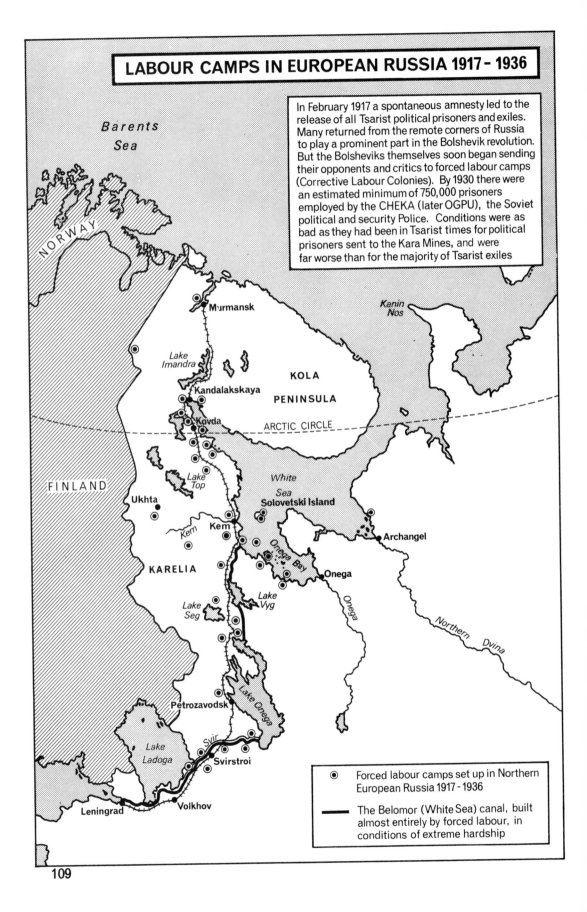

LABOUR CAMPS IN EUROPEAN RUSSIA 1917-1936

In February 1917 a spontaneous amnesty led to the release of all Tsarist political prisoners and exiles. Many returned from the remote corners of Russia to play a prominent part in the Bolshevik revolution. But the Bolsheviks themselves soon began sending their opponents and critics to forced labour camps (Corrective Labour Colonies). By 1930 there were an estimated minimum of 750,000 prisoners employed by the CHEKA (later OGPU), the Soviet political and security Police. Conditions were as bad as they had been in Tsarist times for political prisoners sent to the Kara Mines, and were far worse than for the majority of Tsarist exiles

Barents Sea

NORWAY

Murmansk

Kanin Nos

Lake Imandra

KOLA

Kandalakskaya

PENINSULA

Kovda

ARCTIC CIRCLE

FINLAND

Lake Top

White Sea

Ukhta

Solovetski Island

Kem

Kem

Archangel

KARELIA

Onega Bay

Onega

Lake Vyg

Onega

Lake Seg

Northern Dvina

Petrozavodsk

Lake Onega

Lake Ladoga

Svir

Svirstroi

⊙   Forced labour camps set up in Northern European Russia 1917-1936

Leningrad   Volkhov

━━━   The Belomor (White Sea) canal, built almost entirely by forced labour, in conditions of extreme hardship

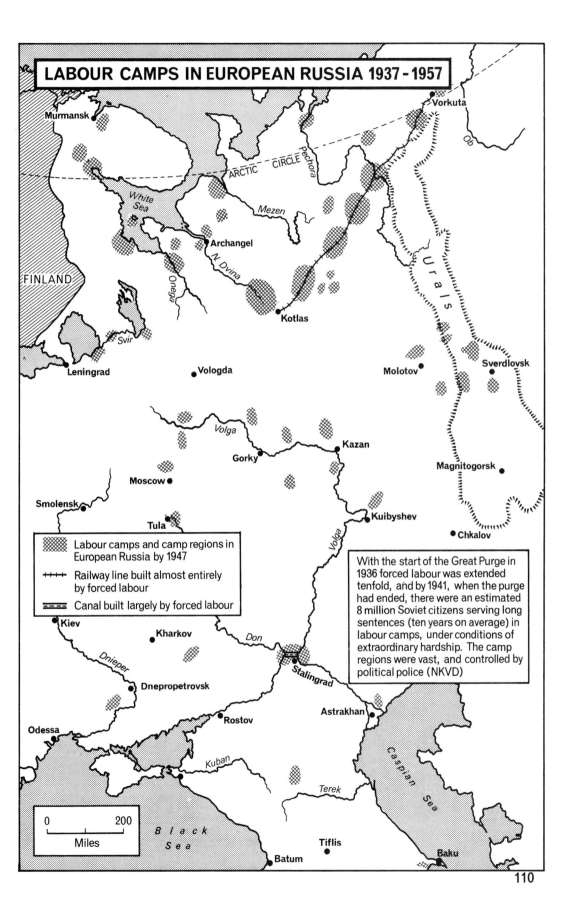

LABOUR CAMPS IN EUROPEAN RUSSIA 1937-1957

Murmansk

Vorkuta

ARCTIC CIRCLE

Pechora

Ob

White Sea

Mezen

Urals

Archangel

N. Dvina

FINLAND

Onega

Kotlas

Svir

Leningrad

Vologda

Molotov

Sverdlovsk

Volga

Gorky

Kazan

Magnitogorsk

Moscow

Smolensk

Kuibyshev

Tula

Chkalov

Volga

Labour camps and camp regions in European Russia by 1947

Railway line built almost entirely by forced labour

Canal built largely by forced labour

Kiev

Kharkov

Don

With the start of the Great Purge in 1936 forced labour was extended tenfold, and by 1941, when the purge had ended, there were an estimated 8 million Soviet citizens serving long sentences (ten years on average) in labour camps, under conditions of extraordinary hardship. The camp regions were vast, and controlled by political police (NKVD)

Dnieper

Dnepropetrovsk

Stalingrad

Astrakhan

Odessa

Rostov

Caspian Sea

Kuban

0   200

Miles

Terek

Black Sea

Tiflis

Baku

Batum

110

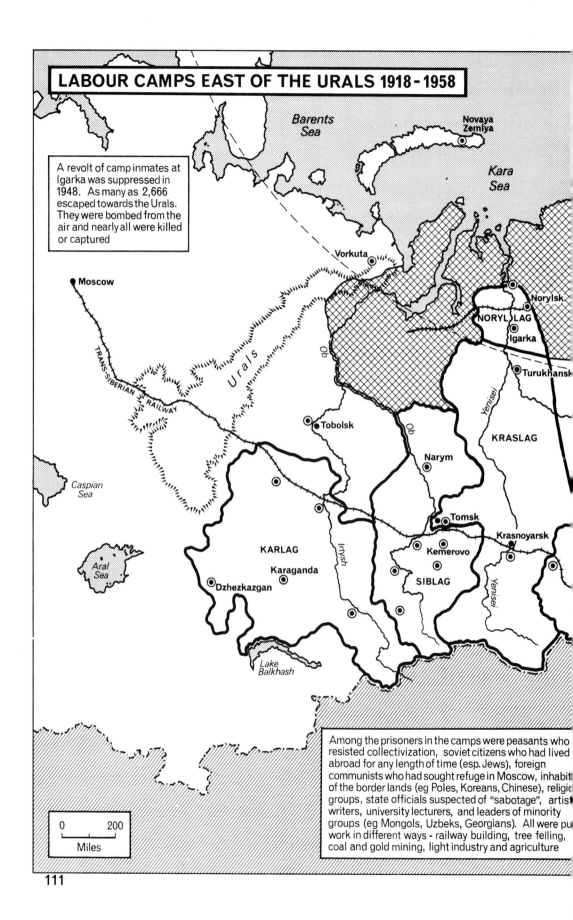

LABOUR CAMPS EAST OF THE URALS 1918-1958

A revolt of camp inmates at Igarka was suppressed in 1948. As many as 2,666 escaped towards the Urals. They were bombed from the air and nearly all were killed or captured

Barents Sea

Kara Sea

Novaya Zemlya

Moscow

Vorkuta

Norylsk

NORYL LAG

Igarka

Turukhansk

TRANS-SIBERIAN RAILWAY

Urals

Ob

Ob

Yenisei

Tobolsk

KRASLAG

Narym

Tomsk

Krasnoyarsk

Caspian Sea

Irtysh

Kemerovo

Aral Sea

KARLAG

Karaganda

SIBLAG

Yenisei

Dzhezkazgan

Lake Balkhash

0   200

Miles

Among the prisoners in the camps were peasants who resisted collectivization, soviet citizens who had lived abroad for any length of time (esp. Jews), foreign communists who had sought refuge in Moscow, inhabit of the border lands (eg Poles, Koreans, Chinese), religi groups, state officials suspected of "sabotage", artis writers, university lecturers, and leaders of minority groups (eg Mongols, Uzbeks, Georgians). All were pu work in different ways - railway building, tree felling, coal and gold mining, light industry and agriculture

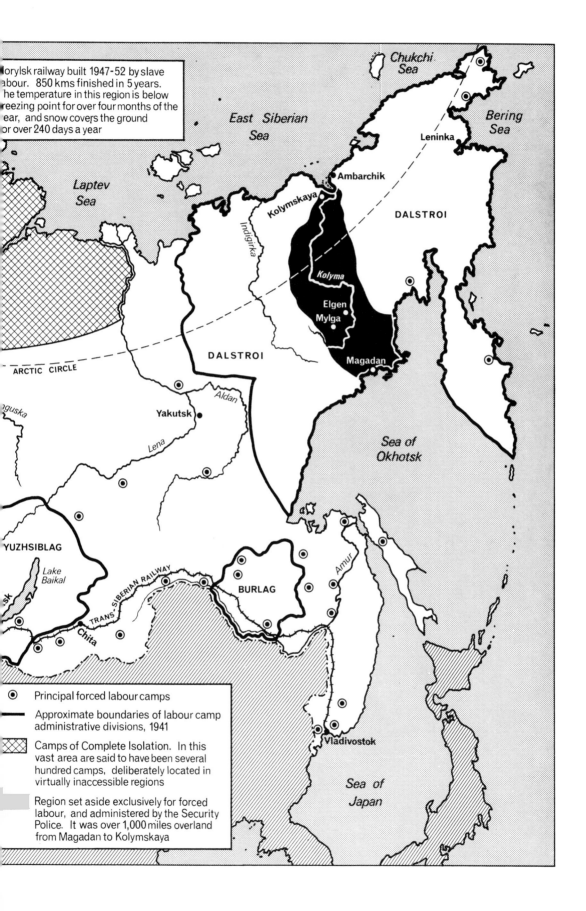

Norylsk railway built 1947-52 by slave
labour. 850 kms finished in 5 years.
The temperature in this region is below
freezing point for over four months of the
year, and snow covers the ground
for over 240 days a year

Chukchi
Sea

Bering
Sea

Leninka

East Siberian
Sea

Laptev
Sea

Ambarchik

Kolymskaya

DALSTROI

Indigirka

Kolyma

Elgen
Mylga

Magadan

ARCTIC CIRCLE

DALSTROI

Aldan

Yakutsk

Sea of
Okhotsk

Lena

nguska

YUZHSIBLAG

Lake
Baikal

TRANS-SIBERIAN RAILWAY

BURLAG

Amur

TRANS-SIBERIAN RAILWAY

Chita

Vladivostok

Sea of
Japan

⊙ Principal forced labour camps

▬ Approximate boundaries of labour camp
administrative divisions, 1941

Camps of Complete Isolation. In this
vast area are said to have been several
hundred camps, deliberately located in
virtually inaccessible regions

Region set aside exclusively for forced
labour, and administered by the Security
Police. It was over 1,000 miles overland
from Magadan to Kolymskaya

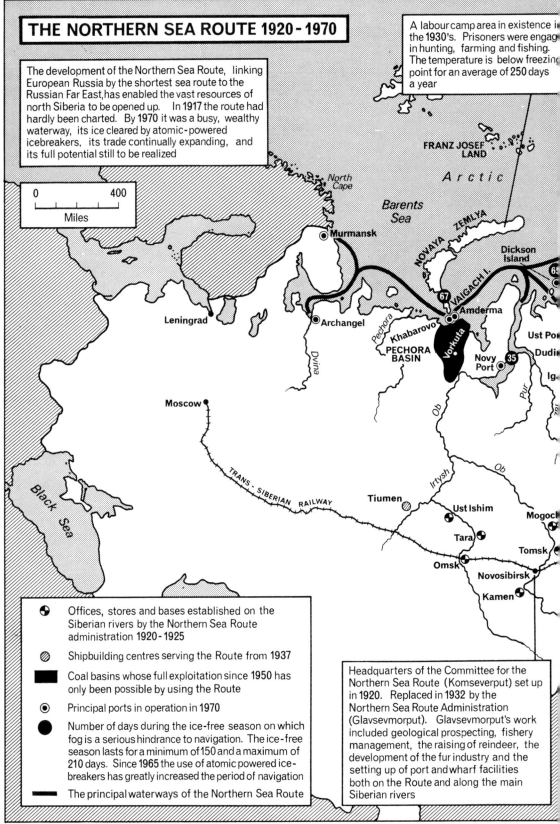

THE NORTHERN SEA ROUTE 1920 - 1970

The development of the Northern Sea Route, linking
European Russia by the shortest sea route to the
Russian Far East, has enabled the vast resources of
north Siberia to be opened up. In 1917 the route had
hardly been charted. By 1970 it was a busy, wealthy
waterway, its ice cleared by atomic-powered
icebreakers, its trade continually expanding, and
its full potential still to be realized

A labour camp area in existence i[n]
the 1930's. Prisoners were engag[ed]
in hunting, farming and fishing.
The temperature is below freezin[g]
point for an average of 250 days
a year

0   400

Miles

FRANZ JOSEF
LAND

North
Cape

Arctic

*Barents
Sea*

Murmansk

NOVAYA ZEMLYA

Dickson
Island

65

VAIGACH I.

67

Amderma

Leningrad

Archangel

Pechora

Khabarovo

PECHORA
BASIN

Vorkuta

Ust Por[t]

Dudi[nka]

Dvina

Novy
Port

35

Ig[arka]

Ob

Pur

Moscow

Irtysh

Ob

TRANS - SIBERIAN RAILWAY

Tiumen

Ust Ishim

Mogoc[ha]

Tara

Tomsk

Black Sea

Omsk

Novosibirsk

Kamen

◐ Offices, stores and bases established on the
  Siberian rivers by the Northern Sea Route
  administration 1920-1925

◎ Shipbuilding centres serving the Route from 1937

■ Coal basins whose full exploitation since 1950 has
  only been possible by using the Route

◉ Principal ports in operation in 1970

● Number of days during the ice-free season on which
  fog is a serious hindrance to navigation. The ice-free
  season lasts for a minimum of 150 and a maximum of
  210 days. Since 1965 the use of atomic powered icebreakers has greatly increased the period of navigation

━ The principal waterways of the Northern Sea Route

Headquarters of the Committee for the
Northern Sea Route (Komseverput) set up
in 1920. Replaced in 1932 by the
Northern Sea Route Administration
(Glavsevmorput). Glavsevmorput's work
included geological prospecting, fishery
management, the raising of reindeer, the
development of the fur industry and the
setting up of port and wharf facilities
both on the Route and along the main
Siberian rivers

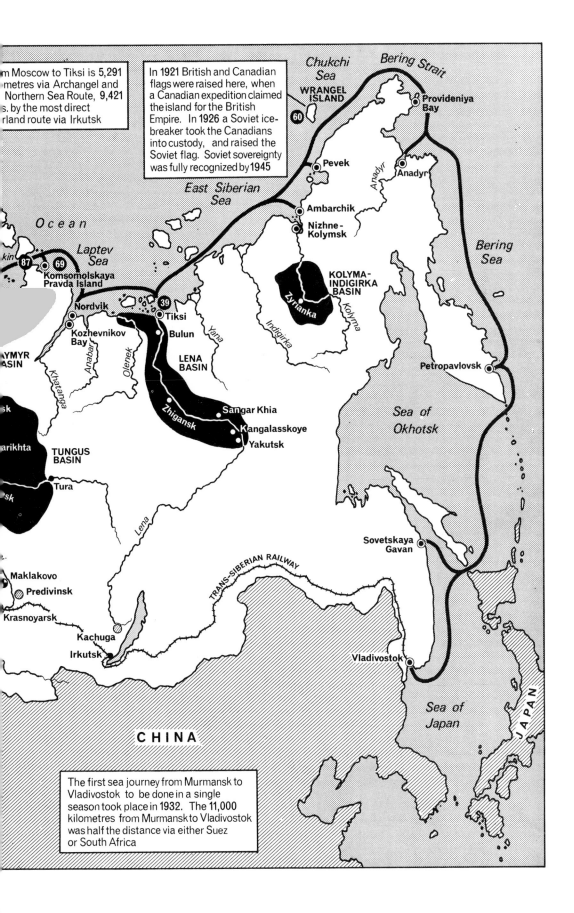

In 1921 British and Canadian flags were raised here, when a Canadian expedition claimed the island for the British Empire. In 1926 a Soviet ice-breaker took the Canadians into custody, and raised the Soviet flag. Soviet sovereignty was fully recognized by 1945

m Moscow to Tiksi is 5,291 metres via Archangel and Northern Sea Route, 9,421 s. by the most direct rland route via Irkutsk

Chukchi Sea

Bering Strait

Providentiya Bay

WRANGEL ISLAND

60

Pevek

Anadyr

East Siberian Sea

Ambarchik

Nizhne-Kolymsk

Ocean

Laptev Sea

Bering Sea

87 69

Komsomolskaya Pravda Island

Nordvik

39 Tiksi

Kozhevnikov Bay

Bulun

KOLYMA-INDIGIRKA BASIN

Zyrianka

Anadyr

Kolyma

AYMYR ASIN

Khatanga

Anabar

Olenek

Yana

Indigirka

LENA BASIN

Petropavlovsk

Zhigansk

Sangar Khia

Kangalasskoye

Yakutsk

Sea of Okhotsk

arikhta

TUNGUS BASIN

Tura

sk

Lena

Maklakovo

Predivinsk

Krasnoyarsk

Kachuga

Irkutsk

TRANS-SIBERIAN RAILWAY

Sovetskaya Gavan

Vladivostok

CHINA

JAPAN

Sea of Japan

The first sea journey from Murmansk to Vladivostok to be done in a single season took place in 1932. The 11,000 kilometres from Murmansk to Vladivostok was half the distance via either Suez or South Africa

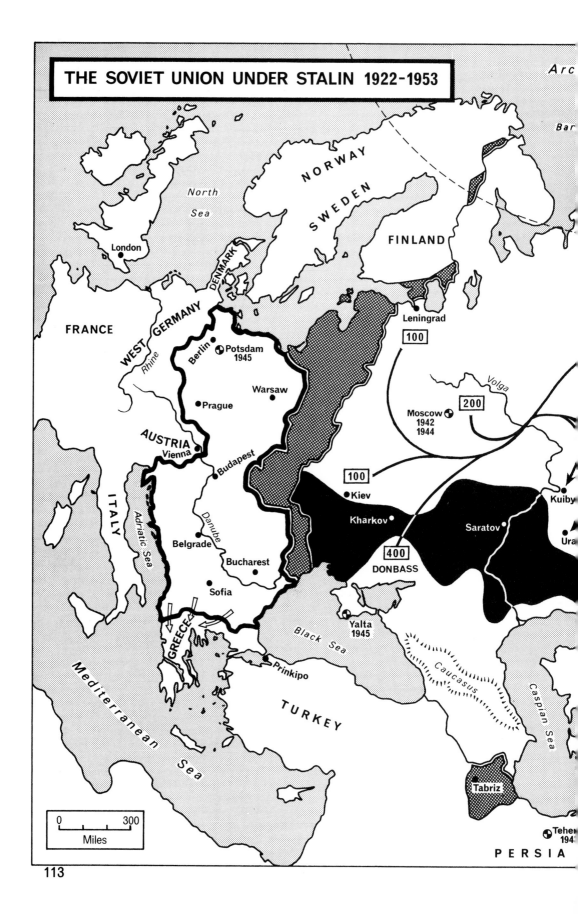

THE SOVIET UNION UNDER STALIN 1922-1953

North Sea

NORWAY

SWEDEN

FINLAND

Arc

Bar

London

FRANCE

WEST GERMANY

DENMARK

Rhine

Berlin

Potsdam 1945

Warsaw

Prague

AUSTRIA

Vienna

Budapest

ITALY

Adriatic Sea

Danube

Belgrade

Bucharest

Sofia

GREECE

Prinkipo

Black Sea

Yalta 1945

Leningrad

100

Volga

Moscow 1942 1944

200

100

Kiev

Kharkov

Saratov

400

DONBASS

Kuiby

Ura

Caucasus

Caspian Sea

TURKEY

Mediterranean Sea

Tabriz

Teher 194

PERSIA

0   300
Miles

113

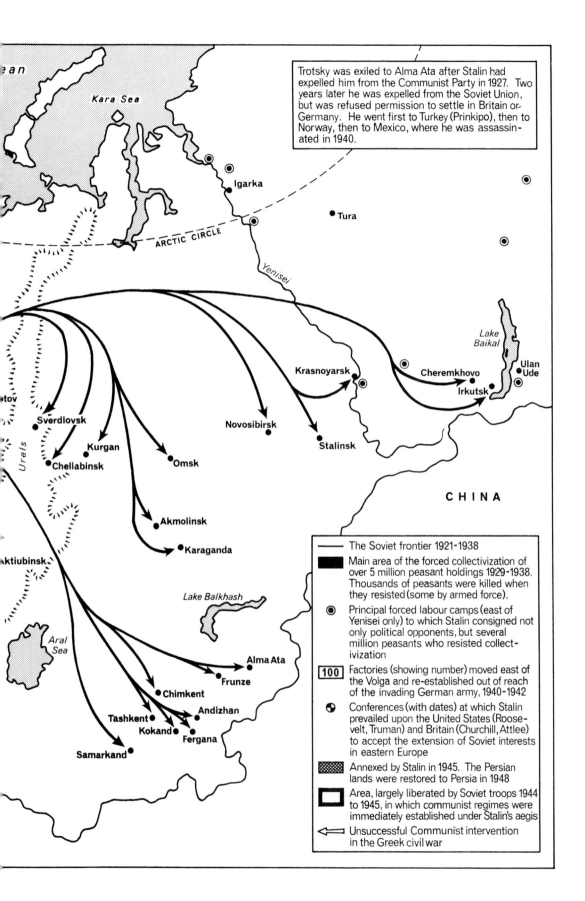

Kara Sea

Trotsky was exiled to Alma Ata after Stalin had expelled him from the Communist Party in 1927. Two years later he was expelled from the Soviet Union, but was refused permission to settle in Britain or Germany. He went first to Turkey (Prinkipo), then to Norway, then to Mexico, where he was assassinated in 1940.

Igarka

Tura

ARCTIC CIRCLE

Yenisei

Lake Baikal

Krasnoyarsk

Cheremkhovo

Ulan Ude

Irkutsk

tov

Sverdlovsk

Novosibirsk

Stalinsk

Kurgan

Cheliabinsk

Omsk

Urals

Akmolinsk

CHINA

ktiubinsk

Karaganda

Lake Balkhash

Aral Sea

Alma Ata

Frunze

Chimkent

Andizhan

Tashkent

Kokand

Fergana

Samarkand

The Soviet frontier 1921-1938

Main area of the forced collectivization of over 5 million peasant holdings 1929-1938. Thousands of peasants were killed when they resisted (some by armed force).

Principal forced labour camps (east of Yenisei only) to which Stalin consigned not only political opponents, but several million peasants who resisted collectivization

100 Factories (showing number) moved east of the Volga and re-established out of reach of the invading German army, 1940-1942

Conferences (with dates) at which Stalin prevailed upon the United States (Roosevelt, Truman) and Britain (Churchill, Attlee) to accept the extension of Soviet interests in eastern Europe

Annexed by Stalin in 1945. The Persian lands were restored to Persia in 1948

Area, largely liberated by Soviet troops 1944 to 1945, in which communist regimes were immediately established under Stalin's aegis

Unsuccessful Communist intervention in the Greek civil war

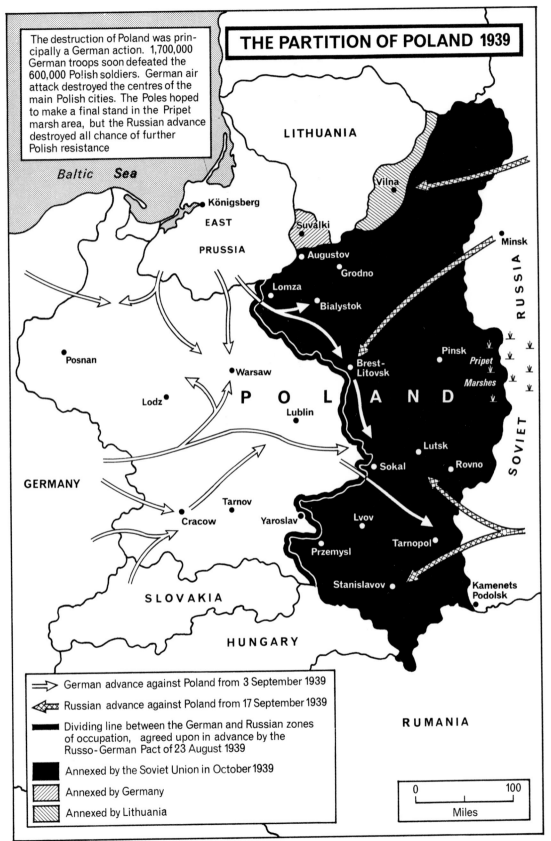

THE PARTITION OF POLAND 1939

The destruction of Poland was principally a German action. 1,700,000 German troops soon defeated the 600,000 Polish soldiers. German air attack destroyed the centres of the main Polish cities. The Poles hoped to make a final stand in the Pripet marsh area, but the Russian advance destroyed all chance of further Polish resistance

Baltic Sea

LITHUANIA

Vilna

Königsberg

EAST
PRUSSIA

Suvalki

Augustov

Grodno

Minsk

Lomza

Bialystok

RUSSIA

Posnan

Warsaw

Pinsk

Pripet

Brest-
Litovsk

Marshes

P O L A N D

Lodz

Lublin

GERMANY

Lutsk

Sokal

Rovno

SOVIET

Tarnov

Cracow

Lvov

Yaroslav

Tarnopol

Przemysl

Stanislavov

Kamenets
Podolsk

SLOVAKIA

HUNGARY

⟹ German advance against Poland from 3 September 1939

⟸ Russian advance against Poland from 17 September 1939

▬ Dividing line between the German and Russian zones of occupation, agreed upon in advance by the Russo-German Pact of 23 August 1939

■ Annexed by the Soviet Union in October 1939

▨ Annexed by Germany

▨ Annexed by Lithuania

RUMANIA

0   100
Miles

114

THE RUSSO – FINNISH WAR 1939 – 1940

Russian fears of Germany and German influence led to the invasion of Finland in November 1939. The Finns had been independent from Russia for 22 years, and fought tenaciously to preserve their independence. French and British volunteers fought on the Finnish side. In March 1940 the Finns agreed to the Treaty of Moscow and the war was over. Russia gained territory around Leningrad and further protection for the Leningrad to Murmansk railway

Atlantic Ocean

NORWAY

SWEDEN

WAR DEAD
Finnish 30,000
Russian 80,000

Petsamo

Murmansk

Kandalaksha

Salla

Kemijaervi

Tornea

Kem

Suomussalmi

Kajaani

S O V I E T

Gulf of Bothnia

Vaasa

FINLAND

Lake Onega

Tampere

Lake Ladoga

U N I O N

Vyborg

Abo

Helsinki

Leningrad

Hango

Gulf of Finland

Tallin

Stockholm

ESTONIA

Baltic Sea

LATVIA

0   100
Miles

▨   Occupied by Russia in October 1939

◀   Russian attacks on Finland in November 1939

▢▭   The Mannerheim Line defences, broken by Russian assaults by land, sea and air

■   Finnish territory ceded to Russia by the Treaty of Moscow

▨   Russia granted access to the Norwegian border by Finland

⊙   Russia given a thirty-year lease on the strategic Hangö Peninsula

115

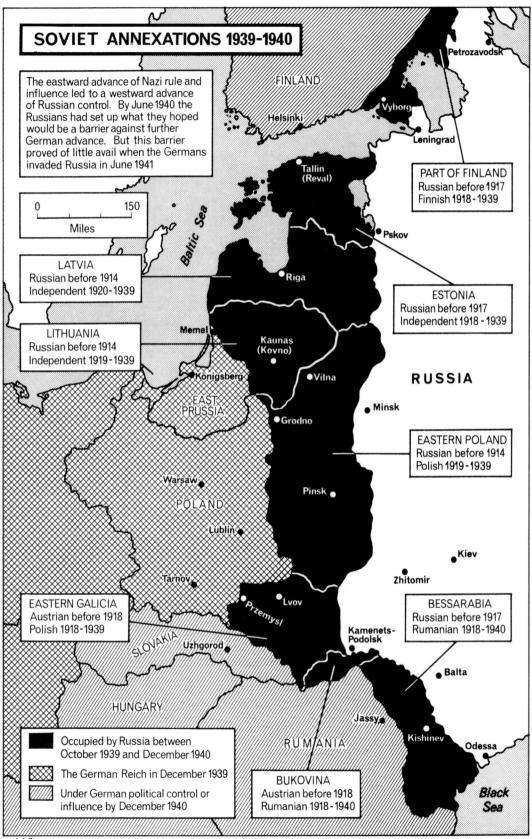

SOVIET ANNEXATIONS 1939-1940

The eastward advance of Nazi rule and influence led to a westward advance of Russian control. By June 1940 the Russians had set up what they hoped would be a barrier against further German advance. But this barrier proved of little avail when the Germans invaded Russia in June 1941

0   150
Miles

FINLAND

Helsinki

Petrozavodsk

Vyborg

Leningrad

Tallin (Reval)

Pskov

PART OF FINLAND
Russian before 1917
Finnish 1918-1939

Baltic Sea

Riga

LATVIA
Russian before 1914
Independent 1920-1939

ESTONIA
Russian before 1917
Independent 1918-1939

Memel

Kaunas (Kovno)

LITHUANIA
Russian before 1914
Independent 1919-1939

Vilna

Königsberg

EAST PRUSSIA

RUSSIA

Minsk

Grodno

EASTERN POLAND
Russian before 1914
Polish 1919-1939

Warsaw

POLAND

Pinsk

Lublin

Kiev

Zhitomir

Tarnov

Lvov

Przemysl

BESSARABIA
Russian before 1917
Rumanian 1918-1940

EASTERN GALICIA
Austrian before 1918
Polish 1918-1939

Kamenets-Podolsk

SLOVAKIA

Uzhgorod

Balta

HUNGARY

Jassy

Kishinev

Odessa

RUMANIA

■ Occupied by Russia between October 1939 and December 1940

▨ The German Reich in December 1939

▨ Under German political control or influence by December 1940

BUKOVINA
Austrian before 1918
Rumanian 1918-1940

Black Sea

116

EUROPE ON 22 JUNE 1941

Archangel

FINLAND

Hango

Leningrad

NORWAY

SWEDEN

Riga

Kovno

Moscow

Vilna

DENMARK

Danzig

SOVIET
UNION

BRITAIN

EIRE

HOLLAND

London

Berlin

Brest-Litovsk

GREATER
GERMANY

Warsaw

Cologne

BELGIUM

Cracow

Lvov

Prague

FRANCE

Munich

SLOVAKIA

SWITZ.

Vienna

HUNGARY

Kishinev

RUMANIA

Odessa

SPAIN

YUGOSLAVIA

BULGARIA

ITALY

ALBANIA

GREECE

TURKEY

The German Reich on 22 June 1941,
the day of the German invasion of Russia

Countries under German rule or
influence by June 1941

Neutral countries

Great Britain, the only state at war with
Germany on 21 June 1941; and the
Soviet Union, to whom Britain
immediately offered all possible help
and alliance in the fight against Nazism

0   300
Miles

117

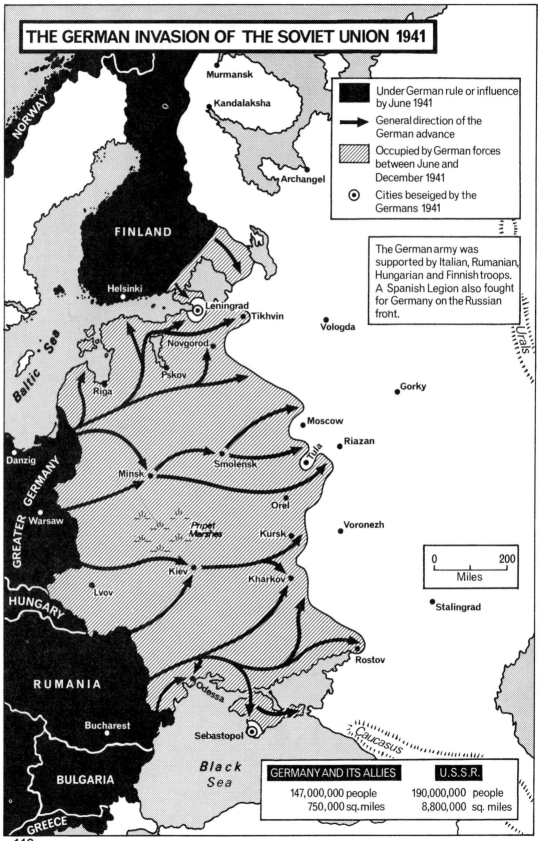

THE GERMAN INVASION OF THE SOVIET UNION 1941

■	Under German rule or influence by June 1941
→	General direction of the German advance
▨	Occupied by German forces between June and December 1941
⊙	Cities beseiged by the Germans 1941

The German army was supported by Italian, Rumanian, Hungarian and Finnish troops. A Spanish Legion also fought for Germany on the Russian front.

NORWAY

Murmansk

Kandalaksha

FINLAND

Archangel

Helsinki

Leningrad

Tikhvin

Vologda

Urals

Novgorod

Baltic Sea

Pskov

Gorky

Riga

Moscow

Danzig

Smolensk

Riazan

GREATER GERMANY

Minsk

Tula

Warsaw

Orel

Voronezh

Pripet Marshes

Kursk

HUNGARY

Kiev

Kharkov

Lvov

Stalingrad

RUMANIA

Rostov

Odessa

0	200
	Miles

Bucharest

Sebastopol

Caucasus

BULGARIA

Black Sea

GREECE

GERMANY AND ITS ALLIES	U.S.S.R.
147,000,000 people	190,000,000 people
750,000 sq. miles	8,800,000 sq. miles

118

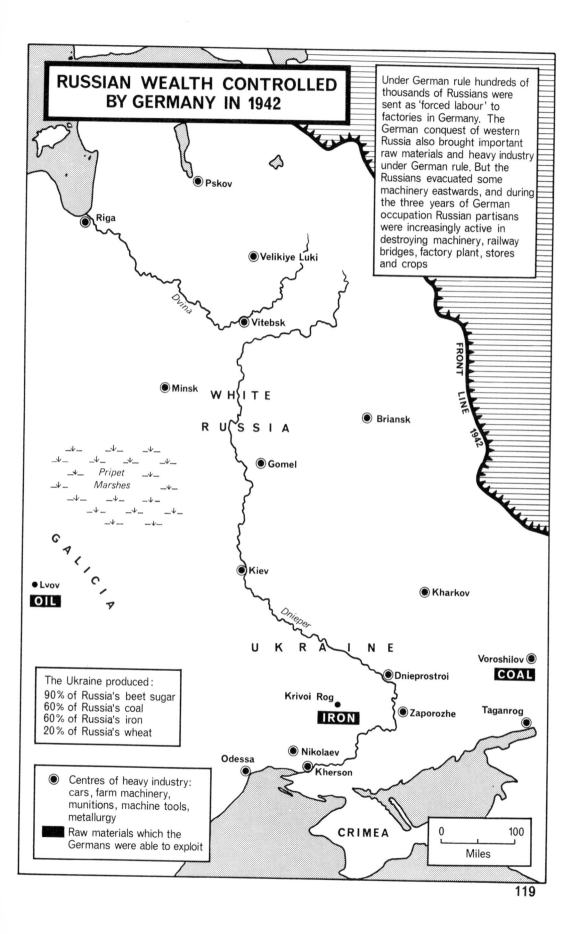

RUSSIAN WEALTH CONTROLLED BY GERMANY IN 1942

Under German rule hundreds of thousands of Russians were sent as 'forced labour' to factories in Germany. The German conquest of western Russia also brought important raw materials and heavy industry under German rule. But the Russians evacuated some machinery eastwards, and during the three years of German occupation Russian partisans were increasingly active in destroying machinery, railway bridges, factory plant, stores and crops

Pskov

Riga

Velikiye Luki

Dvina

Vitebsk

FRONT LINE 1942

Minsk

W H I T E

R U S S I A

Briansk

Gomel

Pripet Marshes

G A L I C I A

Kiev

Dnieper

Kharkov

Lvov
OIL

U K R A I N E

Voroshilov
COAL

Dnieprostroi

Krivoi Rog

IRON

Zaporozhe

Taganrog

The Ukraine produced:
90% of Russia's beet sugar
60% of Russia's coal
60% of Russia's iron
20% of Russia's wheat

Nikolaev

Odessa

Kherson

◉ Centres of heavy industry: cars, farm machinery, munitions, machine tools, metallurgy

■ Raw materials which the Germans were able to exploit

CRIMEA

0   100
Miles

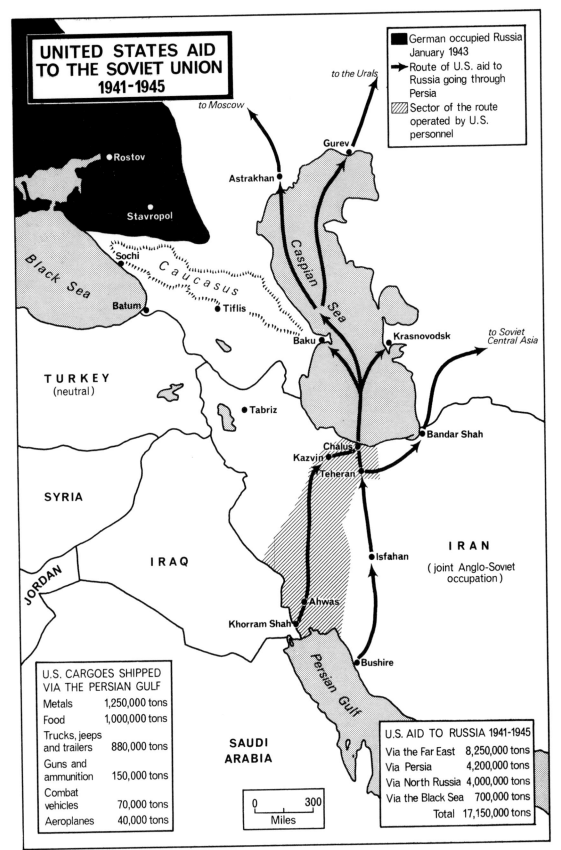

UNITED STATES AID TO THE SOVIET UNION 1941-1945

Legend:
- ■ German occupied Russia January 1943
- → Route of U.S. aid to Russia going through Persia
- ▨ Sector of the route operated by U.S. personnel

to the Urals

to Moscow

●Rostov

●Stavropol

Black Sea

●Sochi

C a u c a s u s

Batum●

●Tiflis

Astrakhan●

Gurev●

Caspian Sea

Baku●

Krasnovodsk●

TURKEY
(neutral)

●Tabriz

to Soviet Central Asia

Bandar Shah●

Chalus●

Kazvin●

Teheran●

SYRIA

IRAN
(joint Anglo-Soviet occupation)

JORDAN

IRAQ

●Isfahan

Ahwas●

Khorram Shah●

●Bushire

Persian Gulf

SAUDI ARABIA

U.S. CARGOES SHIPPED VIA THE PERSIAN GULF

Metals	1,250,000 tons
Food	1,000,000 tons
Trucks, jeeps and trailers	880,000 tons
Guns and ammunition	150,000 tons
Combat vehicles	70,000 tons
Aeroplanes	40,000 tons

0   300
Miles

U.S. AID TO RUSSIA 1941-1945

Via the Far East	8,250,000 tons
Via Persia	4,200,000 tons
Via North Russia	4,000,000 tons
Via the Black Sea	700,000 tons
Total	17,150,000 tons

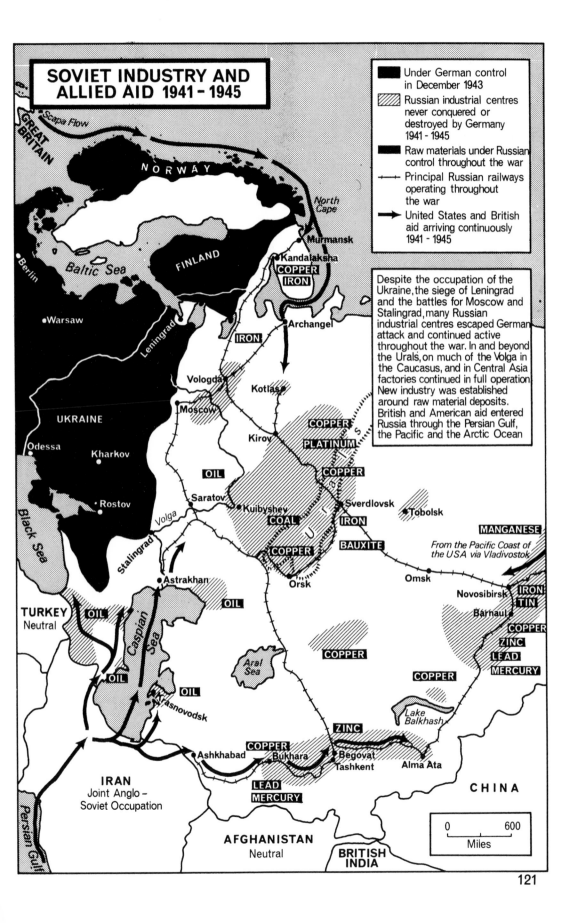

SOVIET INDUSTRY AND ALLIED AID 1941-1945

Under German control in December 1943

Russian industrial centres never conquered or destroyed by Germany 1941 - 1945

Raw materials under Russian control throughout the war

Principal Russian railways operating throughout the war

United States and British aid arriving continuously 1941 - 1945

Despite the occupation of the Ukraine, the siege of Leningrad and the battles for Moscow and Stalingrad, many Russian industrial centres escaped German attack and continued active throughout the war. In and beyond the Urals, on much of the Volga in the Caucasus, and in Central Asia factories continued in full operation. New industry was established around raw material deposits. British and American aid entered Russia through the Persian Gulf, the Pacific and the Arctic Ocean

GREAT BRITAIN

Scapa Flow

NORWAY

North Cape

Murmansk

Baltic Sea

FINLAND

Kandalaksha

COPPER

IRON

Berlin

Warsaw

Leningrad

Archangel

IRON

Vologda

Kotlas

Moscow

UKRAINE

Kirov

COPPER

PLATINUM

COPPER

Odessa

Kharkov

OIL

Sverdlovsk

Tobolsk

Rostov

Saratov

Kuibyshev

COAL

IRON

Volga

COPPER

BAUXITE

MANGANESE

From the Pacific Coast of the USA via Vladivostok

Stalingrad

Orsk

Omsk

Novosibirsk

IRON

TIN

Astrakhan

OIL

Barnaul

Black Sea

COPPER

ZINC

LEAD

MERCURY

TURKEY
Neutral

OIL

Caspian Sea

OIL

Aral Sea

COPPER

COPPER

OIL

Krasnovodsk

Lake Balkhash

ZINC

Ashkhabad

COPPER

Bukhara

Begovat

Tashkent

Alma Ata

IRAN
Joint Anglo - Soviet Occupation

LEAD

MERCURY

CHINA

AFGHANISTAN
Neutral

BRITISH INDIA

Persian Gulf

0   600
Miles

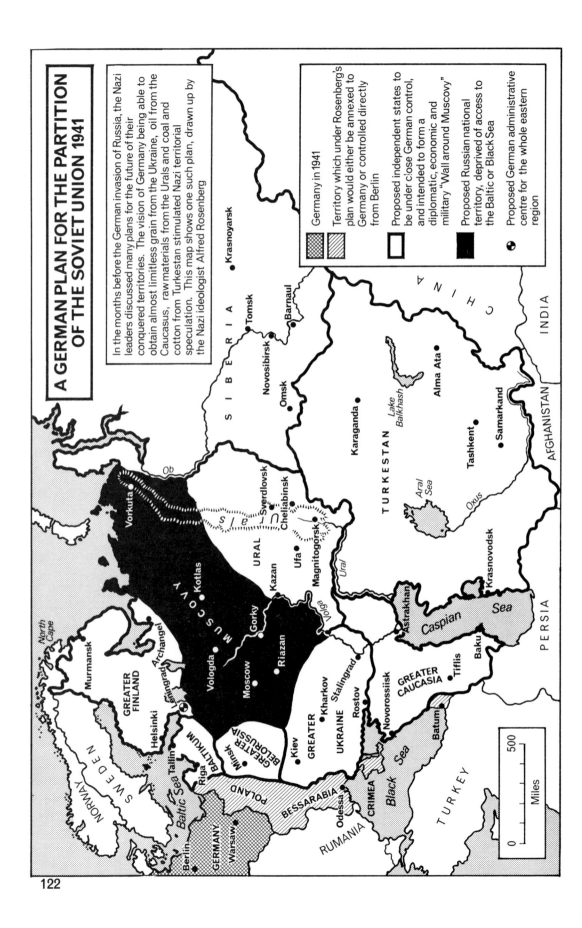

A GERMAN PLAN FOR THE PARTITION OF THE SOVIET UNION 1941

In the months before the German invasion of Russia, the Nazi leaders discussed many plans for the future of their conquered territories. The vision of Germany being able to obtain almost limitless grain from the Ukraine, oil from the Caucasus, raw materials from the Urals and coal and cotton from Turkestan stimulated Nazi territorial speculation. This map shows one such plan, drawn up by the Nazi ideologist Alfred Rosenberg.

Germany in 1941

Territory which under Rosenberg's plan would either be annexed to Germany or controlled directly from Berlin

Proposed independent states to be under close German control and intended to form a diplomatic, economic and military "Wall around Muscovy"

Proposed Russian national territory, deprived of access to the Baltic or Black Sea

Proposed German administrative centre for the whole eastern region

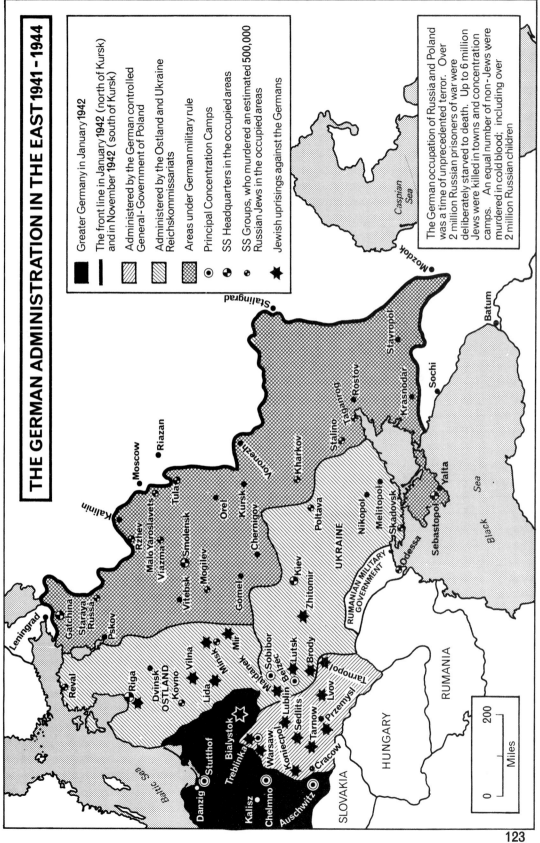

THE GERMAN ADMINISTRATION IN THE EAST 1941–1944

Greater Germany in January 1942

The front line in January 1942 (north of Kursk) and in November 1942 (south of Kursk)

Administered by the German controlled General-Government of Poland

Administered by the Ostland and Ukraine Reichskommissariats

Areas under German military rule

Principal Concentration Camps

SS Headquarters in the occupied areas

SS Groups, who murdered an estimated 500,000 Russian Jews in the occupied areas

Jewish uprisings against the Germans

The German occupation of Russia and Poland was a time of unprecedented terror. Over 2 million Russian prisoners of war were deliberately starved to death. Up to 6 million Jews were killed in towns and concentration camps. An equal number of non-Jews were murdered in cold blood; including over 2 million Russian children

Caspian Sea

Mozdok

Stalingrad

Stavropol

Rostov

Krasnodar

Taganrog

Sochi

Stalino

Batum

Kharkov

Yalta

Poltava

Sebastopol

Black Sea

Voronezh

Kursk

Chernigov

Kiev

Nikopol

UKRAINE

Melitopol

Skadovsk

Odessa

Moscow

Riazan

Kalinin

Rzhev

Malo Yaroslavets

Tula

Orel

Zhitomir

RUMANIAN MILITARY GOVERNMENT

Smolensk

Viazma

Mogilev

Gomel

Leningrad

Gatchina

Staraya Russa

Pskov

Vitebsk

Minsk

Mir

Tarnopol

Reval

Riga

Dvinsk

OSTLAND

Kovno

Vilna

Lida

Sobibor

Lutsk

Brody

Lvov

Przemysl

Baltic Sea

Stutthof

Bialystok

Treblinka

Majdanek

Belzec

Lublin

Sedlits

Tarnow

Danzig

Kalisz

Chelmno

Warsaw

Koniecpol

Cracow

Auschwitz

SLOVAKIA

HUNGARY

RUMANIA

0   200

Miles

123

GERMAN PLANS AND CONQUESTS IN 1942

Despite fierce German efforts, Moscow was not captured in 1941. The Germans planned a more southerly attack for 1942, hoping to capture Stalingrad, drive north along the Volga, and cut off Moscow from the east. This plan failed, as did the one to capture the oil fields of the Caucasus

Gorky •   *Volga*

• Moscow

Kazan •

• Riazan

Smolensk •

Briansk •

Orel •

Kuibyshev •

Kursk •

• Voronezh

Saratov •

Don

• Kiev

Kharkov •

Volga

Stalino •

Stalingrad •

Taganrog •

Rostov

Volga

Astrakhan •

Armavir •

Caspian Sea

Sebastopol •

Maikop •

Grozny •

Black Sea

C a u c a s u s

Batum •

Tiflis •

Baku •

Under German control by June 1942

The objectives of the German General Staff

Hitler's First Plan

Hitler's Second Plan

Russian territory actually conquered by Germany between June and December of 1942. This included the Maikop oilfields, but not the larger oilfields of Baku or Grozny

TURKEY

0   100
Miles

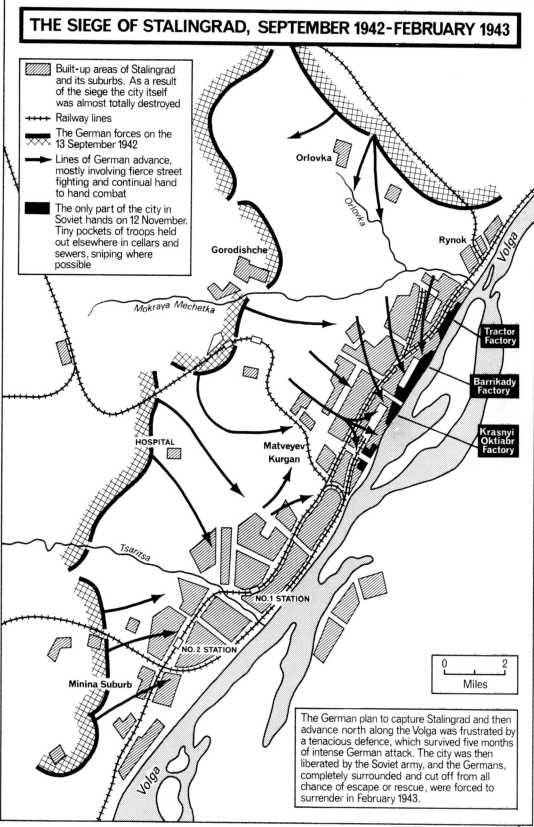

THE SIEGE OF STALINGRAD, SEPTEMBER 1942-FEBRUARY 1943

Built-up areas of Stalingrad and its suburbs. As a result of the siege the city itself was almost totally destroyed

Railway lines

The German forces on the 13 September 1942

Lines of German advance, mostly involving fierce street fighting and continual hand to hand combat

The only part of the city in Soviet hands on 12 November. Tiny pockets of troops held out elsewhere in cellars and sewers, sniping where possible

Orlovka

Orlovka

Rynok

Volga

Gorodishche

Mokraya Mechetka

Tractor Factory

Barrikady Factory

Krasnyi Oktiabr Factory

HOSPITAL

Matveyev Kurgan

Tsaritsa

NO.1 STATION

NO.2 STATION

Minina Suburb

Volga

0   2
Miles

The German plan to capture Stalingrad and then advance north along the Volga was frustrated by a tenacious defence, which survived five months of intense German attack. The city was then liberated by the Soviet army, and the Germans, completely surrounded and cut off from all chance of escape or rescue, were forced to surrender in February 1943.

125

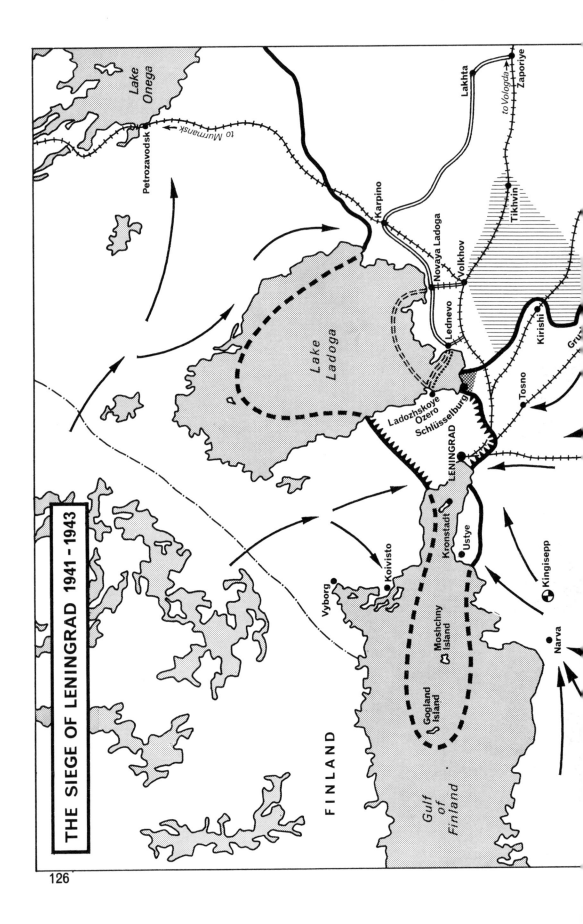

THE SIEGE OF LENINGRAD 1941-1943

Lake Onega

Petrozavodsk

to Murmansk

to Vologda

Zaporiye

Lakhta

Tikhvin

Karpino

Novaya Ladoga

Volkhov

Lednevo

Kirishi

Gru

Lake Ladoga

Tosno

Ladozhskoye Ozero

Schlüsselburg

LENINGRAD

Ustye

Kronstadt

Koivisto

Kingisepp

Vyborg

Mosrichny Island

Narva

Gogland Island

FINLAND

Gulf of Finland

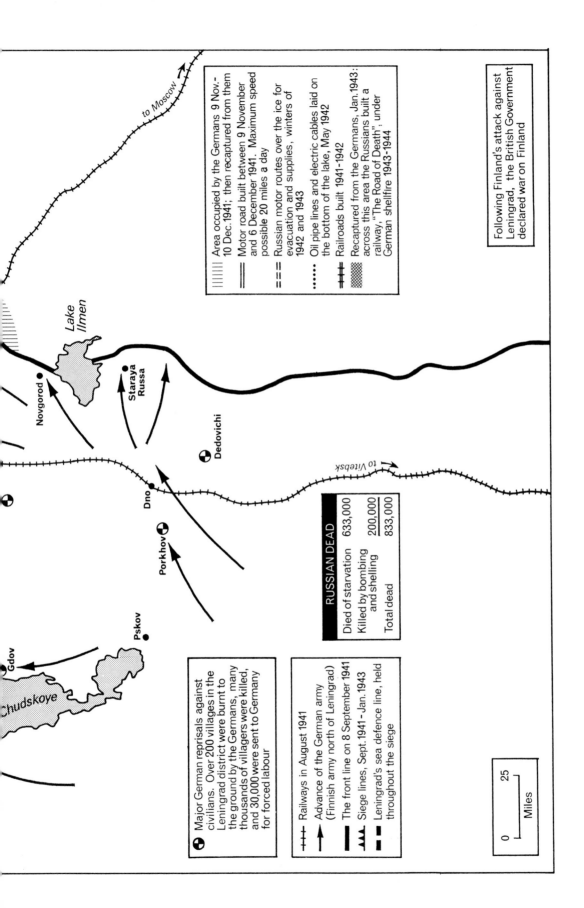

to Moscow

Lake Ilmen

Novgorod

Staraya Russa

Dedovichi

Dno

to Vitebsk

Porkhov

Pskov

Chudskoye

Gdov

RUSSIAN DEAD	
Died of starvation	633,000
Killed by bombing and shelling	200,000
Total dead	833,000

Area occupied by the Germans 9 Nov.-10 Dec.1941; then recaptured from them

Motor road built between 9 November and 6 December 1941. Maximum speed possible 20 miles a day

Russian motor routes over the ice for evacuation and supplies, winters of 1942 and 1943

Oil pipe lines and electric cables laid on the bottom of the lake, May 1942

Railroads built 1941-1942

Recaptured from the Germans, Jan.1943: across this area the Russians built a railway, "The Road of Death", under German shellfire 1943-1944

Following Finland's attack against Leningrad, the British Government declared war on Finland

Major German reprisals against civilians. Over 200 villages in the Leningrad district were burnt to the ground by the Germans, many thousands of villagers were killed, and 30,000 were sent to Germany for forced labour

Railways in August 1941

Advance of the German army (Finnish army north of Leningrad)

The front line on 8 September 1941

Siege lines, Sept. 1941 - Jan. 1943

Leningrad's sea defence line, held throughout the siege

0   25
Miles

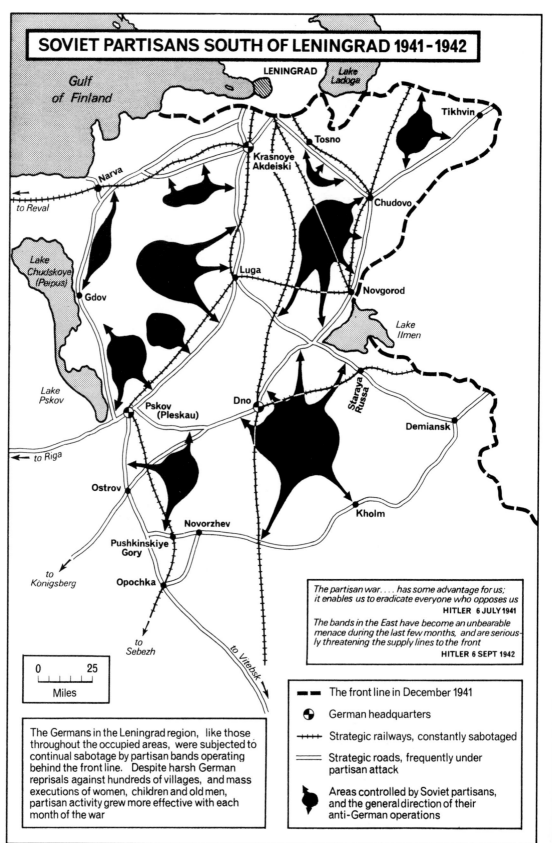

SOVIET PARTISANS SOUTH OF LENINGRAD 1941-1942

Gulf
of Finland

LENINGRAD

Lake
Ladoga

Tikhvin

Tosno

Narva

to Reval

Krasnoye
Akdeiski

Chudovo

Lake
Chudskoye
(Peipus)

Gdov

Luga

Novgorod

Lake
Ilmen

Lake
Pskov

Pskov
(Pleskau)

Dno

Staraya
Russa

Demiansk

to Riga

Ostrov

Novorzhev

Kholm

Pushkinskiye
Gory

to
Königsberg

Opochka

to
Sebezh

to Vitebsk

0   25
Miles

*The partisan war . . . . has some advantage for us;
it enables us to eradicate everyone who opposes us*
HITLER 6 JULY 1941

*The bands in the East have become an unbearable
menace during the last few months, and are serious-
ly threatening the supply lines to the front*
HITLER 6 SEPT 1942

— — The front line in December 1941

🝱 German headquarters

+++ Strategic railways, constantly sabotaged

══ Strategic roads, frequently under
partisan attack

Areas controlled by Soviet partisans,
and the general direction of their
anti-German operations

The Germans in the Leningrad region, like those
throughout the occupied areas, were subjected to
continual sabotage by partisan bands operating
behind the front line. Despite harsh German
reprisals against hundreds of villages, and mass
executions of women, children and old men,
partisan activity grew more effective with each
month of the war

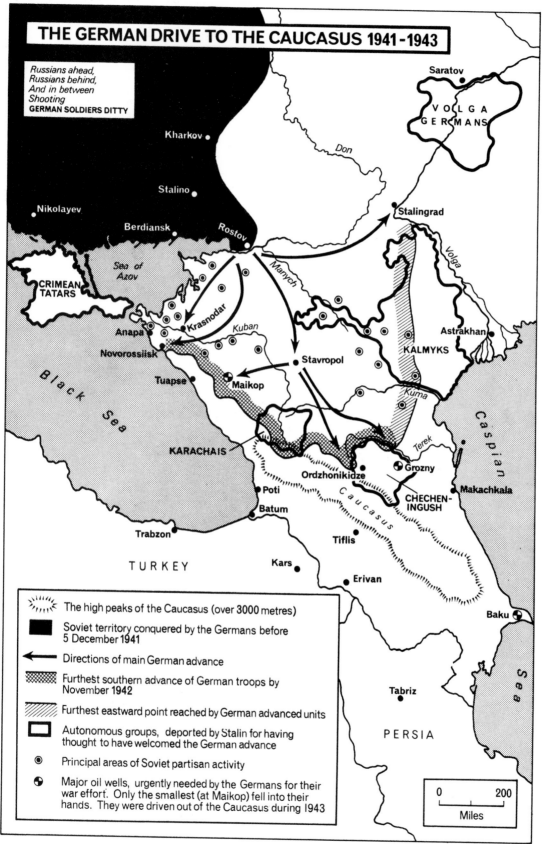

THE GERMAN DRIVE TO THE CAUCASUS 1941-1943

Russians ahead,
Russians behind,
And in between
Shooting
GERMAN SOLDIERS DITTY

Saratov

V O L G A
G E R M A N S

Kharkov

Don

Stalino

Nikolayev

Berdiansk

Rostov

Stalingrad

Sea of
Azov

CRIMEAN
TATARS

Krasnodar

Kuban

Manych

Volga

Astrakhan

KALMYKS

Anapa

Novorossiisk

Stavropol

Tuapse

Maikop

Kuma

B l a c k

S e a

KARACHAIS

Terek

Grozny

Ordzhonikidze

CHECHEN-
INGUSH

Makachkala

C a s p i a n

Poti

C a u c a s u s

Batum

Trabzon

Tiflis

T U R K E Y

Kars

Erivan

Baku

S e a

Tabriz

P E R S I A

〰 The high peaks of the Caucasus (over 3000 metres)

■ Soviet territory conquered by the Germans before
5 December 1941

← Directions of main German advance

▨ Furthest southern advance of German troops by
November 1942

▨ Furthest eastward point reached by German advanced units

□ Autonomous groups, deported by Stalin for having
thought to have welcomed the German advance

◉ Principal areas of Soviet partisan activity

✪ Major oil wells, urgently needed by the Germans for their
war effort. Only the smallest (at Maikop) fell into their
hands. They were driven out of the Caucasus during 1943

0   200

Miles

THE ADVANCE OF THE RED ARMY 1943 – 1944

The Germans ruled western Russia for two years. On 12 July 1943 the Russian Army began the liberation of the conquered territories. Starting along a front over 1,500 miles long, the Russians advanced in the south over 600 miles from Taganrog to the Carpathians. In the north, the siege of Leningrad was ended. Behind the German lines Russian partisans disrupted the German war effort. The Russians killed most of their German prisoners as they advanced. By March 1944 the Germans had been driven out of most of pre-1939 Russia

0   100
Miles

Leningrad

Narva

Luga
Novgorod

Pskov

Kholm

1939 frontier

Polotsk   Nevel

Moscow

Dnieper

Orsha   Smolensk

WHITE   Tula

Minsk

RUSSIA   Briansk   Orel

POLAND

Gomel

Voronezh

Brest-Litovsk
Pinsk   Pripet
Marshes   Chernigov   Kursk

Lutsk
Rovno

GALICIA   Kiev   Kharkov

Lvov   1939 frontier   Zhitomir

Dnieper   Donets

Vinnitsa

UKRAINE   Dnepropetrovsk

Chernovtsy   Dniester   Krivoi Rog   Zaporozhe   Taganrog

Don

Jassy   Berdiansk

BESSARABIA   Kishinev   Nikolaev

Odessa

Carpathians

RUMANIA   Sea of Azov

Territory liberated by July 1943
Territory liberated between
July 1943 and March 1944   CRIMEA

Black Sea   Novorossiisk

Sebastopol

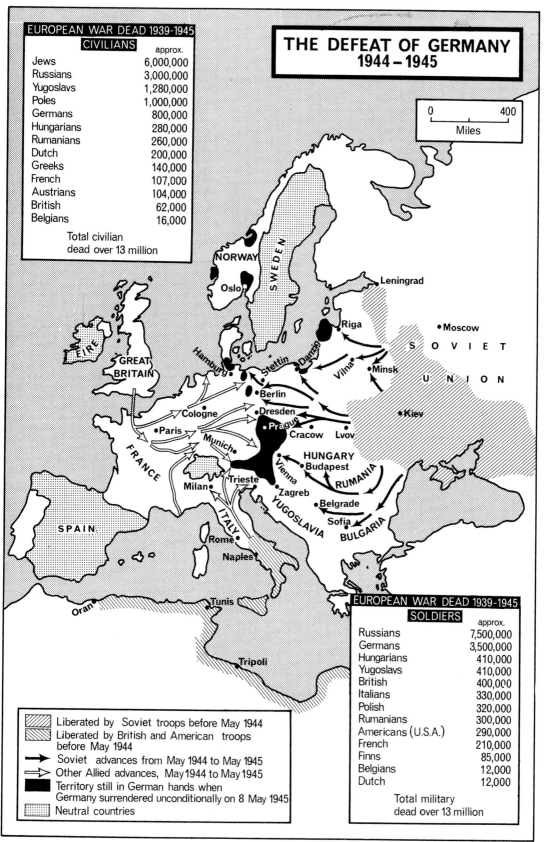

THE DEFEAT OF GERMANY 1944–1945

0 ——— 400
Miles

EUROPEAN WAR DEAD 1939-1945
CIVILIANS

	approx.
Jews	6,000,000
Russians	3,000,000
Yugoslavs	1,280,000
Poles	1,000,000
Germans	800,000
Hungarians	280,000
Rumanians	260,000
Dutch	200,000
Greeks	140,000
French	107,000
Austrians	104,000
British	62,000
Belgians	16,000

Total civilian
dead over 13 million

EUROPEAN WAR DEAD 1939-1945
SOLDIERS

	approx.
Russians	7,500,000
Germans	3,500,000
Hungarians	410,000
Yugoslavs	410,000
British	400,000
Italians	330,000
Polish	320,000
Rumanians	300,000
Americans (U.S.A.)	290,000
French	210,000
Finns	85,000
Belgians	12,000
Dutch	12,000

Total military
dead over 13 million

Liberated by Soviet troops before May 1944
Liberated by British and American troops before May 1944
→ Soviet advances from May 1944 to May 1945
⇒ Other Allied advances, May 1944 to May 1945
Territory still in German hands when Germany surrendered unconditionally on 8 May 1945
Neutral countries

130

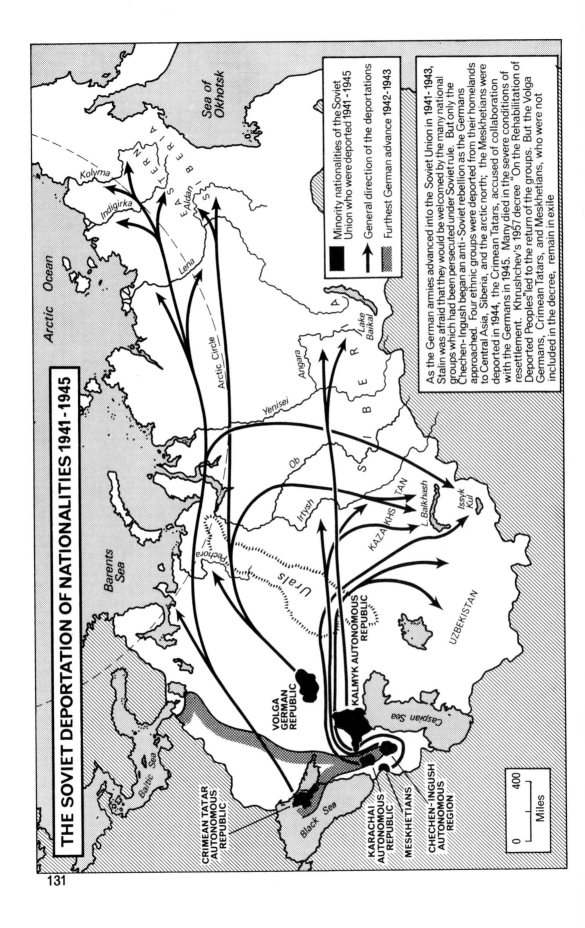

THE SOVIET DEPORTATION OF NATIONALITIES 1941-1945

Arctic Ocean

Barents Sea

Sea of Okhotsk

Kolyma

Indigirka

Lena

Aldan

EASTERN SIBERIA

Arctic Circle

Yenisei

Angara

Lake Baikal

Ob

Irtysh

SIBERIA

Pechora

Urals

KAZAKHSTAN

L. Balkhash

Issyk Kul

UZBEKISTAN

Caspian Sea

KALMYK AUTONOMOUS REPUBLIC

VOLGA GERMAN REPUBLIC

Black Sea

Baltic Sea

CRIMEAN TATAR AUTONOMOUS REPUBLIC

KARACHAI AUTONOMOUS REPUBLIC

MESKHETIANS

CHECHEN-INGUSH AUTONOMOUS REGION

▢ Minority nationalities of the Soviet Union who were deported 1941-1945

→ General direction of the deportations

▨ Furthest German advance 1942-1943

As the German armies advanced into the Soviet Union in 1941-1943, Stalin was afraid that they would be welcomed by the many national groups which had been persecuted under Soviet rule. But only the Chechen-Ingush began an anti-Soviet rebellion as the Germans approached. Four ethnic groups were deported from their homelands to Central Asia, Siberia, and the arctic north; the Meskhetians were deported in 1944, the Crimean Tatars, accused of collaboration with the Germans in 1945. Many died in the severe conditions of resettlement. Khrushchev's 1957 decree "On the Rehabilitation of Deported Peoples" led to the return of the groups. But the Volga Germans, Crimean Tatars, and Meskhetians, who were not included in the decree, remain in exile

0 400
Miles

131

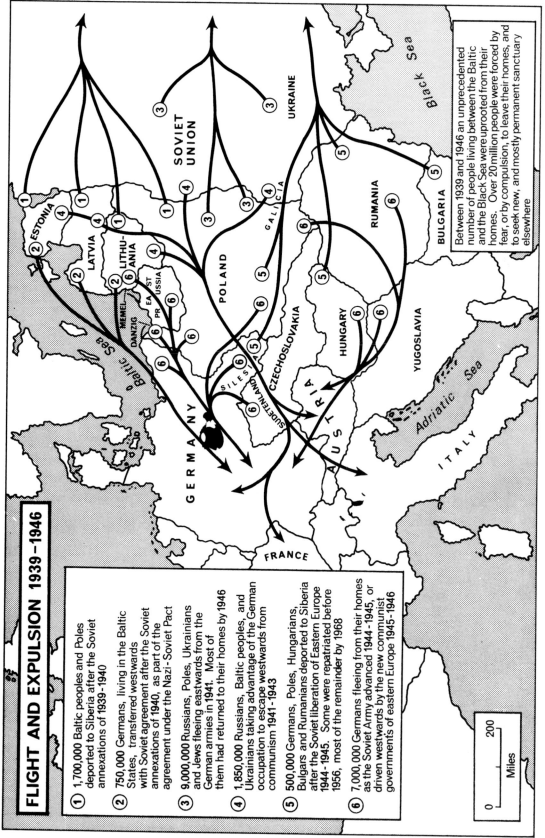

FLIGHT AND EXPULSION 1939–1946

① 1,700,000 Baltic peoples and Poles deported to Siberia after the Soviet annexations of 1939–1940

② 750,000 Germans, living in the Baltic States, transferred westwards with Soviet agreement after the Soviet annexations of 1940, as part of the agreement under the Nazi-Soviet Pact

③ 9,000,000 Russians, Poles, Ukrainians and Jews fleeing eastwards from the German armies in 1941. Most of them had returned to their homes by 1946

④ 1,850,000 Russians, Baltic peoples, and Ukrainians taking advantage of the German occupation to escape westwards from communism 1941-1943

⑤ 500,000 Germans, Poles, Hungarians, Bulgars and Rumanians deported to Siberia after the Soviet liberation of Eastern Europe 1944-1945. Some were repatriated before 1956, most of the remainder by 1968

⑥ 7,000,000 Germans fleeing from their homes as the Soviet Army advanced 1944-1945, or driven westwards by the new communist governments of eastern Europe 1945-1946

Between 1939 and 1946 an unprecedented number of people living between the Baltic and the Black Sea were uprooted from their homes. Over 20 million people were forced by fear, or by compulsion, to leave their homes, and to seek new, and mostly permanent sanctuary elsewhere

0   200
Miles

132

THE SOVIET UNION IN EASTERN EUROPE 1945 - 1948

Territory annexed by Russia 1939-1940, and re-incorporated in Russia in 1945

Former German and Czechoslovak territory annexed by Russia in 1945

States liberated by the Soviet army, and in which Communist regimes came to power between 1945 and 1948

Russian occupation zones in Austria (evacuated 1950) and Germany

British, French and American occupation zones

The 'Iron Curtain' in 1948

FINLAND

North Sea

SWEDEN

Baltic Sea

Vyborg

Leningrad

Reval

ESTONIA

Pskov

Riga

LATVIA

Memel

Königsberg

LITHUANIA

EAST PRUSSIA

Kovno

Vilna

Minsk

Bremen

Stettin

annexed by Poland from Germany

Bialystok

SOVIET

Berlin

Posnan

Warsaw

Pinsk

GERMANY

Erfurt

POLAND

UNION

Bonn

Dresden

SILESIA

Breslau

Cracow

Nuremburg

Przemysl

Lvov

GALICIA

Chernovtsy

FRANCE

Prague

CZECHOSLOVAKIA

Munich

Vienna

AUSTRIA

Uzhgorod

BESSARABIA

SWITZ.

Budapest

Jassy

Kishinev

HUNGARY

RUMANIA

Trieste

Belgrade

YUGOSLAVIA

Bucharest

ITALY

Adriatic Sea

Sofia

BULGARIA

Black Sea

ALBANIA

Tirana

GREECE

Ægean Sea

TURKEY

The Russian liberation of Eastern Europe was quickly followed by the establishment of communist regimes, and an 'Iron Curtain' from the Baltic to the Adriatic. Communist rule brought national subservience to Russian policy, and the subordination of personal liberty. The cities of Berlin and Vienna were divided into Russian, British, French and American sectors

0   200
Miles

133

THE SOVIET UNION IN EASTERN EUROPE 1949-1968

0 — 200
Miles

North Sea

Baltic Sea

FINLAND

Vyborg

SWEDEN

Leningrad

Tallin (Reval)

Riga

Klaypeda (Memel)

Kaliningrad

SOVIET UNION

Rostock

Gdansk

East Berlin

Szczecin

POLAND

Warsaw

EAST GERMANY

Posnan

Halle

Lodz

Dresden

Wroclaw

Lublin

Kiev

WEST GERMANY

Prague

CZECHOSLOVAKIA

Cracow

FRANCE

Brno

Przemysl

Lvov

Kosice

Bratislava

SWITZ.

AUSTRIA

Debrecen

Györ

Budapest

Jassy

Cluj

Odessa

HUNGARY

Zagreb

Pécs

Arad

RUMANIA

Rijeka

Belgrade

Constanza

YUGOSLAVIA

Bucharest

Adriatic Sea

Split

Nish

Varna

ITALY

Kotor

BULGARIA

Black Sea

Tirana

ALBANIA

Sofia

Burgas

Durres

Vlone

TURKEY

GREECE

Aegean Sea

— Frontiers of communist states since 1945

▨ Only European communist state entirely free from Soviet direction of foreign, economic and domestic policy since 1949

▧ Only communist state within the Soviet bloc pursuing a relatively independent foreign policy since 1968

▨ Only communist state in Europe aligned with China and refusing all contact with the Soviet Union since 1961

▢ Only European communist state to accept Soviet guidance with equanimity

■ Principal areas of anti-Soviet protest and revolt 1953-1968, crushed by Soviet military intervention (East Germany, Hungary, Czechoslovakia) and by strong political pressure (Poland)

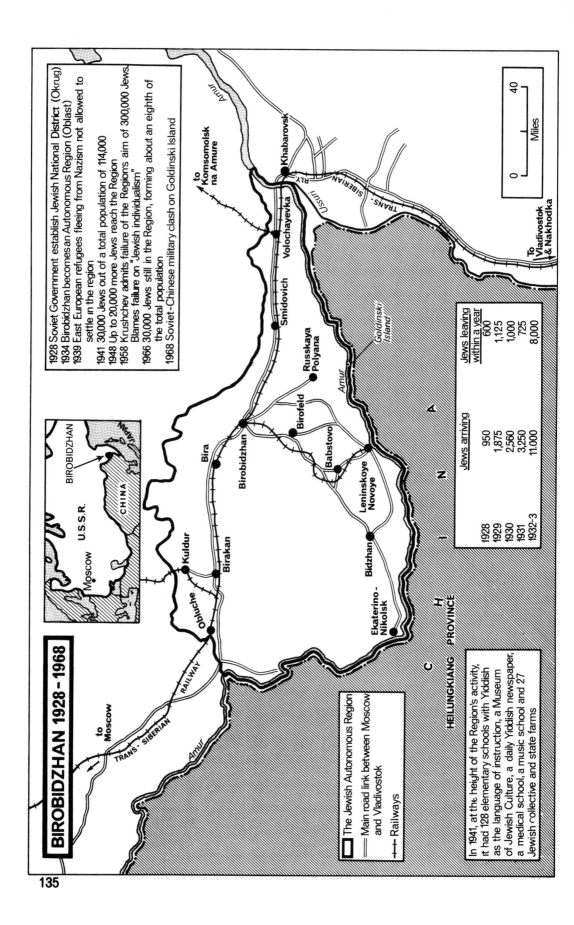

BIROBIDZHAN 1928 – 1968

1928 Soviet Government establish Jewish National District (Okrug)
1934 Birobidzhan becomes an Autonomous Region (Oblast)
1939 East European refugees fleeing from Nazism not allowed to settle in the region
1941 30,000 Jews out of a total population of 114,000
1948 Up to 20,000 more Jews reach the Region
1958 Krushchev admits failure of the Region's aim of 300,000 Jews. Blames failure on "Jewish individualism"
1966 30,000 Jews still in the Region, forming about an eighth of the total population
1968 Soviet-Chinese military clash on Goldinski Island

	Jews arriving	Jews leaving within a year
1928	950	600
1929	1,875	1,125
1930	2,560	1,000
1931	3,250	725
1932-3	11,000	8,000

In 1941, at the height of the Region's activity, it had 128 elementary schools with Yiddish as the language of instruction, a Museum of Jewish Culture, a daily Yiddish newspaper, a medical school, a music school and 27 Jewish collective and state farms

☐ The Jewish Autonomous Region

══ Main road link between Moscow and Vladivostok

+++ Railways

0   40
Miles

HEILUNGKIANG PROVINCE

to Komsomolsk na Amure

To Vladivostok & Nakhodka

to Moscow

Khabarovsk
Volochayevka
Smidovich
Russkaya Polyana
Birofeld
Babstovo
Leninskoye
Novoye
Bidzhan
Ekaterino-Nikolsk
Bira
Birobidzhan
Birakan
Kuldur
Obluche

Goldinski Island

Amur
Ussuri
TRANS-SIBERIAN R'LY
TRANS-SIBERIAN RAILWAY

CHINA

U.S.S.R.
Moscow
BIROBIDZHAN

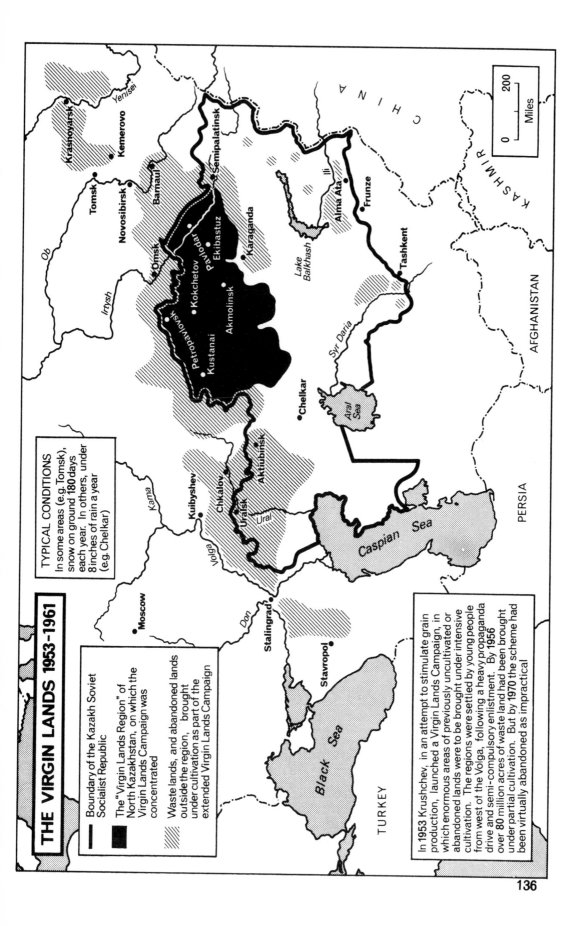

THE VIRGIN LANDS 1953–1961

Boundary of the Kazakh Soviet Socialist Republic

The "Virgin Lands Region" of North Kazakhstan, on which the Virgin Lands Campaign was concentrated

Waste lands, and abandoned lands outside the region, brought under cultivation as part of the extended Virgin Lands Campaign

TYPICAL CONDITIONS
In some areas (e.g. Tomsk), snow on ground 180 days each year. In others, under 8 inches of rain a year (e.g. Chelkar)

In 1953 Krushchev, in an attempt to stimulate grain production, launched a Virgin Lands Campaign, in which enormous areas of previously uncultivated or abandoned lands were to be brought under intensive cultivation. The regions were settled by young people from west of the Volga, following a heavy propaganda drive and semi-compulsory enlistment. By 1956 over 80 million acres of waste land had been brought under partial cultivation. But by 1970 the scheme had been virtually abandoned as impractical

CHINA

KASHMIR

AFGHANISTAN

PERSIA

TURKEY

Krasnoyarsk

Kemerovo

Tomsk

Novosibirsk

Barnaul

Semipalatinsk

Omsk

Kokchetov

Pavlodar

Ekibastuz

Karaganda

Akmolinsk

Petropavlovsk

Kustanai

Alma Ata

Frunze

Tashkent

Chelkar

Kuibyshev

Chkalov

Aktiubinsk

Uralsk

Moscow

Stalingrad

Stavropol

Yenisei

Ob

Irtysh

Ili

Lake Balkhash

Syr Daria

Aral Sea

Caspian Sea

Black Sea

Kama

Volga

Ural

Don

0   200
Miles

136

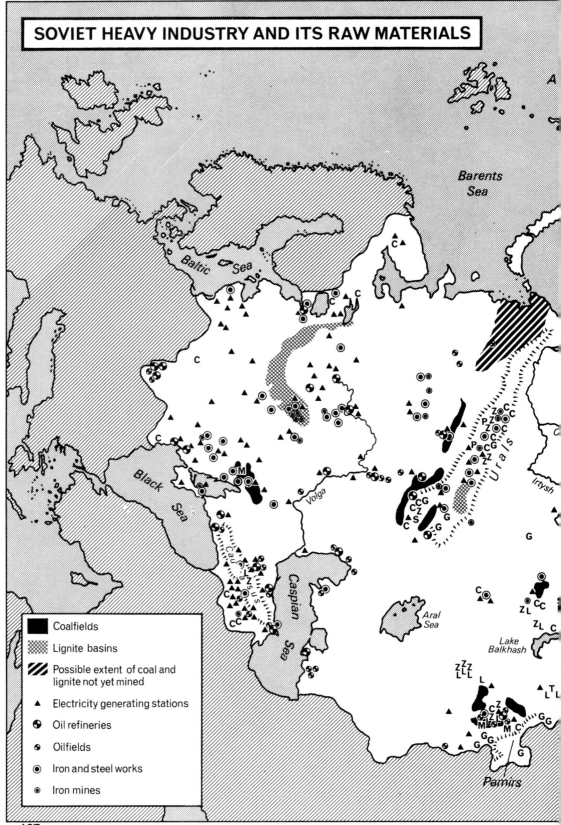

SOVIET HEAVY INDUSTRY AND ITS RAW MATERIALS

Barents Sea

Baltic Sea

Black Sea

Caspian Sea

Volga

Caucasus

Aral Sea

Lake Balkhash

Urals

Irtysh

Pamirs

Coalfields

Lignite basins

Possible extent of coal and lignite not yet mined

▲ Electricity generating stations

🜨 Oil refineries

◉ Oilfields

◉ Iron and steel works

◉ Iron mines

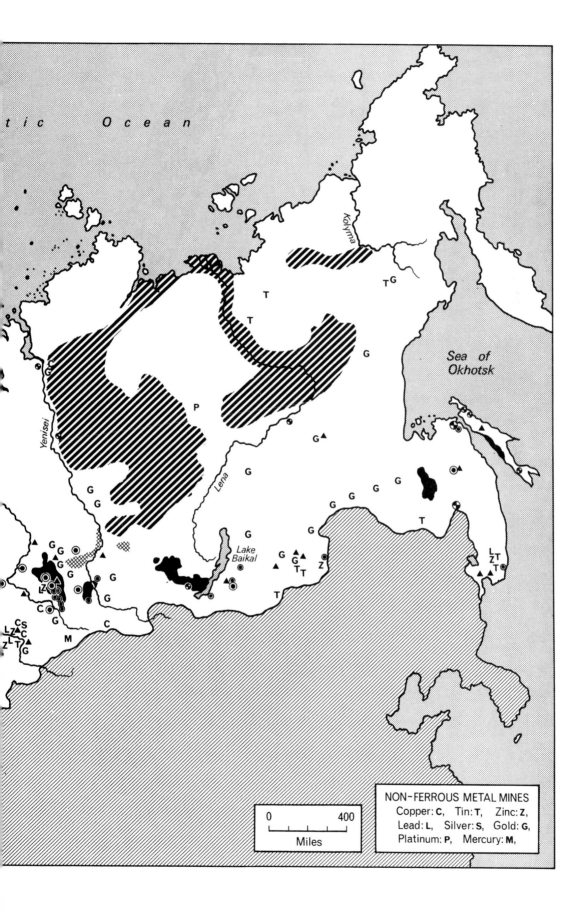

tic   O c e a n

Kolyma

T G

Sea of
Okhotsk

T

T

G

P

G

G

G

G

G

G

G

G

G

Lena

G

Lake
Baikal

G

G

T
T

Z

T

L
Z
T
T

G
G
G
G
G
G

G

G

G

L
Z
S

C

G

L
Z
T
G

C S
C

M

C

Yenisei

NON-FERROUS METAL MINES
Copper: **C**, Tin: **T**, Zinc: **Z**,
Lead: **L**, Silver: **S**, Gold: **G**,
Platinum: **P**, Mercury: **M**,

0   400

Miles

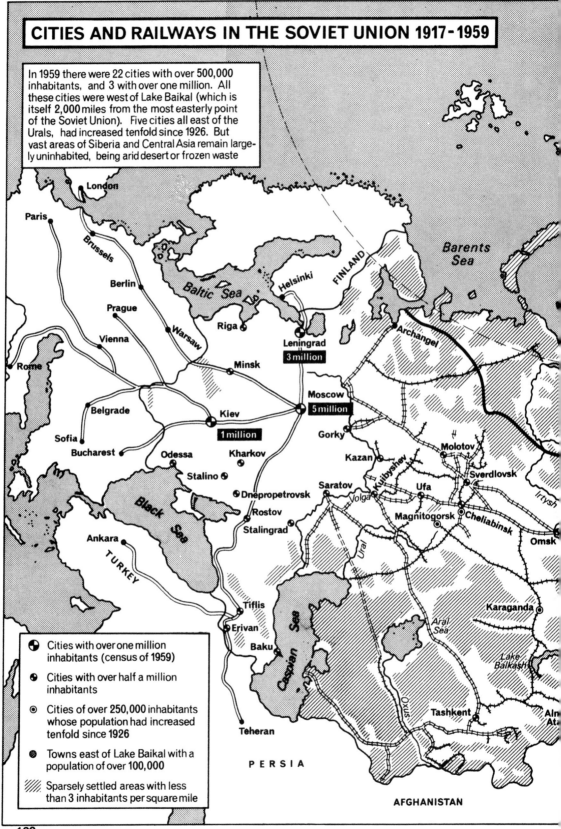

CITIES AND RAILWAYS IN THE SOVIET UNION 1917-1959

In 1959 there were 22 cities with over 500,000 inhabitants, and 3 with over one million. All these cities were west of Lake Baikal (which is itself 2,000 miles from the most easterly point of the Soviet Union). Five cities all east of the Urals, had increased tenfold since 1926. But vast areas of Siberia and Central Asia remain largely uninhabited, being arid desert or frozen waste

London

Paris

Brussels

Berlin

Prague

Vienna

Rome

Warsaw

Helsinki

FINLAND

Barents Sea

Baltic Sea

Riga

Leningrad
3 million

Minsk

Moscow
5 million

Archangel

Belgrade

Kiev
1 million

Sofia

Bucharest

Odessa

Kharkov

Stalino

Dnepropetrovsk

Rostov

Stalingrad

Ankara

TURKEY

Black Sea

Gorky

Kazan

Saratov

Volga

Kuibyshev

Molotov

Sverdlovsk

Ufa

Magnitogorsk

Cheliabinsk

Irtysh

Ural

Omsk

Tiflis

Erivan

Baku

Caspian Sea

Aral Sea

Oxus

Karaganda

Lake Balkash

Tashkent

Alma Ata

Teheran

PERSIA

AFGHANISTAN

Cities with over one million inhabitants (census of 1959)

Cities with over half a million inhabitants

Cities of over 250,000 inhabitants whose population had increased tenfold since 1926

Towns east of Lake Baikal with a population of over 100,000

Sparsely settled areas with less than 3 inhabitants per square mile

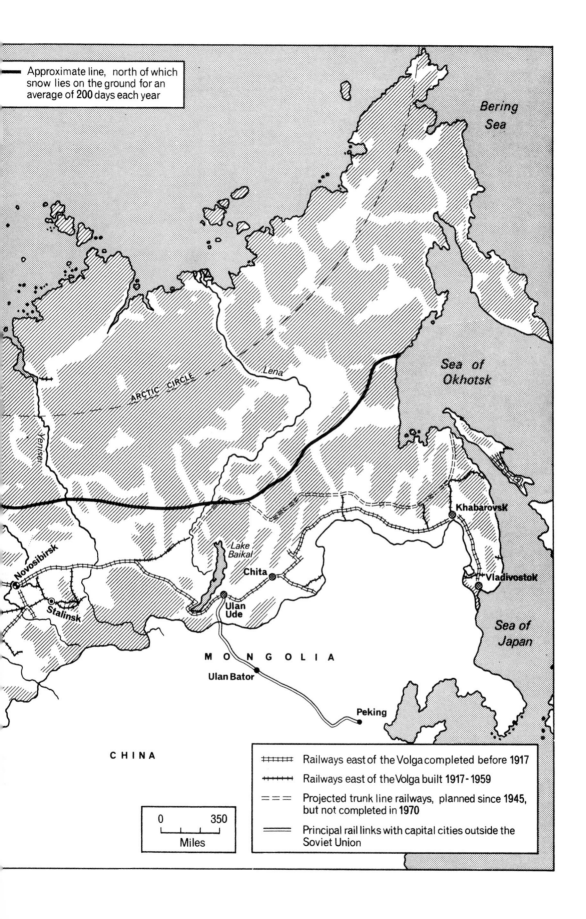

Approximate line, north of which
snow lies on the ground for an
average of **200** days each year

*Bering
Sea*

Lena

ARCTIC CIRCLE

Yenisei

*Sea of
Okhotsk*

Khabarovsk

*Lake
Baikal*

Chita

Novosibirsk

Stalinsk

**Ulan
Ude**

Vladivostok

*Sea of
Japan*

M O N G O L I A

Ulan Bator

Peking

C H I N A

| | Railways east of the Volga completed before 1917 |
| Railways east of the Volga built 1917-1959 |
| Projected trunk line railways, planned since 1945, but not completed in 1970 |
| Principal rail links with capital cities outside the Soviet Union |

0   350
Miles

THE CHANGING NAMES OF SOVIET CITIES 1917-1961

Petrograd
Leningrad

Königsberg
Kaliningrad

Tver
Kalinin

Viat
Kira

Nizhnii-Novgorod
Gorky

Volga

Bobriki
Stalinogorsk

Stavropol
Toliatti

Elizavetgrad
Kirovo

Pokrovsk
Engels

Ekateri
enstadt
Marx

Yuzovo
Stalino

Lugansk
Voroshilov

Chistiakovo
Torez

Tsaritsyn
Stalingrad

Mariupol
Zhdanov

Don

Ekaterinodar
Krasnodar

Black

Stavropol
Voroshilovsk

Sea

Caspian

Vladikavkaz
Ordzhonikidze

Alexandropol
Leninakan

Sea

Between 1930 and his death in 1953 Stalin
was commemorated in over a thousand place
names including: Stalina, Stalino, Stalinsk,
Stalinskii, Stalinskaya, Stalinskoye,
Stalinogorsk, Stalingrad and Stalinabad.
Since 1953 all have been renamed; the last
two as Dushanbe and Volgograd

Elizavetpol
Kirovabad

● Towns founded before 1917, which changed
their names after 1917

▬ New names chosen since 1917 (some have already
reverted to their original name e.g. Perm)

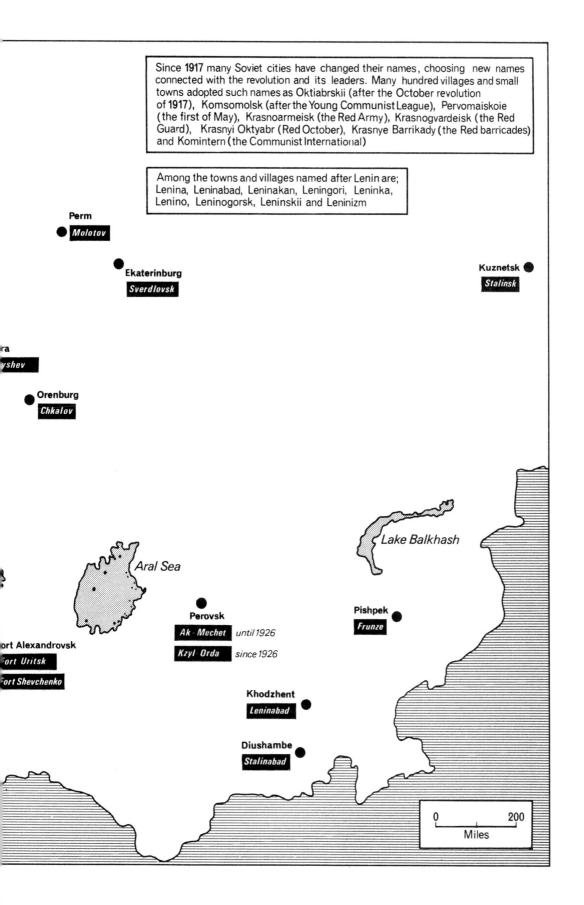

Since 1917 many Soviet cities have changed their names, choosing new names connected with the revolution and its leaders. Many hundred villages and small towns adopted such names as Oktiabrskii (after the October revolution of 1917), Komsomolsk (after the Young Communist League), Pervomaiskoie (the first of May), Krasnoarmeisk (the Red Army), Krasnogvardeisk (the Red Guard), Krasnyi Oktyabr (Red October), Krasnye Barrikady (the Red barricades) and Komintern (the Communist International)

Among the towns and villages named after Lenin are;
Lenina, Leninabad, Leninakan, Leningori, Leninka,
Lenino, Leninogorsk, Leninskii and Leninizm

Perm
Molotov

Ekaterinburg
Sverdlovsk

Kuznetsk
Stalinsk

ra
yshev

Orenburg
Chkalov

Aral Sea

Lake Balkhash

Perovsk
Ak - Mechet *until 1926*
Kzyl - Orda *since 1926*

Pishpek
Frunze

ort Alexandrovsk
ort Uritsk
ort Shevchenko

Khodzhent
Leninabad

Diushambe
Stalinabad

0   200
Miles

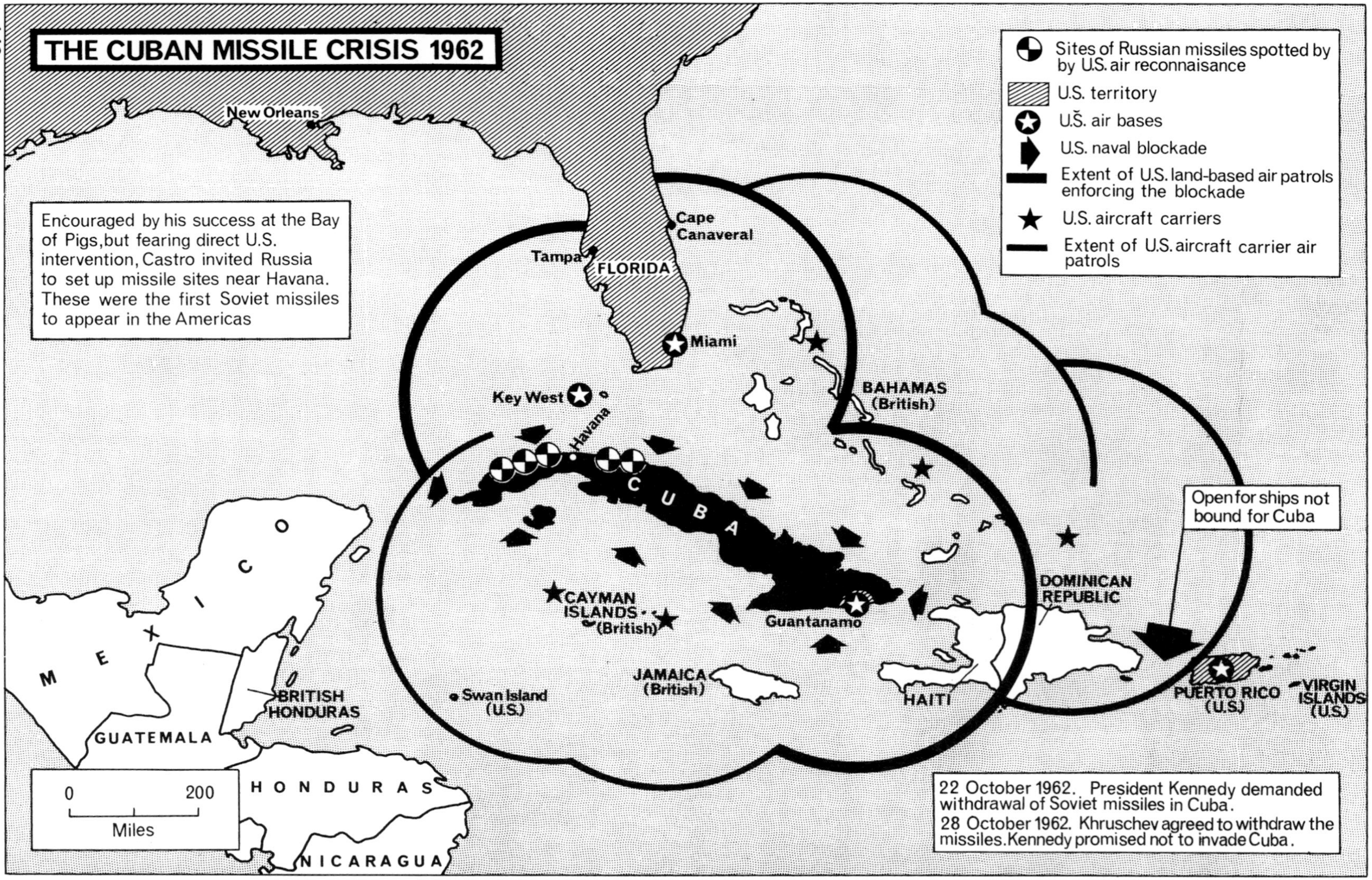
THE CUBAN MISSILE CRISIS 1962
Sites of Russian missiles spotted by by U.S. air reconnaisance
U.S. territory
U.S. air bases
U.S. naval blockade
Extent of U.S. land-based air patrols enforcing the blockade
U.S. aircraft carriers
Extent of U.S. aircraft carrier air patrols
Encouraged by his success at the Bay of Pigs, but fearing direct U.S. intervention, Castro invited Russia to set up missile sites near Havana. These were the first Soviet missiles to appear in the Americas
New Orleans
Tampa
FLORIDA
Cape Canaveral
Miami
Key West
Havana
BAHAMAS (British)
C U B A
CAYMAN ISLANDS (British)
Guantanamo
JAMAICA (British)
Swan Island (U.S.)
HAITI
DOMINICAN REPUBLIC
Open for ships not bound for Cuba
PUERTO RICO (U.S.)
VIRGIN ISLANDS (U.S.)
M E X I C O
BRITISH HONDURAS
GUATEMALA
H O N D U R A S
N I C A R A G U A
0
200
Miles
22 October 1962. President Kennedy demanded withdrawal of Soviet missiles in Cuba.
28 October 1962. Khruschev agreed to withdraw the missiles. Kennedy promised not to invade Cuba.

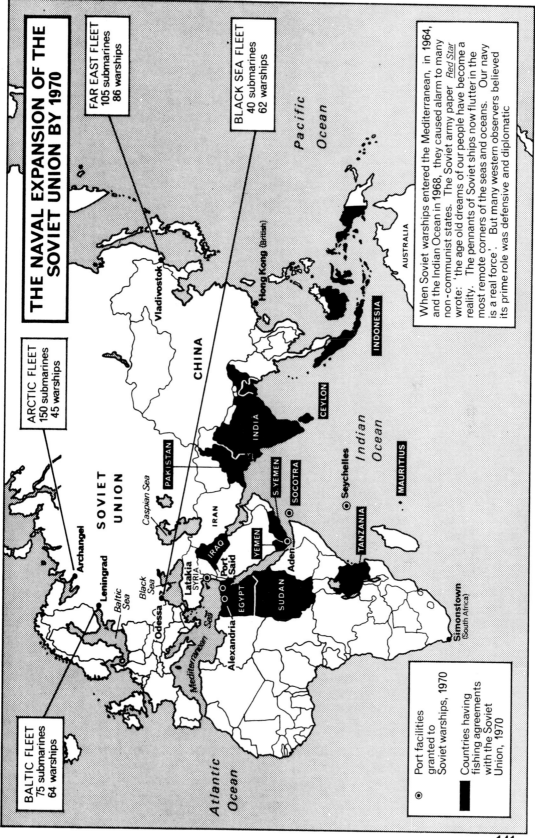

THE NAVAL EXPANSION OF THE SOVIET UNION BY 1970

FAR EAST FLEET
105 submarines
86 warships

BLACK SEA FLEET
40 submarines
62 warships

ARCTIC FLEET
150 submarines
45 warships

BALTIC FLEET
75 submarines
64 warships

Pacific Ocean

AUSTRALIA

When Soviet warships entered the Mediterranean, in 1964, and the Indian Ocean in 1968, they caused alarm to many non-communist states. The Soviet army paper *Red Star* wrote: 'the age old dreams of our people have become a reality. The pennants of Soviet ships now flutter in the most remote corners of the seas and oceans. Our navy is a real force'. But many western observers believed its prime role was defensive and diplomatic

INDONESIA

Vladivostok

CHINA

Hong Kong (British)

Archangel

SOVIET UNION

Caspian Sea

INDIA

CEYLON

Indian Ocean

Leningrad

Baltic Sea

PAKISTAN

IRAN

S. YEMEN

SOCOTRA

Seychelles

MAURITIUS

Black Sea

Odessa

IRAQ

Port Said

YEMEN

Aden

TANZANIA

Latakia
SYRIA

Alexandria

EGYPT

SUDAN

Simonstown
(South Africa)

Mediterranean Sea

Atlantic Ocean

⊙ Port facilities
granted to
Soviet warships, 1970

■ Countries having
fishing agreements
with the Soviet
Union, 1970

141

THE SOVIET UNION AND CHINA 1860-1970

The Chinese Communist Party was founded in 1921. But the Soviet Union preferred to support the Kuomintang under Chiang Kai Shek, to which it gave substantial military aid to establish its power 1923-1927, and to fight the Japanese 1937-1941 (when Stalin formed a Non-Aggression pact with Japan). In 1945 Soviet troops drove the Japanese from Northern China. In 1949 the Chinese Communists came to power. From a policy of considerable Soviet aid to China in the 1950's, the two nations became increasingly hostile. By 1960 the rift was open, and soon led to armed skirmishes on the frontier

TANNU TUVA

1914 Russian protectorate
1921 Independent "Peoples' Republic" allied with the Soviet Union
1944 Annexed by the Soviet Union

SINKIANG

1760-1920 Chinese
1921-1949 Under Soviet influence and partial occupation
Since 1949 Chinese. Heavily colonized by Chinese settlers

SOVIET UNION

Irkut

TANNU TUVA

MONGO

Lake Balkhash

Alma Ata

Urumchi

Hami

Tashkent

Kashgar

SINKIANG

Lop Nor

Yarkand

AFGHANISTAN

Khotan

Kabul

Gilgit

KASHMIR

C   H

PAKISTAN

Lahore

TIBET

INDIA

Lhasa

NEPAL

SIKKIM

BHUTAN

INDIA

INDIA

EAST PAKISTAN

BURMA

⬛⬛⬛ Territory annexed by Russia 1858-1860

◉ Communist Party cells established under Moscow's instructions 1920-1924 and urged to collaborate with the Kuomintang (nationalists)

◑ Soviet air units defending Kuomintang strongholds against Japan 1941

➡ Soviet military advances across China in the war against Japan 1945

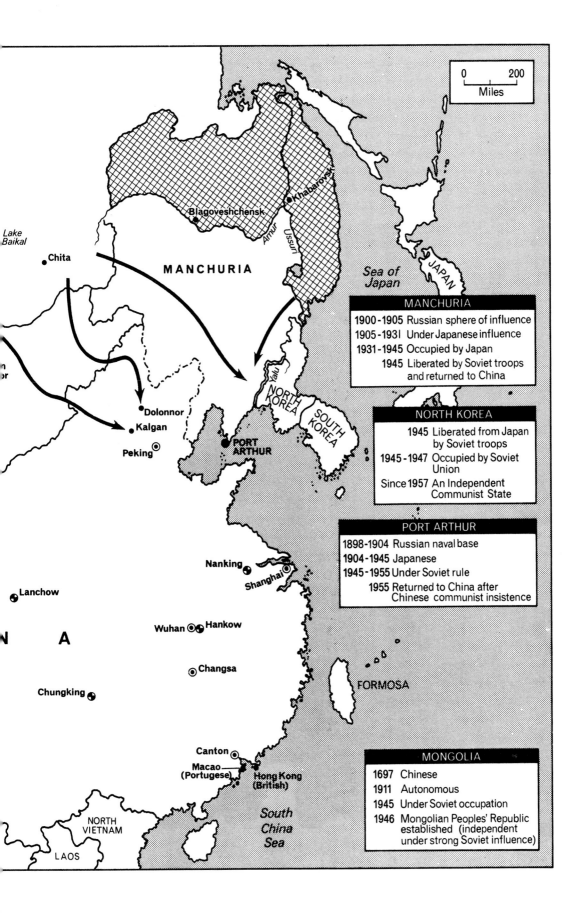

0 200
Miles

Lake
Baikal

● Chita

● Blagoveshchensk

● Khabarovsk

Amur

Ussuri

MANCHURIA

Sea of Japan

JAPAN

● Dolonnor

● Kalgan

Yalu

NORTH KOREA

SOUTH KOREA

● Peking

PORT ARTHUR

MANCHURIA
1900-1905 Russian sphere of influence
1905-1931 Under Japanese influence
1931-1945 Occupied by Japan
1945 Liberated by Soviet troops and returned to China

NORTH KOREA
1945 Liberated from Japan by Soviet troops
1945-1947 Occupied by Soviet Union
Since 1957 An Independent Communist State

PORT ARTHUR
1898-1904 Russian naval base
1904-1945 Japanese
1945-1955 Under Soviet rule
1955 Returned to China after Chinese communist insistence

● **Nanking**
● **Shanghai**

● **Lanchow**

● **Wuhan** ● **Hankow**

● **Changsa**

Chungking ●

N A

● **Canton**
Macao (Portugese) — ● **Hong Kong (British)**

FORMOSA

South China Sea

MONGOLIA
1697 Chinese
1911 Autonomous
1945 Under Soviet occupation
1946 Mongolian Peoples' Republic established (independent under strong Soviet influence)

NORTH VIETNAM

LAOS

THE SOVIET-CHINESE BORDERLANDS 1970

——	The Soviet-Chinese border
—·—·—	Other international borders
++++++	Soviet, Mongolian and Chinese railways in the border area
▨	Land over 2000 metres (6562 feet)
⊕	Main airfields

Caspian Sea

Aral Sea

S O V I E T

to Moscow

Omsk

TRANS-SIBERIAN RAILWAY

Novosibirsk ⊕

Barnaul

Karaganda ⊕

Achinsk

Krasnoyarsk ⊕

Rubtsovsk

Bilsk

Semipalatinsk ⊕

Abakan

Leninogorsk

Lake Balkash

Aktogai

Lake Zaisan

Lake Markakol

Urdzhar

Tashkent ⊕

Lugovoi

Zaisan

Samarkand

Frunze

Panfilov

L. Alakol

Tahcheng

PERSIA

Diushambe

Dzhalal Abad

Rybachye

Alma Ata

Issyk Kul

Ebi Nor

Kuldja

Ulyungur Nor

Osh

Urumchi ⊕

AFGHANISTAN

Kashgar

Aksu

PAKISTAN

KASHMIR

Lop Nor

I N D I A

Lanchow

C H I

M

0	250

Miles

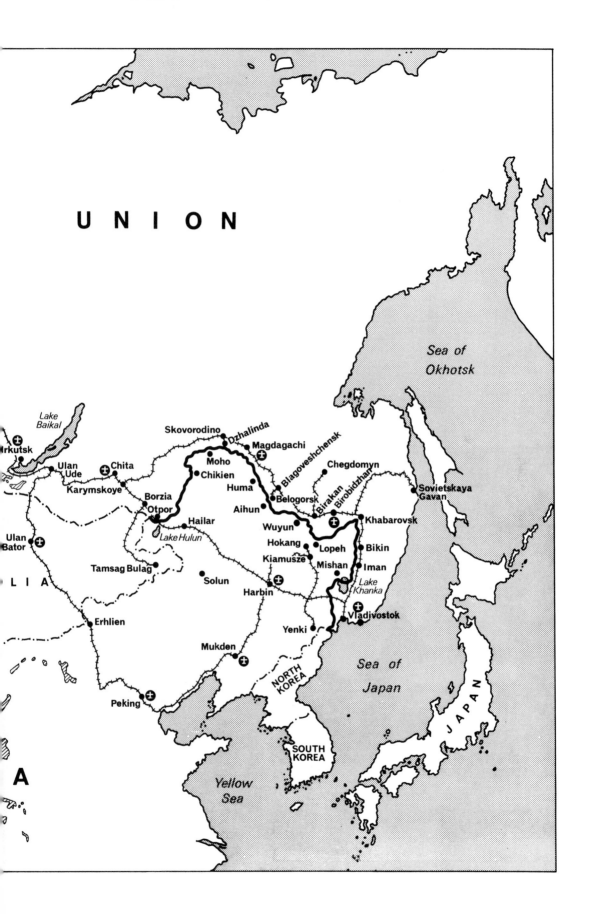

THE REPUBLICS AND AUTONOMOUS REGIONS OF THE SOVIET UNION IN 1970

North Sea

Arctic

North Cape

LATVIAN S.S.R.   ESTONIA S.S.R.

Baltic Sea

LITHUANIA S.S.R.

Part of the RSFSR

BELORUSSIAN S.S.R.

UKRAINIAN S.S.R.

Karelian A.S.S.R.

Nenets N.O.

RUSSIAN

Moscow

Komi A.S.S.R.

Yam Nene N.O.

Chuvash A.S.S.R.   Mary A.S.S.R.   Komi-Permyak N.O.

MOLDAVIAN S.S.R.

Mordovian A.S.S.R.   Udmurt A.S.S.R.   Khanty-Mansi N.O.

Tatar A.S.S.R.

Black Sea

Bashkir A.S.S.R.

SOVIET

Adyge A.O.

Abkhaz A.S.S.R.   Cherkess A.O.
N.Ossetian A.O.
S.Ossetian A.O.   Dagestan A.S.S.R.

Adzhar A.S.S.R.

Kara-Kalpak A.S.S.R.

GEORGIAN S.S.R.

ARMENIAN S.S.R.

Nakhichevan A.S.S.R.

Caspian Sea

AZERBAIDZAN S.S.R.

Nagorno-Karabakh A.O.

TURKMEN S.S.R.

KIRGIZ S.S.

Gorno-Badakhshan

0   400
Miles

UZBEK S.S.R.   TADZHIK S.S.

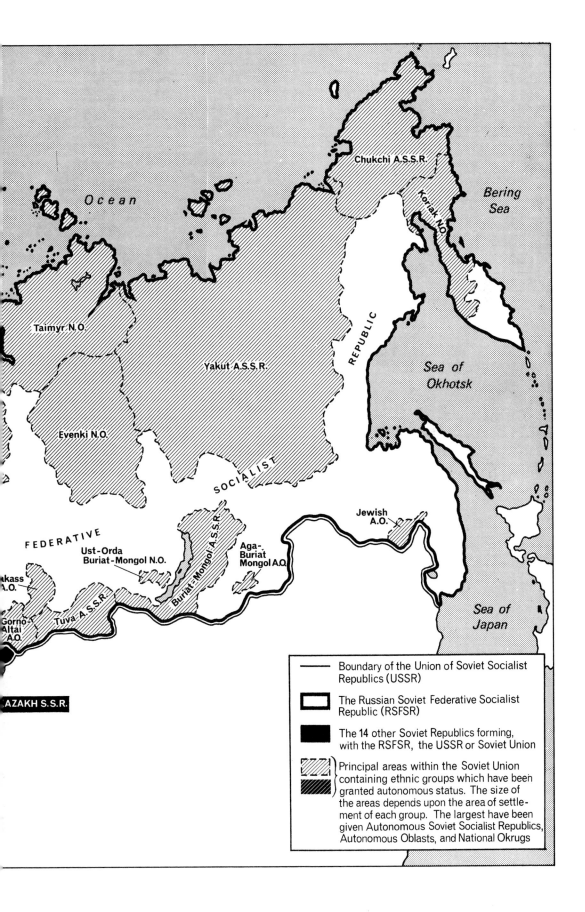

Chukchi A.S.S.R.

Ocean

Bering Sea

Koriak N.O.

Taimyr N.O.

R
E
P
U
B
L
I
C

Sea of Okhotsk

Yakut A.S.S.R.

Evenki N.O.

S
O
C
I
A
L
I
S
T

Jewish A.O.

FEDERATIVE

Ust-Orda
Buriat-Mongol N.O.

Aga-
Buriat
Mongol A.O.

Buriat-Mongol A.S.S.R.

kass
.O.

Sea of Japan

Gorno-
Altai
A.O.

Tuva A.S.S.R.

AZAKH S.S.R.

Boundary of the Union of Soviet Socialist Republics (USSR)

The Russian Soviet Federative Socialist Republic (RSFSR)

The 14 other Soviet Republics forming, with the RSFSR, the USSR or Soviet Union

Principal areas within the Soviet Union containing ethnic groups which have been granted autonomous status. The size of the areas depends upon the area of settlement of each group. The largest have been given Autonomous Soviet Socialist Republics, Autonomous Oblasts, and National Okrugs

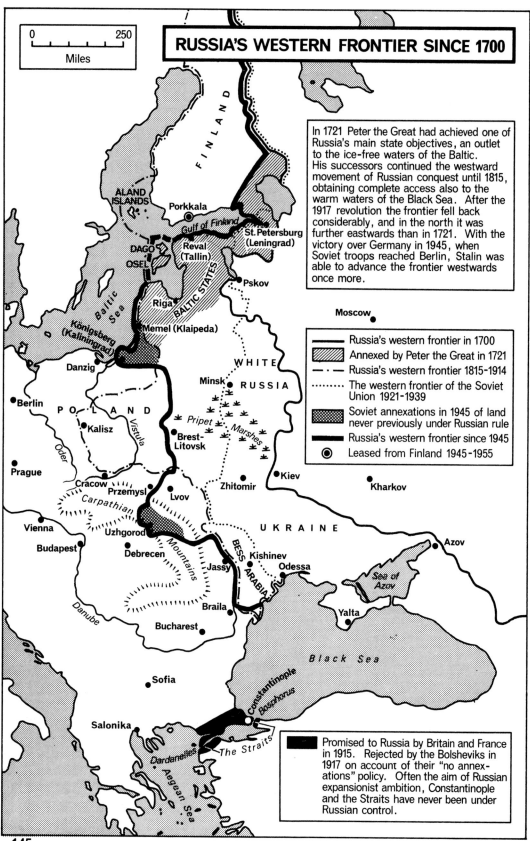

RUSSIA'S WESTERN FRONTIER SINCE 1700

0 — 250
Miles

In 1721 Peter the Great had achieved one of Russia's main state objectives, an outlet to the ice-free waters of the Baltic. His successors continued the westward movement of Russian conquest until 1815, obtaining complete access also to the warm waters of the Black Sea. After the 1917 revolution the frontier fell back considerably, and in the north it was further eastwards than in 1721. With the victory over Germany in 1945, when Soviet troops reached Berlin, Stalin was able to advance the frontier westwards once more.

Moscow

—— Russia's western frontier in 1700

▨ Annexed by Peter the Great in 1721

–·–· Russia's western frontier 1815-1914

········ The western frontier of the Soviet Union 1921-1939

▧ Soviet annexations in 1945 of land never previously under Russian rule

━━ Russia's western frontier since 1945

◉ Leased from Finland 1945-1955

FINLAND

ALAND ISLANDS

Porkkala

Gulf of Finland

St. Petersburg (Leningrad)

DAGO (Tallin)
OSEL
Reval (Tallin)

Pskov

Riga

BALTIC STATES

Baltic Sea

Memel (Klaipeda)

Königsberg (Kaliningrad)

Danzig

WHITE

Minsk

RUSSIA

Berlin

P O L A N D

Kalisz

Vistula

Pripet

Marshes

Brest-Litovsk

Oder

Prague

Cracow

Przemysl

Lvov

Zhitomir

Kiev

Kharkov

Carpathian

Vienna

Uzhgorod

U K R A I N E

Budapest

Debrecen

Mountains

Jassy

BESS-ARABIA

Kishinev

Odessa

Azov

Sea of Azov

Danube

Braila

Yalta

Bucharest

Black Sea

Sofia

Constantinople

Bosphorus

Salonika

The Straits

Dardanelles

Aegean Sea

Promised to Russia by Britain and France in 1915. Rejected by the Bolsheviks in 1917 on account of their "no annexations" policy. Often the aim of Russian expansionist ambition, Constantinople and the Straits have never been under Russian control.

145

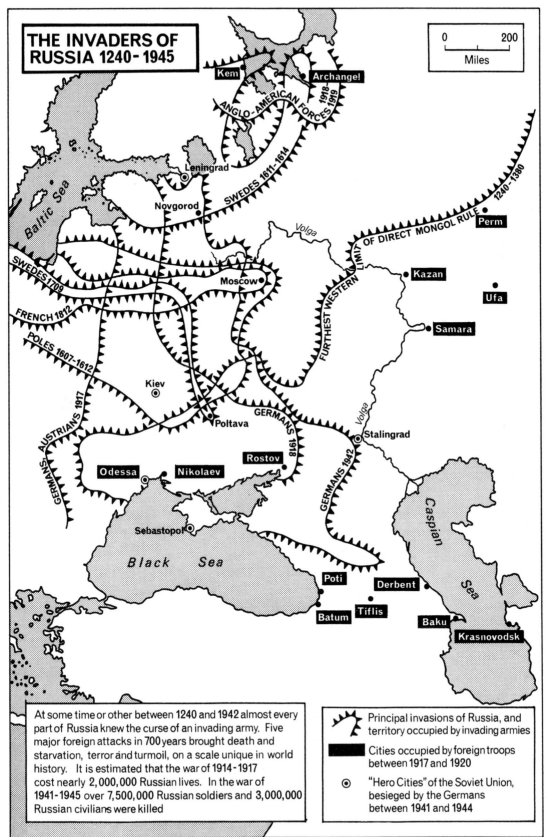

THE INVADERS OF RUSSIA 1240-1945

0   200

Miles

Kem

Archangel

1918-1919

ANGLO-AMERICAN FORCES

Leningrad

SWEDES 1611-1614

LIMIT OF DIRECT MONGOL RULE

1240-1380

Perm

Novgorod

Volga

SWEDES 1709

Kazan

Ufa

Moscow

FURTHEST WESTERN

FRENCH 1812

Samara

POLES 1607-1612

Kiev

Volga

GERMANS 1918

Stalingrad

AUSTRIANS 1917

Poltava

GERMANS

Rostov

Odessa

Nikolaev

Caspian

GERMANS 1942

Sebastopol

Sea

Black   Sea

Poti

Derbent

Batum   Tiflis

Baku

Krasnovodsk

At some time or other between 1240 and 1942 almost every part of Russia knew the curse of an invading army. Five major foreign attacks in 700 years brought death and starvation, terror and turmoil, on a scale unique in world history. It is estimated that the war of 1914-1917 cost nearly 2,000,000 Russian lives. In the war of 1941-1945 over 7,500,000 Russian soldiers and 3,000,000 Russian civilians were killed

Principal invasions of Russia, and territory occupied by invading armies

Cities occupied by foreign troops between 1917 and 1920

⊙   "Hero Cities" of the Soviet Union, besieged by the Germans between 1941 and 1944

GREAT POWER CONFRONTATION AND CONCILIATION, 1972-1986

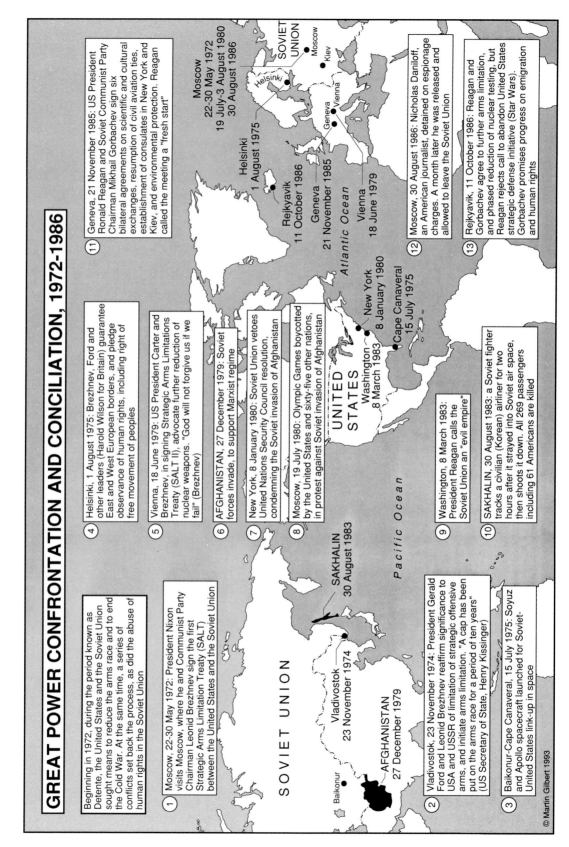

Beginning in 1972, during the period known as Detente, the United States and the Soviet Union sought means to reduce the arms race and to end the Cold War. At the same time, a series of conflicts set back the process, as did the abuse of human rights in the Soviet Union

1 Moscow, 22-30 May 1972: President Nixon visits Moscow, where he and Communist Party Chairman Leonid Brezhnev sign the first Strategic Arms Limitation Treaty (SALT) between the United States and the Soviet Union

2 Vladivostok, 23 November 1974: President Gerald Ford and Leonid Brezhnev reaffirm significance to USA and USSR of limitation of strategic offensive arms, and initiate arms limitation. "A cap has been put on the arms race for a period of ten years" (US Secretary of State, Henry Kissinger)

3 Baikonur-Cape Canaveral, 15 July 1975: Soyuz and Apollo spacecraft launched for Soviet-United States link-up in space

4 Helsinki, 1 August 1975: Brezhnev, Ford and other leaders (Harold Wilson for Britain) guarantee East and West European borders, and pledge observance of human rights, including right of free movement of peoples

5 Vienna, 18 June 1979: US President Carter and Brezhnev, in signing Strategic Arms Limitations Treaty (SALT II), advocate further reduction of nuclear weapons. "God will not forgive us if we fail" (Brezhnev)

6 AFGHANISTAN, 27 December 1979: Soviet forces invade, to support Marxist regime

7 New York, 8 January 1980: Soviet Union vetoes United Nations Security Council resolution, condemning the Soviet invasion of Afghanistan

8 Moscow, 19 July 1980: Olympic Games boycotted by the United States and sixty-five other nations, in protest against Soviet invasion of Afghanistan

9 Washington, 8 March 1983: President Reagan calls the Soviet Union an "evil empire"

10 SAKHALIN, 30 August 1983: a Soviet fighter tracks a civilian (Korean) airliner for two hours after it strayed into Soviet air space, then shoots it down. All 269 passengers including 61 Americans are killed

11 Geneva, 21 November 1985: US President Ronald Reagan and Soviet Communist Party Chairman Mikhail Gorbachev sign six bilateral agreements on scientific and cultural exchanges, resumption of civil aviation ties, establishment of consulates in New York and Kiev, and environmental protection. Reagan called the meeting a "fresh start"

12 Moscow, 30 August 1986: Nicholas Daniloff, an American journalist, detained on espionage charges. A month later he was released and allowed to leave the Soviet Union

13 Reijkyavik, 11 October 1986: Reagan and Gorbachev agree to further arms limitation, and phased reduction of nuclear testing, but Reagan rejects call to abandon United States strategic defense initiative (Star Wars). Gorbachev promises progress on emigration and human rights

© Martin Gilbert 1993

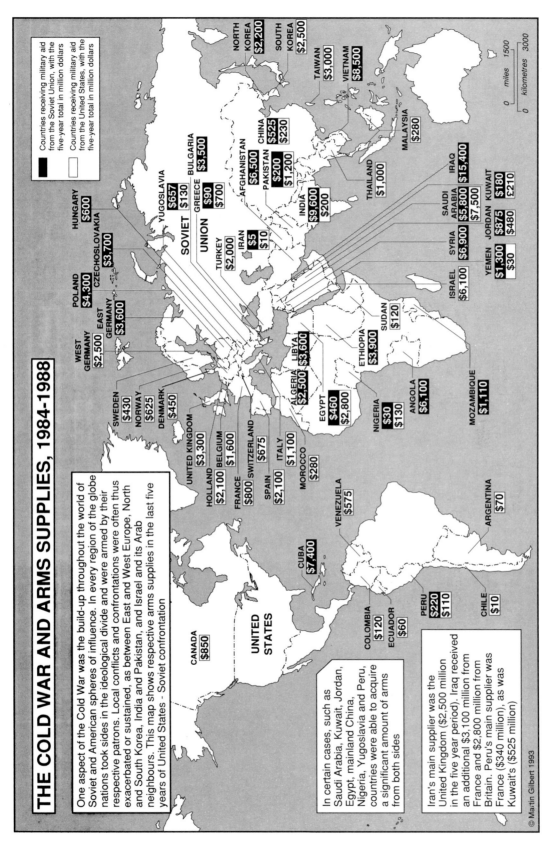

THE COLD WAR AND ARMS SUPPLIES, 1984-1988

One aspect of the Cold War was the build-up throughout the world of Soviet and American spheres of influence. In every region of the globe nations took sides in the ideological divide and were armed by their respective patrons. Local conflicts and confrontations were often thus exacerbated or sustained, as between East and West Europe, North and South Korea, India and Pakistan, and Israel and its Arab neighbours. This map shows respective arms supplies in the last five years of United States - Soviet confrontation

Countries receiving military aid from the Soviet Union, with the five-year total in million dollars

Countries receiving military aid from the United States, with the five-year total in million dollars

In certain cases, such as Saudi Arabia, Kuwait, Jordan, Egypt, mainland China, Nigeria, Yugoslavia and Peru, countries were able to acquire a significant amount of arms from both sides

Iran's main supplier was the United Kingdom ($2,500 million in the five year period). Iraq received an additional $3,100 million from France and $2,800 million from Britain. Peru's main supplier was France ($340 million), as was Kuwait's ($525 million)

CANADA $850

UNITED STATES

CUBA $7,400

COLOMBIA $120
ECUADOR $60
PERU $220 $110
VENEZUELA $575
CHILE $10
ARGENTINA $70

SWEDEN $430
NORWAY $625
DENMARK $450
UNITED KINGDOM $3,300
HOLLAND $2,100
BELGIUM $1,600
FRANCE $800
SWITZERLAND $675
SPAIN $2,100
ITALY $1,100
MOROCCO $280

WEST GERMANY $2,500
EAST GERMANY $3,600
POLAND $4,300
CZECHOSLOVAKIA $3,700
HUNGARY $600
YUGOSLAVIA $657 $130
SOVIET UNION
GREECE $90 $700
BULGARIA $3,500

ALGERIA $2,500
LIBYA $3,600
EGYPT $460 $2,800
NIGERIA $30 $130
SUDAN $120
ETHIOPIA $3,900
ANGOLA $6,100
MOZAMBIQUE $1,110

TURKEY $2,000
IRAN $5 $10
AFGHANISTAN $6,500
PAKISTAN $200 $1,200
INDIA $9,600 $200
CHINA $525 $230

ISRAEL $6,100
SYRIA $6,900
YEMEN $1,300 $30
JORDAN $875 $480
KUWAIT $180 £210
SAUDI ARABIA $5,800 $7,500
IRAQ $15,400

THAILAND $1,000
MALAYSIA $280

NORTH KOREA $2,200
SOUTH KOREA $2,500
TAIWAN $3,000
VIETNAM $8,500

0   miles   1500
0   kilometres   3000

© Martin Gilbert 1993

148

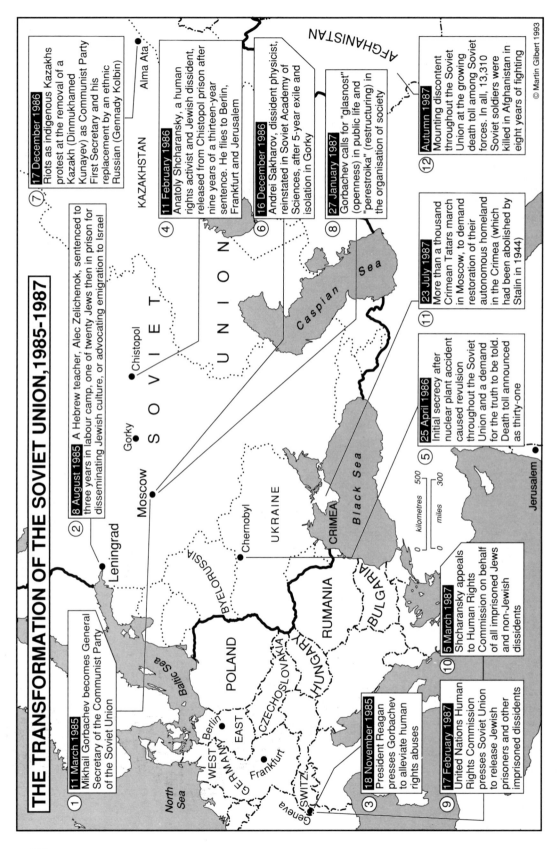

THE TRANSFORMATION OF THE SOVIET UNION, 1985-1987

① 11 March 1985 Mikhail Gorbachev becomes General Secretary of the Communist Party of the Soviet Union

② 8 August 1985 A Hebrew teacher, Alec Zelichenok, sentenced to three years in labour camp, one of twenty Jews then in prison for disseminating Jewish culture, or advocating emigration to Israel

⑦ 17 December 1986 Riots as indigenous Kazakhs protest at the removal of a Kazakh (Dinmukhamed Kunayev) as Communist Party First Secretary and his replacement by an ethnic Russian (Gennady Kolbin)

④ 11 February 1986 Anatoly Shcharansky, a human rights activist and Jewish dissident, released from Chistopol prison after nine years of a thirteen-year sentence. He flies to Berlin, Frankfurt and Jerusalem

⑥ 16 December 1986 Andrei Sakharov, dissident physicist, reinstated in Soviet Academy of Sciences, after 5-year exile and isolation in Gorky

⑧ 27 January 1987 Gorbachev calls for "glasnost" (openness) in public life and "perestroika" (restructuring) in the organisation of society

⑫ Autumn 1987 Mounting discontent throughout the Soviet Union at the growing death toll among Soviet forces. In all, 13,310 Soviet soldiers were killed in Afghanistan in eight years of fighting

⑪ 23 July 1987 More than a thousand Crimean Tatars march in Moscow, to demand restoration of their autonomous homeland in the Crimea (which had been abolished by Stalin in 1944)

⑤ 25 April 1986 Initial secrecy after nuclear plant accident caused revulsion throughout the Soviet Union and a demand for the truth to be told. Death toll announced as thirty-one

③ 18 November 1985 President Reagan presses Gorbachev to alleviate human rights abuses

⑩ 5 March 1987 Shcharansky appeals to Human Rights Commission on behalf of all imprisoned Jews and non-Jewish dissidents

⑨ 17 February 1987 United Nations Human Rights Commission presses Soviet Union to release Jewish prisoners and other imprisoned dissidents

AFGHANISTAN

KAZAKHSTAN

Alma Ata

Chistopol

Gorky

Moscow

S O V I E T   U N I O N

Caspian Sea

Leningrad

BYELORUSSIA

UKRAINE

Chernobyl

CRIMEA

Black Sea

RUMANIA

BULGARIA

POLAND

CZECHOSLOVAKIA

HUNGARY

Baltic Sea

EAST GERMANY

WEST GERMANY

Berlin

Frankfurt

Geneva (SWITZ.)

North Sea

Jerusalem

kilometres   0   500
miles   0   300

© Martin Gilbert 1993

149

THE END OF THE COLD WAR, 1987-1993

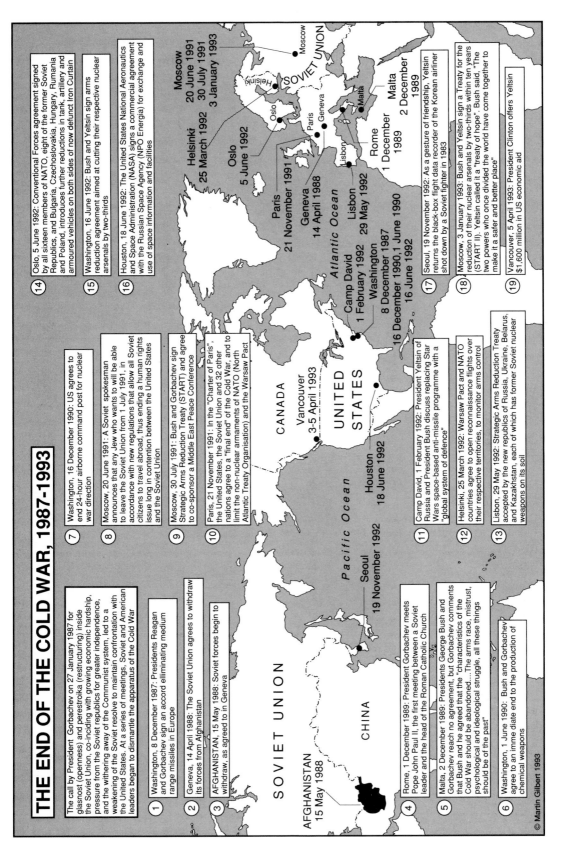

(1) The call by President Gorbachev on 27 January 1987 for glasnost (openness) and perestroika (restructuring) inside the Soviet Union, co-inciding with growing economic hardship, pressure from the Soviet republics for greater independence, and the withering away of the Communist system, led to a weakening of the Soviet resolve to maintain confrontation with the United States. At a series of meetings, Soviet and American leaders began to dismantle the apparatus of the Cold War

(2) Geneva, 14 April 1988: The Soviet Union agrees to withdraw its forces from Afghanistan

(3) AFGHANISTAN, 15 May 1988: Soviet forces begin to withdraw, as agreed to in Geneva

(4) Rome, 1 December 1989: President Gorbachev meets Pope John Paul II, the first meeting between a Soviet leader and the head of the Roman Catholic Church

(5) Malta, 2 December 1989: Presidents George Bush and Gorbachev reach no agreement, but Gorbachev comments that Bush and he agreed that the "characteristics of the Cold War should be abandoned....The arms race, mistrust, psychological and ideological struggle, all these things should be of the past"

(6) Washington, 1 June 1990: Bush and Gorbachev agree to an imme diate end to the production of chemical weapons

(7) Washington, 16 December 1990: US agrees to end 24-hour airborne command post for nuclear war direction

(8) Moscow, 20 June 1991: A Soviet spokesman announces that any Jew who wants to will be able to leave the Soviet Union from 1 July 1991, in accordance with new regulations that allow all Soviet citizens to travel abroad, thus ending a human rights issue long in contention between the United States and the Soviet Union

(9) Moscow, 30 July 1991: Bush and Gorbachev sign Strategic Arms Reduction Treaty (START) and agree to co-sponsor a Middle East Peace Conference

(10) Paris, 21 November 1991: In the "Charter of Paris", the United States, the Soviet Union and 32 other nations agree to a "final end" of the Cold War, and to limit the non-nuclear armaments of NATO (North Atlantic Treaty Organisation) and the Warsaw Pact

(11) Camp David, 1 February 1992: President Yeltsin of Russia and President Bush discuss replacing Star Wars space-based anti-missile programme with a "global system of defence"

(12) Helsinki, 25 March 1992: Warsaw Pact and NATO countries agree to open reconnaissance flights over their respective territories, to monitor arms control

(13) Lisbon, 29 May 1992: Strategic Arms Reduction Treaty accepted by the new republics of Russia, Ukraine, Belarus, and Kazakhstan, each of which has former Soviet nuclear weapons on its soil

(14) Oslo, 5 June 1992: Conventional Forces agreement signed by all sixteen members of NATO, eight of the former Soviet Republics, and Bulgaria, Czechoslovakia, Hungary, Rumania and Poland, introduces further reductions in tank, artillery and armoured vehicles on both sides of now defunct Iron Curtain

(15) Washington, 16 June 1992: Bush and Yeltsin sign arms reduction agreement aimed at cutting their respective nuclear arsenals by two-thirds

(16) Houston, 18 June 1992: The United States National Aeronautics and Space Administration (NASA) signs a commercial agreement with the Russian Space Agency (NPO Energia) for exchange and use of space information and facilities

(17) Seoul, 19 November 1992: As a gesture of friendship, Yeltsin returns the black-box flight data recorder of the Korean airliner shot down by a Soviet fighter in 1983

(18) Moscow, 3 January 1993: Bush and Yeltsin sign a Treaty for the reduction of their nuclear arsenals by two-thirds within ten years (START II). Yeltsin called it a "treaty of hope". Bush said, "The two powers who once divided the world have come together to make it a safer and better place"

(19) Vancouver, 5 April 1993: President Clinton offers Yeltsin $1,600 million in US economic aid

AFGHANISTAN
15 May 1988

SOVIET UNION

CHINA

Pacific Ocean

Seoul
19 November 1992

CANADA

Vancouver
3-5 April 1993

UNITED STATES

Houston
18 June 1992

Camp David
1 February 1992

Washington
8 December 1987
16 December 1990, 1 June 1990
16 June 1992

Atlantic Ocean

Lisbon
29 May 1992

Geneva
14 April 1988

Paris
21 November 1991

Oslo
5 June 1992

Helsinki
25 March 1992

Rome
1 December 1989

Lisbon

Malta
2 December 1989

SOVIET UNION

Moscow

Moscow
20 June 1991
30 July 1991
3 January 1993

Helsinki

Oslo

Paris

Geneva

Malta

© Martin Gilbert 1993

150

THE TRANSFORMATION OF THE SOVIET UNION, 1988-1989

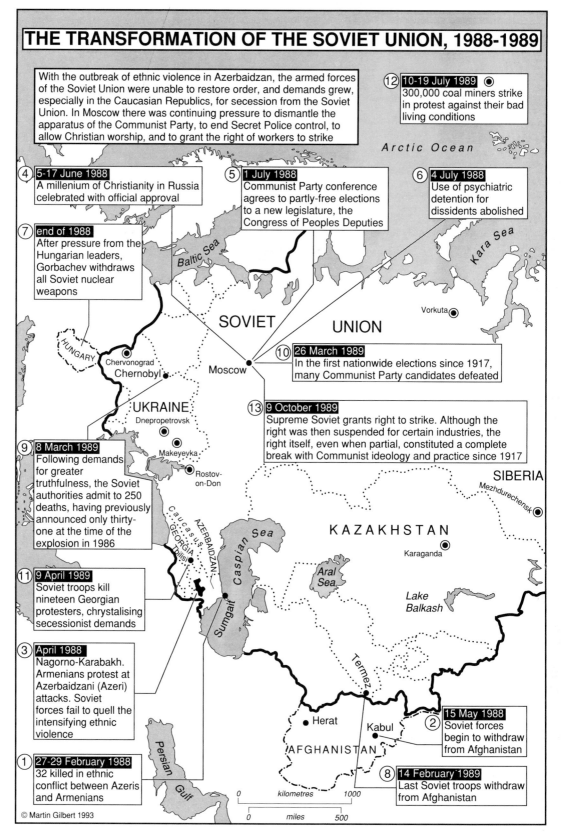

With the outbreak of ethnic violence in Azerbaidzan, the armed forces of the Soviet Union were unable to restore order, and demands grew, especially in the Caucasian Republics, for secession from the Soviet Union. In Moscow there was continuing pressure to dismantle the apparatus of the Communist Party, to end Secret Police control, to allow Christian worship, and to grant the right of workers to strike

(12) 10-19 July 1989 ◉
300,000 coal miners strike in protest against their bad living conditions

Arctic Ocean

(4) 5-17 June 1988
A millenium of Christianity in Russia celebrated with official approval

(5) 1 July 1988
Communist Party conference agrees to partly-free elections to a new legislature, the Congress of Peoples Deputies

(6) 4 July 1988
Use of psychiatric detention for dissidents abolished

Kara Sea

(7) end of 1988
After pressure from the Hungarian leaders, Gorbachev withdraws all Soviet nuclear weapons

Baltic Sea

SOVIET   UNION

Vorkuta ◉

HUNGARY

Chervonograd
Chernobyl·

Moscow ●

(10) 26 March 1989
In the first nationwide elections since 1917, many Communist Party candidates defeated

UKRAINE
Dnepropetrovsk ◉

(13) 9 October 1989
Supreme Soviet grants right to strike. Although the right was then suspended for certain industries, the right itself, even when partial, constituted a complete break with Communist ideology and practice since 1917

SIBERIA

(9) 8 March 1989
Following demands for greater truthfulness, the Soviet authorities admit to 250 deaths, having previously announced only thirty-one at the time of the explosion in 1986

Makeyevka ◉

Rostov-on-Don ◉

Mezhdurechensk ◉

Caucasus
GEORGIA
AZERBAIDZAN
Tbilisi

Caspian Sea

K A Z A K H S T A N

Karaganda ◉

Aral Sea

Lake Balkash

(11) 9 April 1989
Soviet troops kill nineteen Georgian protesters, chrystalising secessionist demands

Sumgait

(3) April 1988
Nagorno-Karabakh. Armenians protest at Azerbaidzani (Azeri) attacks. Soviet forces fail to quell the intensifying ethnic violence

Termez

Herat ●

Kabul ●

(2) 15 May 1988
Soviet forces begin to withdraw from Afghanistan

Persian Gulf

AFGHANISTAN

(1) 27-29 February 1988
32 killed in ethnic conflict between Azeris and Armenians

0   kilometres   1000

(8) 14 February 1989
Last Soviet troops withdraw from Afghanistan

0   miles   500

© Martin Gilbert 1993

151

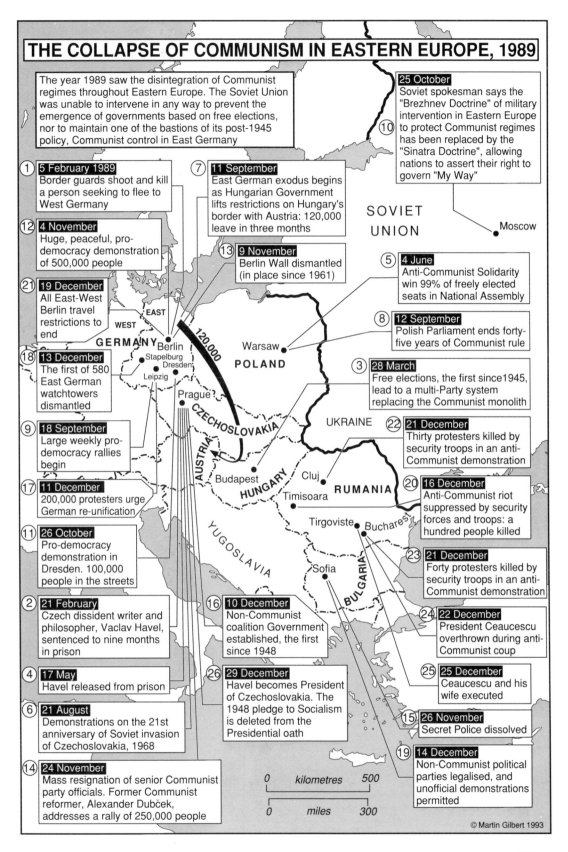

THE COLLAPSE OF COMMUNISM IN EASTERN EUROPE, 1989

The year 1989 saw the disintegration of Communist regimes throughout Eastern Europe. The Soviet Union was unable to intervene in any way to prevent the emergence of governments based on free elections, nor to maintain one of the bastions of its post-1945 policy, Communist control in East Germany

25 October
Soviet spokesman says the "Brezhnev Doctrine" of military intervention in Eastern Europe to protect Communist regimes has been replaced by the "Sinatra Doctrine", allowing nations to assert their right to govern "My Way"

(10)

SOVIET UNION

Moscow

① **5 February 1989**
Border guards shoot and kill a person seeking to flee to West Germany

⑦ **11 September**
East German exodus begins as Hungarian Government lifts restrictions on Hungary's border with Austria: 120,000 leave in three months

⑫ **4 November**
Huge, peaceful, pro-democracy demonstration of 500,000 people

⑬ **9 November**
Berlin Wall dismantled (in place since 1961)

⑤ **4 June**
Anti-Communist Solidarity win 99% of freely elected seats in National Assembly

㉑ **19 December**
All East-West Berlin travel restrictions to end

EAST
WEST
GERMANY Berlin
Stapelburg
Dresden
Leipzig
120,000

⑧ **12 September**
Polish Parliament ends forty-five years of Communist rule

⑱ **13 December**
The first of 580 East German watchtowers dismantled

Warsaw
POLAND

Prague
CZECHOSLOVAKIA

③ **28 March**
Free elections, the first since 1945, lead to a multi-Party system replacing the Communist monolith

⑨ **18 September**
Large weekly pro-democracy rallies begin

UKRAINE

㉒ **21 December**
Thirty protesters killed by security troops in an anti-Communist demonstration

⑰ **11 December**
200,000 protesters urge German re-unification

AUSTRIA

Budapest
HUNGARY
Cluj
Timisoara
RUMANIA

⑳ **16 December**
Anti-Communist riot suppressed by security forces and troops: a hundred people killed

⑪ **26 October**
Pro-democracy demonstration in Dresden. 100,000 people in the streets

YUGOSLAVIA

Tirgoviste Bucharest

㉓ **21 December**
Forty protesters killed by security troops in an anti-Communist demonstration

② **21 February**
Czech dissident writer and philosopher, Vaclav Havel, sentenced to nine months in prison

Sofia
BULGARIA

⑯ **10 December**
Non-Communist coalition Government established, the first since 1948

㉔ **22 December**
President Ceaucescu overthrown during anti-Communist coup

④ **17 May**
Havel released from prison

㉖ **29 December**
Havel becomes President of Czechoslovakia. The 1948 pledge to Socialism is deleted from the Presidential oath

㉕ **25 December**
Ceaucescu and his wife executed

⑥ **21 August**
Demonstrations on the 21st anniversary of Soviet invasion of Czechoslovakia, 1968

⑮ **26 November**
Secret Police dissolved

⑲ **14 December**
Non-Communist political parties legalised, and unofficial demonstrations permitted

⑭ **24 November**
Mass resignation of senior Communist party officials. Former Communist reformer, Alexander Dubček, addresses a rally of 250,000 people

0   kilometres   500

0   miles   300

© Martin Gilbert 1993

152

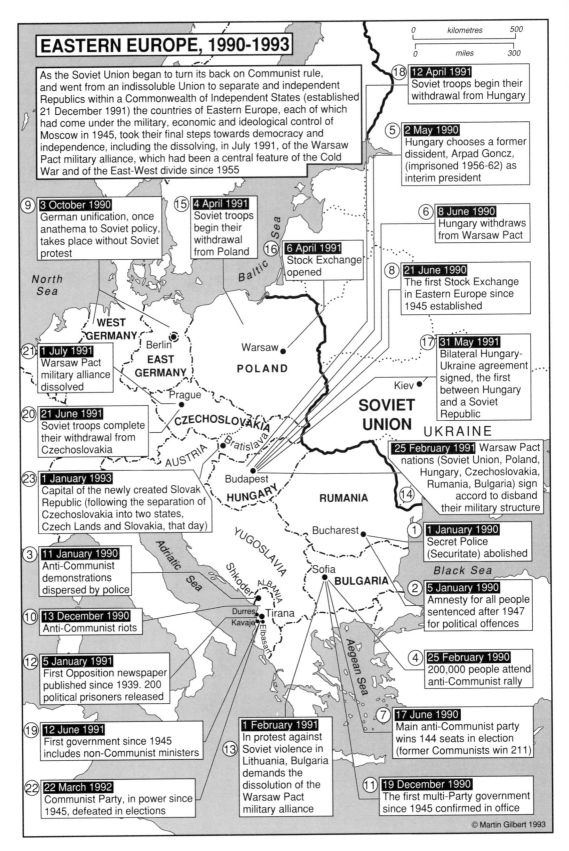

EASTERN EUROPE, 1990-1993

As the Soviet Union began to turn its back on Communist rule, and went from an indissoluble Union to separate and independent Republics within a Commonwealth of Independent States (established 21 December 1991) the countries of Eastern Europe, each of which had come under the military, economic and ideological control of Moscow in 1945, took their final steps towards democracy and independence, including the dissolving, in July 1991, of the Warsaw Pact military alliance, which had been a central feature of the Cold War and of the East-West divide since 1955

18 12 April 1991
Soviet troops begin their withdrawal from Hungary

5 2 May 1990
Hungary chooses a former dissident, Arpad Goncz, (imprisoned 1956-62) as interim president

9 3 October 1990
German unification, once anathema to Soviet policy, takes place without Soviet protest

15 4 April 1991
Soviet troops begin their withdrawal from Poland

16 6 April 1991
Stock Exchange opened

6 8 June 1990
Hungary withdraws from Warsaw Pact

8 21 June 1990
The first Stock Exchange in Eastern Europe since 1945 established

17 31 May 1991
Bilateral Hungary-Ukraine agreement signed, the first between Hungary and a Soviet Republic

21 1 July 1991
Warsaw Pact military alliance dissolved

20 21 June 1991
Soviet troops complete their withdrawal from Czechoslovakia

23 1 January 1993
Capital of the newly created Slovak Republic (following the separation of Czechoslovakia into two states, Czech Lands and Slovakia, that day)

25 February 1991 Warsaw Pact nations (Soviet Union, Poland, Hungary, Czechoslovakia, Rumania, Bulgaria) sign accord to disband their military structure

14

1 1 January 1990
Secret Police (Securitate) abolished

3 11 January 1990
Anti-Communist demonstrations dispersed by police

10 13 December 1990
Anti-Communist riots

2 5 January 1990
Amnesty for all people sentenced after 1947 for political offences

4 25 February 1990
200,000 people attend anti-Communist rally

12 5 January 1991
First Opposition newspaper published since 1939. 200 political prisoners released

7 17 June 1990
Main anti-Communist party wins 144 seats in election (former Communists win 211)

19 12 June 1991
First government since 1945 includes non-Communist ministers

13 1 February 1991
In protest against Soviet violence in Lithuania, Bulgaria demands the dissolution of the Warsaw Pact military alliance

11 19 December 1990
The first multi-Party government since 1945 confirmed in office

22 22 March 1992
Communist Party, in power since 1945, defeated in elections

North Sea

WEST GERMANY
Berlin
EAST GERMANY
Prague
CZECHOSLOVAKIA
Bratislava
AUSTRIA
Budapest
HUNGARY

Baltic Sea

Warsaw
POLAND

SOVIET UNION
Kiev
UKRAINE

RUMANIA
Bucharest

Black Sea

YUGOSLAVIA
Adriatic Sea
Shkoder
ALBANIA
Durres
Kavaje
Elbasan
Tirana

Sofia
BULGARIA

Aegean Sea

0   kilometres   500
0   miles   300

© Martin Gilbert 1993

153

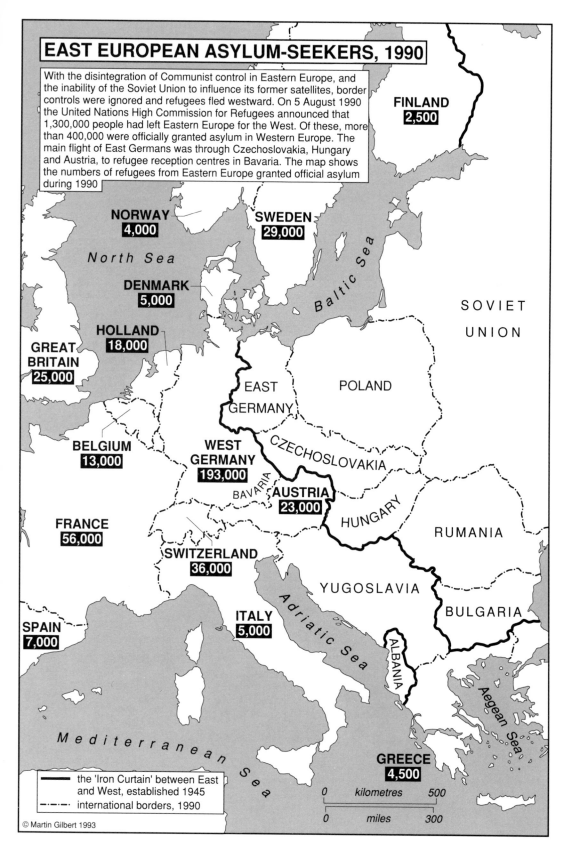

EAST EUROPEAN ASYLUM-SEEKERS, 1990

With the disintegration of Communist control in Eastern Europe, and the inability of the Soviet Union to influence its former satellites, border controls were ignored and refugees fled westward. On 5 August 1990 the United Nations High Commission for Refugees announced that 1,300,000 people had left Eastern Europe for the West. Of these, more than 400,000 were officially granted asylum in Western Europe. The main flight of East Germans was through Czechoslovakia, Hungary and Austria, to refugee reception centres in Bavaria. The map shows the numbers of refugees from Eastern Europe granted official asylum during 1990

FINLAND 2,500

NORWAY 4,000

SWEDEN 29,000

North Sea

Baltic Sea

DENMARK 5,000

SOVIET UNION

HOLLAND 18,000

GREAT BRITAIN 25,000

EAST GERMANY

POLAND

BELGIUM 13,000

WEST GERMANY 193,000

CZECHOSLOVAKIA

BAVARIA

AUSTRIA 23,000

HUNGARY

FRANCE 56,000

RUMANIA

SWITZERLAND 36,000

Adriatic Sea

YUGOSLAVIA

BULGARIA

ITALY 5,000

SPAIN 7,000

ALBANIA

Aegean Sea

Mediterranean Sea

GREECE 4,500

——— the 'Iron Curtain' between East and West, established 1945
—·—·— international borders, 1990

0   kilometres   500
0   miles   300

© Martin Gilbert 1993

154

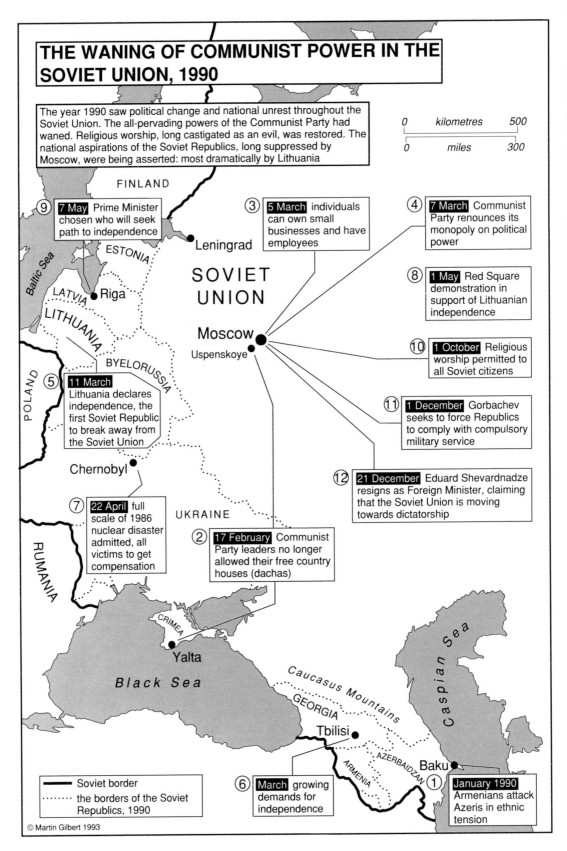

THE WANING OF COMMUNIST POWER IN THE SOVIET UNION, 1990

The year 1990 saw political change and national unrest throughout the Soviet Union. The all-pervading powers of the Communist Party had waned. Religious worship, long castigated as an evil, was restored. The national aspirations of the Soviet Republics, long suppressed by Moscow, were being asserted: most dramatically by Lithuania

0   kilometres   500

0   miles   300

FINLAND

⑨ **7 May** Prime Minister chosen who will seek path to independence

③ **5 March** individuals can own small businesses and have employees

④ **7 March** Communist Party renounces its monopoly on political power

ESTONIA

Leningrad

⑧ **1 May** Red Square demonstration in support of Lithuanian independence

SOVIET
UNION

Baltic Sea

LATVIA · Riga

LITHUANIA

Moscow

Uspenskoye

⑩ **1 October** Religious worship permitted to all Soviet citizens

BYELORUSSIA

POLAND

⑤ **11 March** Lithuania declares independence, the first Soviet Republic to break away from the Soviet Union

⑪ **1 December** Gorbachev seeks to force Republics to comply with compulsory military service

Chernobyl

⑫ **21 December** Eduard Shevardnadze resigns as Foreign Minister, claiming that the Soviet Union is moving towards dictatorship

⑦ **22 April** full scale of 1986 nuclear disaster admitted, all victims to get compensation

UKRAINE

② **17 February** Communist Party leaders no longer allowed their free country houses (dachas)

RUMANIA

CRIMEA

Yalta

Black Sea

Caucasus Mountains

Caspian Sea

GEORGIA

Tbilisi

AZERBAIDZAN

Baku

ARMENIA

① **January 1990** Armenians attack Azeris in ethnic tension

⑥ **March** growing demands for independence

—— Soviet border

········· the borders of the Soviet Republics, 1990

© Martin Gilbert 1993

155

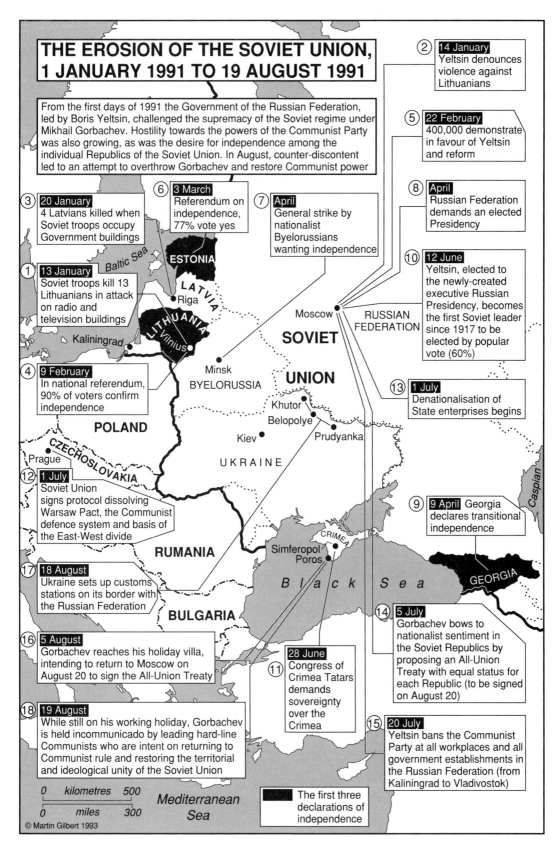

THE EROSION OF THE SOVIET UNION, 1 JANUARY 1991 TO 19 AUGUST 1991

From the first days of 1991 the Government of the Russian Federation, led by Boris Yeltsin, challenged the supremacy of the Soviet regime under Mikhail Gorbachev. Hostility towards the powers of the Communist Party was also growing, as was the desire for independence among the individual Republics of the Soviet Union. In August, counter-discontent led to an attempt to overthrow Gorbachev and restore Communist power

② **14 January** Yeltsin denounces violence against Lithuanians

⑤ **22 February** 400,000 demonstrate in favour of Yeltsin and reform

⑧ **April** Russian Federation demands an elected Presidency

③ **20 January** 4 Latvians killed when Soviet troops occupy Government buildings

⑥ **3 March** Referendum on independence, 77% vote yes

⑦ **April** General strike by nationalist Byelorussians wanting independence

⑩ **12 June** Yeltsin, elected to the newly-created executive Russian Presidency, becomes the first Soviet leader since 1917 to be elected by popular vote (60%)

① **13 January** Soviet troops kill 13 Lithuanians in attack on radio and television buildings

④ **9 February** In national referendum, 90% of voters confirm independence

⑬ **1 July** Denationalisation of State enterprises begins

⑫ **1 July** Soviet Union signs protocol dissolving Warsaw Pact, the Communist defence system and basis of the East-West divide

⑨ **9 April** Georgia declares transitional independence

⑰ **18 August** Ukraine sets up customs stations on its border with the Russian Federation

⑪ **28 June** Congress of Crimea Tatars demands sovereignty over the Crimea

⑭ **5 July** Gorbachev bows to nationalist sentiment in the Soviet Republics by proposing an All-Union Treaty with equal status for each Republic (to be signed on August 20)

⑯ **5 August** Gorbachev reaches his holiday villa, intending to return to Moscow on August 20 to sign the All-Union Treaty

⑱ **19 August** While still on his working holiday, Gorbachev is held incommunicado by leading hard-line Communists who are intent on returning to Communist rule and restoring the territorial and ideological unity of the Soviet Union

⑮ **20 July** Yeltsin bans the Communist Party at all workplaces and all government establishments in the Russian Federation (from Kaliningrad to Vladivostok)

Baltic Sea

ESTONIA

LATVIA

Riga

LITHUANIA

Vilnius

Kaliningrad

Moscow

RUSSIAN FEDERATION

SOVIET

UNION

Minsk

BYELORUSSIA

Khutor

Belopolye

Kiev

Prudyanka

UKRAINE

POLAND

CZECHOSLOVAKIA

Prague

RUMANIA

BULGARIA

CRIMEA

Simferopol

Poros

B l a c k   S e a

GEORGIA

Caspian

0   kilometres   500

0   miles   300

Mediterranean Sea

The first three declarations of independence

© Martin Gilbert 1993

156

THE ATTEMPTED COUP AND ITS AFTERMATH, 19 AUGUST 1991 TO 26 DECEMBER 1991

As more Soviet Republics moved towards independence, and the powers and institutions of the Communist Party were being progressively dismantled, a group of leading Communists tried to seize power in Moscow, intent upon the restoration of Communism, and of the Soviet Union. But in Moscow itself, the head of the Russian Federation, Boris Yeltsin, rallied the forces for change, and forestalled the take-over. Within four and a half months, the Soviet Union had ceased to exist

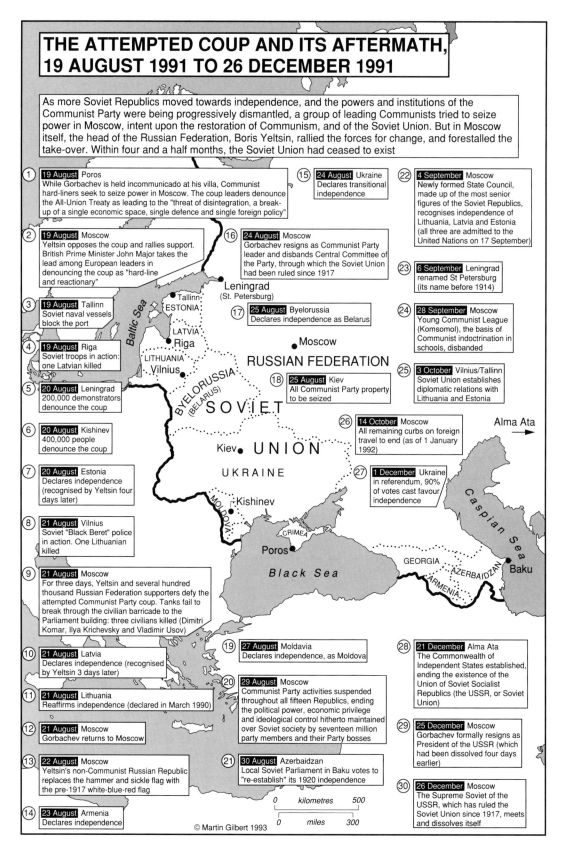

(1) **19 August** Poros
While Gorbachev is held incommunicado at his villa, Communist hard-liners seek to seize power in Moscow. The coup leaders denounce the All-Union Treaty as leading to the "threat of disintegration, a break-up of a single economic space, single defence and single foreign policy"

(2) **19 August** Moscow
Yeltsin opposes the coup and rallies support. British Prime Minister John Major takes the lead among European leaders in denouncing the coup as "hard-line and reactionary"

(3) **19 August** Tallinn
Soviet naval vessels block the port

(4) **19 August** Riga
Soviet troops in action: one Latvian killed

(5) **20 August** Leningrad
200,000 demonstrators denounce the coup

(6) **20 August** Kishinev
400,000 people denounce the coup

(7) **20 August** Estonia
Declares independence (recognised by Yeltsin four days later)

(8) **21 August** Vilnius
Soviet "Black Beret" police in action. One Lithuanian killed

(9) **21 August** Moscow
For three days, Yeltsin and several hundred thousand Russian Federation supporters defy the attempted Communist Party coup. Tanks fail to break through the civilian barricade to the Parliament building: three civilians killed (Dimitri Komar, Ilya Krichevsky and Vladimir Usov)

(10) **21 August** Latvia
Declares independence (recognised by Yeltsin 3 days later)

(11) **21 August** Lithuania
Reaffirms independence (declared in March 1990)

(12) **21 August** Moscow
Gorbachev returns to Moscow

(13) **22 August** Moscow
Yeltsin's non-Communist Russian Republic replaces the hammer and sickle flag with the pre-1917 white-blue-red flag

(14) **23 August** Armenia
Declares independence

(15) **24 August** Ukraine
Declares transitional independence

(16) **24 August** Moscow
Gorbachev resigns as Communist Party leader and disbands Central Committee of the Party, through which the Soviet Union had been ruled since 1917

(17) **25 August** Byelorussia
Declares independence as Belarus

(18) **25 August** Kiev
All Communist Party property to be seized

(19) **27 August** Moldavia
Declares independence, as Moldova

(20) **29 August** Moscow
Communist Party activities suspended throughout all fifteen Republics, ending the political power, economic privilege and ideological control hitherto maintained over Soviet society by seventeen million party members and their Party bosses

(21) **30 August** Azerbaidzan
Local Soviet Parliament in Baku votes to "re-establish" its 1920 independence

(22) **4 September** Moscow
Newly formed State Council, made up of the most senior figures of the Soviet Republics, recognises independence of Lithuania, Latvia and Estonia (all three are admitted to the United Nations on 17 September)

(23) **6 September** Leningrad
renamed St Petersburg (its name before 1914)

(24) **28 September** Moscow
Young Communist League (Komsomol), the basis of Communist indoctrination in schools, disbanded

(25) **3 October** Vilnius/Tallinn
Soviet Union establishes diplomatic relations with Lithuania and Estonia

(26) **14 October** Moscow
All remaining curbs on foreign travel to end (as of 1 January 1992)

(27) **1 December** Ukraine
in referendum, 90% of votes cast favour independence

(28) **21 December** Alma Ata
The Commonwealth of Independent States established, ending the existence of the Union of Soviet Socialist Republics (the USSR, or Soviet Union)

(29) **25 December** Moscow
Gorbachev formally resigns as President of the USSR (which had been dissolved four days earlier)

(30) **26 December** Moscow
The Supreme Soviet of the USSR, which has ruled the Soviet Union since 1917, meets and dissolves itself

© Martin Gilbert 1993

0 kilometres 500

0 miles 300

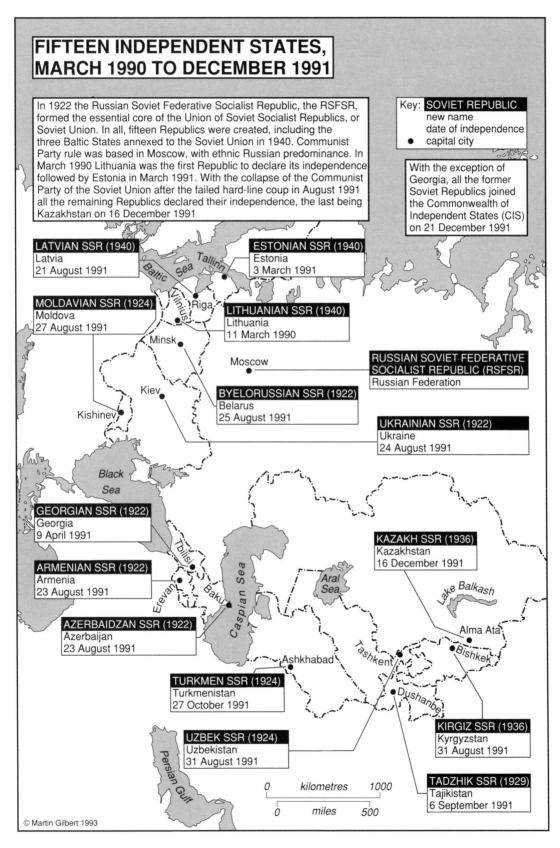

FIFTEEN INDEPENDENT STATES, MARCH 1990 TO DECEMBER 1991

In 1922 the Russian Soviet Federative Socialist Republic, the RSFSR, formed the essential core of the Union of Soviet Socialist Republics, or Soviet Union. In all, fifteen Republics were created, including the three Baltic States annexed to the Soviet Union in 1940. Communist Party rule was based in Moscow, with ethnic Russian predominance. In March 1990 Lithuania was the first Republic to declare its independence followed by Estonia in March 1991. With the collapse of the Communist Party of the Soviet Union after the failed hard-line coup in August 1991 all the remaining Republics declared their independence, the last being Kazakhstan on 16 December 1991

Key: **SOVIET REPUBLIC**
new name
date of independence
● capital city

With the exception of Georgia, all the former Soviet Republics joined the Commonwealth of Independent States (CIS) on 21 December 1991

LATVIAN SSR (1940)
Latvia
21 August 1991

ESTONIAN SSR (1940)
Estonia
3 March 1991

MOLDAVIAN SSR (1924)
Moldova
27 August 1991

LITHUANIAN SSR (1940)
Lithuania
11 March 1990

RUSSIAN SOVIET FEDERATIVE SOCIALIST REPUBLIC (RSFSR)
Russian Federation

BYELORUSSIAN SSR (1922)
Belarus
25 August 1991

UKRAINIAN SSR (1922)
Ukraine
24 August 1991

GEORGIAN SSR (1922)
Georgia
9 April 1991

KAZAKH SSR (1936)
Kazakhstan
16 December 1991

ARMENIAN SSR (1922)
Armenia
23 August 1991

AZERBAIDZAN SSR (1922)
Azerbaijan
23 August 1991

TURKMEN SSR (1924)
Turkmenistan
27 October 1991

KIRGIZ SSR (1936)
Kyrgyzstan
31 August 1991

UZBEK SSR (1924)
Uzbekistan
31 August 1991

TADZHIK SSR (1929)
Tajikistan
6 September 1991

Baltic Sea
Tallinn
Vilnius
Riga
Minsk
Moscow
Kiev
Kishinev
Black Sea
Tbilisi
Erevan
Baku
Caspian Sea
Aral Sea
Lake Balkash
Alma Ata
Bishkek
Ashkhabad
Tashkent
Dushanbe
Persian Gulf

0   kilometres   1000
0   miles   500

© Martin Gilbert 1993

158

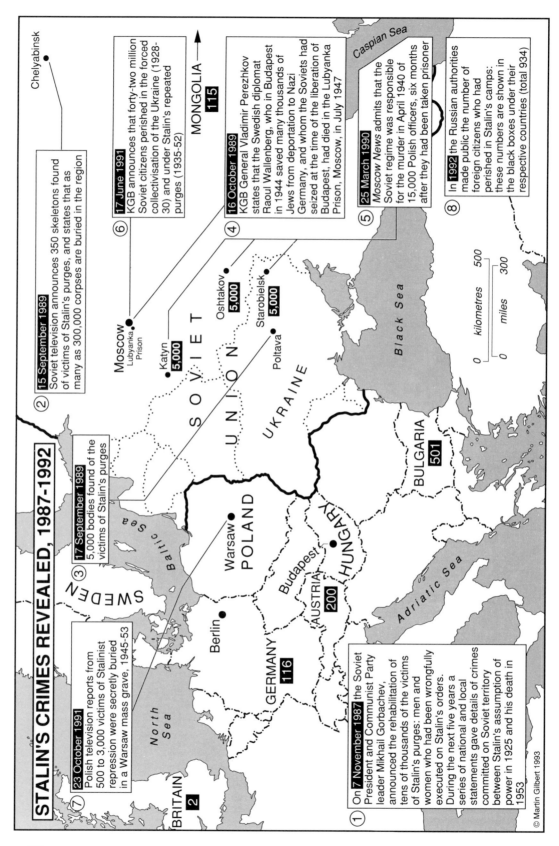

STALIN'S CRIMES REVEALED, 1987-1992

② **15 September 1989**
Soviet television announces 350 skeletons found of victims of Stalin's purges, and states that as many as 300,000 corpses are buried in the region

⑥ **17 June 1991**
KGB announces that forty-two million Soviet citizens perished in the forced collectivisation of the Ukraine (1928-30) and under Stalin's repeated purges (1935-52)

④ **16 October 1989**
KGB General Vladimir Perezhkov states that the Swedish diplomat Raoul Wallenberg, who in Budapest in 1944 saved many thousands of Jews from deportation to Nazi Germany, and whom the Soviets had seized at the time of the liberation of Budapest, had died in the Lubyanka Prison, Moscow, in July 1947

⑤ **25 March 1990**
Moscow News admits that the Soviet regime was responsible for the murder in April 1940 of 15,000 Polish officers, six months after they had been taken prisoner

⑧ In 1992 the Russian authorities made public the number of foreign citizens who had perished in Stalin's camps: these numbers are shown in the black boxes under their respective countries (total 934)

③ **17 September 1989**
5,000 bodies found of the victims of Stalin's purges

⑦ **23 October 1991**
Polish television reports from 500 to 3,000 victims of Stalinist repression were secretly buried in a Warsaw mass grave, 1945-53

① On **7 November 1987** the Soviet President and Communist Party leader Mikhail Gorbachev, announced the rehabilitation of tens of thousands of the victims of Stalin's purges: men and women who had been wrongfully executed on Stalin's orders. During the next five years a series of national and local statements gave details of crimes committed on Soviet territory between Stalin's assumption of power in 1925 and his death in 1953

Chelyabinsk

MONGOLIA **115**

Caspian Sea

Moscow
Lubyanka Prison

Katyn **5,000**

Oshtakov **5,000**

Starobielsk **5,000**

Poltava

SOVIET UNION

UKRAINE

Black Sea

SWEDEN

Baltic Sea

North Sea

Berlin

GERMANY **116**

Warsaw
POLAND

Budapest
HUNGARY

AUSTRIA **200**

BULGARIA **501**

Adriatic Sea

BRITAIN **2**

0   kilometres   500
0   miles   300

© Martin Gilbert 1993

159

THE COMMONWEALTH OF INDEPENDENT STATES, 1992

(9) **7 February** Yeltsin and Mitterand sign Franco-Russian Treaty

(26) **9 November** Yeltsin and Major sign Anglo-Russian Treaty

(1) Established on **21 December 1991**, the Commonwealth of Independent States had a stormy first year, but its structure survived, and it was gradually accepted by the international community, to which its member States appealed at different times for economic help, and with which its members began to establish bilateral working relationships at diplomatic and economic levels

(3) **8 January 1992** European Community (under Britain's presidency) agrees on 2 December 1991, to emergency food aid worth $263 million. Russia accepts this on 8 January 1992

(23) **25 July** Eleven members of the Commonwealth of Independent States combined to send a "Unified Team" to the Olympic Games in Barcelona, winning the largest number of Gold Medals (45) as against the United States (37), the recently united East and West Germany (33), and China (16)

(10) **10 February** 'Operation Provide Hope', the United States airlift to the CIS, begins. Fifty-four flights in all, with 17,000 tons of food and medical supplies (left over from the Gulf War)

(4) **13 January** Poland and Lithuania recognise existing borders and agree to non-interference in internal affairs

(5) **14 January** Estonia and Russia establish diplomatic relations

(15) **2 March** Polish-Belarus diplomatic relations established. Belarus agrees to set up Polish language schools for its Polish minority

(17) **6 March** Trade links inaugurated

(8) **1 February** The Commonwealth of Independent States agrees to withdraw all its troops, principally Russians, from the Baltic Republics

(21) **22 April** Exposing the scale of former Soviet deception, Ukraine declares that between **6,000** and **8,000** people died as a result of the nuclear plant explosion in 1986

(6) **16 January** Hungary and Moldova establish diplomatic relations (Moldova's first)

(12) **21 February** Yeltsin agrees to re-establish a German National District on the Volga (abolished by Stalin in the 1930s)

(7) **29 January** Ukraine signs barter deal with Iran: gas and oil from Ukraine in return for chemicals, concrete and steel piping

(13) **24 February** 3 dead when construction battalion riots suppressed

(24) **3 August** Russia and Ukraine agree to divide the former Soviet Black Sea Fleet after three years joint control

(20) **28 March** 18 dead in fighting between pro- and anti-Russia factions. Five thousand flee to the Odessa region

(25) **14-16 August** 50 dead as secessionist Abkhazians fight Georgians **26 August.** Georgians set up interim government over Abkhazians (250,00 Georgians and 160,000 Abkhazians live in region)

(22) **15 May** Mutual Security Treaty signed (Russia, Kazakhstan, Armenia, Turkmenistan, Uzbekistan and Tajikistan), recognising each others borders and pledging common defence against aggression

(2) **6 January** **113 killed** since late December in civil war

(14) **25 February** Azeris claim 1,000 killed by Armenians

(18) **9 March** Last Russian troops evacuated from Armenian enclave of Nagorno-Karabakh, after 3 soldiers killed

(17) **15 March** Armenian-Azerbaijan truce signed

(27) **23 December** Thousands of Tajiks flee into Afghanistan during fighting between local Tajik ex-Communist and Islamic forces

(11) **17 February** The six Muslim Republics of the CIS join the Muslim trading group, the Economic Co-operation Organisation

(16) **4 March** Joint Turkmenistan-Iran Chamber of Commerce established

0 kilometres 1000

0 miles 500

© Martin Gilbert 1993

160

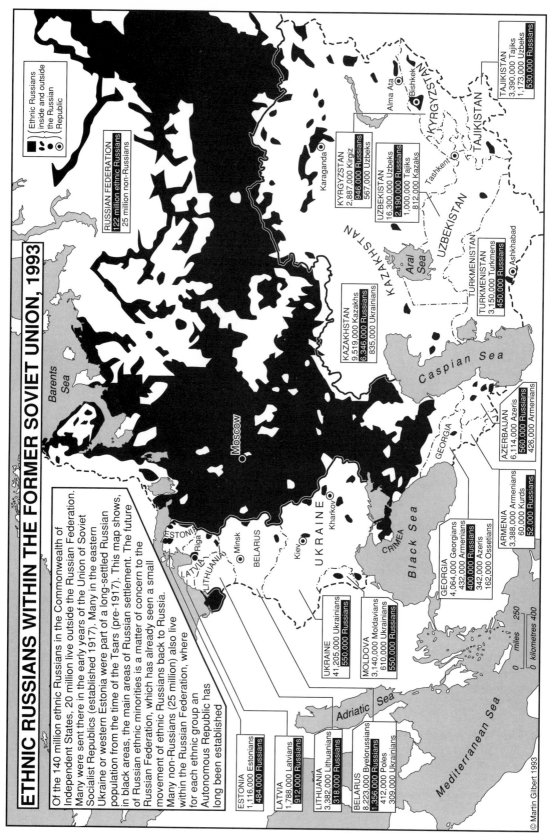

ETHNIC RUSSIANS WITHIN THE FORMER SOVIET UNION, 1993

Of the 140 million ethnic Russians in the Commonwealth of Independent States, 20 million live outside the Russian Federation. Many were sent there in the early years of the Union of Soviet Socialist Republics (established 1917). Many in the eastern Ukraine or western Estonia were part of a long-settled Russian population from the time of the Tsars (pre-1917). This map shows, in black areas, the main areas of Russian settlement. The future of Russian ethnic minorities is a matter of concern to the Russian Federation, which has already seen a small movement of ethnic Russians back to Russia. Many non-Russians (25 million) also live within the Russian Federation, where for each ethnic group an Autonomous Republic has long been established

Ethnic Russians inside and outside the Russian Republic

RUSSIAN FEDERATION
122 million ethnic Russians
25 million non-Russians

KYRGYZSTAN
2,887,000 Kirgiz
946,000 Russians
567,000 Uzbek

UZBEKISTAN
16,300,000 Uzbeks
2,190,000 Russians
1,000,000 Tajiks
812,000 Kazaks

TAJIKISTAN
3,390,000 Tajiks
1,173,000 Uzbeks
530,000 Russians

KAZAKHSTAN
9,519,000 Kazakhs
6,346,000 Russians
835,000 Ukrainians

TURKMENISTAN
3,150,000 Turkmens
450,000 Russians

AZERBAIJAN
6,114,000 Azeris
560,000 Russians
426,000 Armenians

ARMENIA
3,388,000 Armenians
60,000 Kurds
52,000 Russians

GEORGIA
4,064,000 Georgians
432,000 Armenians
400,000 Russians
342,000 Azeris
162,000 Ossetians

UKRAINE
41,205,000 Ukrainians
550,000 Russians

MOLDOVA
3,140,000 Moldavians
610,000 Ukrainians
550,000 Russians

ESTONIA
1,116,000 Estonians
484,000 Russians

LATVIA
1,788,000 Latvians
912,000 Russians

LITHUANIA
3,382,000 Lithuanians
318,000 Russians

BELARUS
8,223,000 Byelorussians
1,356,000 Russians
412,000 Poles
309,000 Ukrainians

Barents Sea

Moscow

ESTONIA
Riga
LATVIA
LITHUANIA
Minsk
BELARUS
Kiev
UKRAINE
Kharkov
CRIMEA

Black Sea

Caspian Sea

Aral Sea

KAZAKHSTAN

Karaganda

Alma Ata
Bishkek
KYRGYZSTAN
Tashkent
UZBEKISTAN
TAJIKISTAN

TURKMENISTAN
Ashkhabad

GEORGIA
AZERBAIJAN
ARMENIA

Adriatic Sea

Mediterranean Sea

0   250
miles   400
0 kilometres

© Martin Gilbert 1993

161

Bibliography of Works Consulted

(i) ATLASES

Baratov, R. B. (and others), *Atlas Tadzhikskoi Sovetskoi Sotsialisticheskoi Respubliki* (Dushanbe and Moscow, 1968)

Bartholomew, John (ed), *The Times Atlas of the World*, 5 vols (London, 1959)

Bazilevich, K. V., Golubtsov, I. A. and Zinoviev, M. A., *Atlas Istorii SSSR*, 3 vols (Moscow, 1949–54)

Beloglazova, O. A. (ed), *Atlas SSSR* (Moscow, 1954)

Czapliński, Wladislaw and Ladogórski, Tadeusz, *Atlas Historyczny Polski* (Warsaw, 1968)

Droysens, G., *Historischer Handatlas* (Bielefeld and Leipzig, 1886)

Durov, A. G. (General editor), *Atlas Leningradskoi Oblasti* (Moscow, 1967)

Engel, Joseph, *Grosser Historischer Weltatlas* (Munich, 1962)

Grosier, L'Abbé, *Atlas Générale de la Chine* (Paris 1785)

Hudson, G. F. and Rajchman, Marthe, *An Atlas of Far Eastern Politics* (London, 1938)

Kalesnik, S. V. (and others), *Peterburg–Leningrad* (Leningrad, 1957)

Kosev, Dimiter (and others), *Atlas Po Bulgarska Istoriya* (Sofia, 1963)

Kubijovyć, Volodymyr, *Atlas of Ukraine and Adjoining Countries* (Lvov, 1937)

Kudriashov, K. V., *Russkii Istoricheskii Atlas* (Leningrad, 1928)

Kovalevsky, Pierre, *Atlas Historique et Culturel de la Russie et du Monde Slave* (Paris, 1961)

McEvedy, Colin, *The Penguin Atlas of Medieval History* (London, 1961)

Penkala, Maria, *A Correlated History of the Far East* (The Hague and Paris, 1966)

Oxford Regional Economic Atlas: The USSR and Eastern Europe (Oxford, 1956)

Sochava, V. B. (Principal ed), *Atlas Zabaikalia* (Moscow and Irkutsk, 1967)

Taaffe, Robert N. and Kingsbury, Robert C., *An Atlas of Soviet Affairs* (London, 1965)

Terekhov, N. M. (senior editor), *Atlas Volgogradskoi Oblasti* (Moscow, 1967)

Toynbee, Arnold J. and Myers, Edward D., *Historical Atlas and Gazetteer* (London, 1959)

Voznesenski (and others), *Atlas Razvitiya Khoziastva i Kultury SSSR* (Moscow, 1967)

Westermann, Georg, *Atlas zur Weltgeschichte* (Braunschweig, 1956)

Zamyslovski, Igor E., *Uchebnii Atlas po Russkoi Istorii* (St Petersburg, 1887)

(ii) MAPS

Atanasiu, A. D., *La Bessarabie* (Paris, 1919)

Bazewicz, J. M., *Polska w Trzech Zaborach* (Warsaw, n.d.)

Bazileva, Z. P., *Rossiiskaya Imperia 1801–1861* (Moscow, 1960)

British G.H.Q., Constantinople, *Ethnographical Map of Caucasus* (Constantinople, 1920)

Fedorovskaya, G. P. (publisher), *Promyshlennost Rossii 1913; Promyshlennost Soyuza SSR 1940* (Moscow, 1962)

Filonenko, W. J., *Volkstumkarte der Krim* (Vienna, 1932)

Kuchborskaya, E. P., *Rossiiskaya Imperia 1725–1801* (Moscow, 1959)

Stanford, Edward, *Sketch of the Acquisitions of Russia* (London, 1876)

Wyld, James, *Wyld's Military Staff Map of Central Asia, Turkistan and Afghanistan* (London, 1878)

(iii) ENCYCLOPAEDIAS, REFERENCE BOOKS AND GENERAL WORKS

Baedeker, Karl, *Russland* (Leipzig, 1912)

Cole, J. P., *Geography of the USSR* (London, 1967)

Florinsky, Michael T. (ed), *Encyclopaedia of Russia and the Soviet Union* (New York, 1961)

Katzenelson, Y. L. and Gintsburg, D. G. (eds), *Evreiskaya Entsiklopediya,* 16 vols (St Petersburg, 1906–13)

Kubijovyć, Volodymyr (ed), *Ukraine: A Concise Encyclopaedia* (Toronto, 1963)

Pares, Bernard, *A History of Russia* (London, 1926)

Parker, W. H., *An Historical Georgraphy of Russia* (London, 1968)

Sumner, B. H., *Survey of Russian History* (London, 1944)

Utechin, S. V., *Everyman's Concise Encyclopaedia of Russia* (London, 1961)

Zhukov, E. M. (ed), *Sovetskaya Istoricheskaya Entsiklopediya,* vols 1–12 (Moscow, 1961–69)

(iv) BOOKS ON SPECIAL TOPICS

Allen, W. E. D., *The Ukraine: A History* (Cambridge, 1940)

Allen, W. E. D. and Muratov, P., *Caucasian Battlefields: A History of the Wars on the Turco-Caucasian Border 1828–1921* (London, 1953)

Allilueva, A. S., *Iz Vospominanii* (Moscow, 1946)

Armstrong, John A. (ed), *Soviet Partisans in World War II* (Madison, 1964)

Armstrong, Terence E., *The Northern Sea Route* (Cambridge, 1952)

Avalishvili, Zourab, *The Independence of Georgia in International Politics 1918–1921* (London, 1940)

Baddeley, John F., *The Russian Conquest of the Caucasus* (London, 1908)

Baddeley, John F., *Russia, Mongolia, China*, 2 vols (London, 1919)

Caroe, Olaf, *Soviet Empire: The Turks of Central Asia and Stalinism* (London, 1953)

Chamberlin, William Henry, *The Russian Revolution 1917–1921*, 2 vols (New York, 1935)

Clark, Alan, *Barbarossa: The Russo-German Conflict 1941–1945* (London, 1965)

Conquest, Robert, *The Soviet Deportation of Nationalities* (London, 1960)

Cresson, W. P., *The Cossacks, their History and Country* (New York, 1919)

Dallin, Alexander, *German Rule in Russia 1941–1945* (London, 1957)

Dallin, David J., *The Rise of Russia in Asia* (London, 1950)

Dallin, David J. and Nicolaevsky, Boris I., *Forced Labour in Soviet Russia* (London, 1948)

Dixon, C. Aubrey and Heilbrunn, Otto, *Communist Guerilla Warfare* (London, 1954)

Dubnow, S. M., *History of the Jews in Russia and Poland* (Philadelphia, 1916–20)

Eudin, X. J. and Fisher, H. H., *Soviet Russia and the West 1920–1927: A Documentary Survey* (Stanford, 1957)

Fennell, J. L. I., *Ivan the Great of Moscow* (London, 1963)

Fennell, J. L. I., *The Emergence of Moscow 1304–1359* (London, 1968)

Fischer, Louis, *The Soviets in World Affairs,* 2 vols (London, 1930)

Fischer, Louis, *The Life of Lenin* (London, 1964)

Freund, Gerald, *Unholy Alliance: Russian-German relations from the Treaty of Brest-Litovsk to the Treaty of Berlin* (London, 1957)

Futrell, Michael, *Northern Underground: Episodes of Russian Revolutionary Transport and Communications through Scandinavia and Finland 1863–1917* (London, 1963)

Greenberg, Louis, *The Jews in Russia: The Struggle For Emancipation,* 2 vols (New Haven, 1944, 1951)

Höhne, Heinz, *The Order of the Death's Head: The Story of Hitler's S.S.* (London, 1969)

Indian Officer, An (anon), *Russia's March Towards India*, 2 vols (London, 1894)

Jackson, W. A. Douglas, *Russo-Chinese Borderlands* (Princeton, 1962)

Joll, James, *The Anarchists* (London, 1964)

Kamenetsky, Ihor, *Hitler's Occupation of Ukraine 1941–1944: A study of Totalitarian imperialism* (Milwaukee, 1956)

Kazemzadeh, F., *The Struggle for Transcaucasia* (New York, 1951)

Katkov, George, *Russia 1917: The February Revolution* (London, 1967)

Kennan, George, *Siberia and the Exile System* (New York, 1891)

Kerner, Robert J., *The Urge to the Sea: The Course of Russian History* (Berkeley and Los Angeles, 1946)

Kirchner, Walther, *Commercial Relations Between Russia and Europe 1400 to 1800* (Bloomington, Indiana, 1966)

Klyuchevskii, Vasilii Osipovich, *Peter the Great* (London, 1958)

Kochan, Lionel, *Russia in Revolution 1890–1918* (London, 1966)

Kolarz, Walter, *Russia and her Colonies* (London, 1952)

Krypton, Constantine, *The Northern Sea Route* (New York, 1953)

Lang, D. M., *A Modern History of Georgia* (London, 1962)

Leslie, R. F., *Reform and Insurrection in Russian Poland* (London, 1963)

Lias, Godfrey, *Kazak Exodus* (London, 1956)

Liubavskii, M. K., *Ocherk Istorii Litovsko-Russkovo Gosudarstva* (Moscow, 1910; Russian Reprint Series, The Hague, 1966)

Lorimer, F., *The Population of the Soviet Union: History and Prospects* (Geneva, 1946)

Lyashchenko, Peter I., *History of the National Economy of Russia to the 1917 Revolution* (New York, 1949)

Maksimov, S., *Sibir i Katorga,* 3 vols (St Petersburg, 1871)

Malozemoff, A., *Russian Far-Eastern Policy 1881–1904* (Los Angeles, 1958)

Manning, Clarence A., *Twentieth-Century Ukraine* (New York, 1951)

Mazour, Anatole G., *The First Russian Revolution, 1825: the Decembrist movement* (Stanford, 1961)

Mikhailov, V., *Pamiatnaya Knizhka Sotsialista-Revoliutsionera*, 2 vols (Paris, 1911, 1914)

Miller, Margaret, *The Economic Development of Russia 1905–1914* (London, 1926)

Mora, Sylvestre and Zwierniak, Pierre, *La Justice Sovietique* (Rome, 1945)

Nasonov, A. N., *Russkaya Zemlia* (Moscow, 1951)

Nikitin, M. N. and Vagin, P. I., *The Crimes of the German Fascists in the Leningrad Region: Materials and Documents* (London, 1947)

Nosenko, A. K. (ed), *V. I. Lenin 1870–1924* (Kiev, n.d.). A collection of photographs, with 2 maps

Obolenski, Prince Eugene, *Souvenirs D'Un Exilé en Sibérie* (Leipzig, 1862)

Owen, Launcelot A., *The Russian Peasant Movement 1906–17* (London, 1937)

Park, Alexander G., *Bolshevism in Turkestan 1917–1927* (New York, 1957)

Philippi, Alfred and Heim, Ferdinand, *Der Feldzug gegen Sowjetrussland 1941–1945* (Stuttgart, 1962)

Pierce, Richard A., *Russian Central Asia 1867–1917* (Berkeley and Los Angeles, 1960)

Pipes, Richard, *The Formation of the Soviet Union: Communism and Nationalism 1917–1923* (Cambridge, Massachusetts, 1954)

Platonov, S. F., *Ocherki Po Istorii Smuti v Moskovskom Gosudarstve* (Moscow, 1937)

Pospelov, P. N., *Istoriya Kommunisticheskoi Partii Sovetskovo Soyuza,* 6 vols (Moscow, 1964–68)

Pounds, Norman J. G., *Poland Between East and West* (Princeton, 1964)

Radkey, Oliver H., *The Agrarian Foes of Bolshevism* (New York, 1958)

Rapport du Parti Socialiste Revolutionnaire de Russie au Congres Socialiste International de Stuttgart (Ghent, 1907)

Reddaway, W. R., Penson, J. H., Halecki, O. and Dyboski, R. (eds), *Cambridge History of Poland*, 2 vols (Cambridge, 1941, 1950)

Reitlinger, Gerald, *The House Built on Sand: The Conflicts of German Policy in Russia 1939–1945* (London, 1960)

Riasanovsky, Nicholas V., *A History of Russia* (New York, 1963)

Rosen, Baron A., *Russian Conspirators in Siberia* (London, 1872)

Rostovtzeff, M., *The Iranians and Greeks in South Russia* (Oxford, 1922)

Salisbury, Harrison E., *The Siege of Leningrad* (London, 1969)

Schuyler, Eugene, *Peter the Great: Emperor of Russia,* 2 vols (London, 1844)

Schwarz, Solomon M., *The Russian Revolution of 1905* (Chicago, 1967)

Serge, Victor, *Memoirs of a Revolutionary 1901–1941* (London, 1963)

Seton-Watson, Hugh, *The Russian Empire 1801–1917* (London, 1967)

Shukman, Harold, *Lenin and the Russian Revolution* (London, 1966)

Simpson, Sir John Hope, *The Refugee Problem* (London, 1939)

Skazkin, S. D. (and others), *Istoriya Vizantii*, 3 vols (Moscow, 1967)

Slusser, Robert M. and Triska Jan F., *A Calendar of Soviet Treaties 1917–1957* (Stanford, 1959)

Squire, P. S., *The Third Department: The establishment and practices of the political police in the Russia of Nicholas I* (Cambridge, 1968)

Stephan, John J., *Sakhalin* (Oxford, 1971)

Sullivant, Robert S., *Soviet Politics and the Ukraine 1917–1957* (New York, 1962)

Sumner, B. H., *Peter the Great and the Ottoman Empire* (Oxford, 1949)

Sumner, B. H., *Peter the Great and the Emergence of Russia* (London, 1950)

Suprunenko, M. I. (and others), *Istoria Ukrainskoi RSR* (Kiev, 1958)

Tikhonov, Nikolai (and others), *The Defence of Leningrad: Eye-witness Accounts of the Siege* (London, 1944)

Treadgold, Donald W., *The Great Siberian Migration* (Princeton, 1957)

Trotsky, Leon, *My Life* (London, 1930)

Vernadsky, George, *The Mongols and Russia* (London, 1953)

Wheeler, G., *The Modern History of Soviet Central Asia* (London, 1964)

Woodward, David, *The Russians at Sea* (London, 1965)

Yarmolinski, Avram, *The Road to Revolution: A Century of Russian Radicalism* (London, 1957)

Yaroslavsky, E., *History of Anarchism in Russia* (London, 1937)

Zimin, A. A., *Reformy Ivana Groznovo* (Moscow, 1960)

(v) ARTICLES

Anon, 'How the Bear Learned to Swim', *The Economist* (London, 24–30 October 1970)

Bealby, John Thomas, Kropotkin, Prince Peter Alexeivitch, Philips, Walter Alison and Wallace, Sir Donald Mackenzie, 'Russia', *The Encyclopaedia Britannica* (Eleventh edition, London and New York, 1910)

Carsten, F. L., 'The Reichswehr and the Red Army 1920–1933', *Survey* (London, 1962)

Dziewanowski, M. K., 'Pilsudski's Federal Policy 1919–21', *Journal of Central European Affairs* (London, 1950)

Footman, David, 'Nestor Makno', *St Antony's Papers No. 6: Soviet Affairs No. 2* (Oxford, 1959)

Lobanov-Rostovsky, A., 'Anglo-Russian Relations through the Centuries', *Russian Review*, vol 7 (New York, 1948)

Parkes, Harry, 'Report on the Russian Caravan Trade with China', *Journal of the Royal Geographic Society*, vol 25 (London, 1854)

Stanhope, Henry, 'Soviet Strength at Sea', *The Times* (London, 25 January 1971)

Sullivan, Joseph L., 'Decembrists in Exile', *Harvard Slavic Studies,* vol 4 (The Hague, 1954)

Wildes, Harry Emerson, 'Russia's Attempts to Open Japan', *Russian Review,* vol 5 (New York, 1945)

Yakunskiy, V. K. 'La Révolution Industrielle en Russie', *Cahiers du Monde Russe et Sovietique* (The Hague, 1961)

Index

European Russia, 27; a shipbuilding centre (by 1800), 34; administrative centre of a Province established by Peter the Great, 38; industrial growth of (by 1860), 56; Bolshevik propaganda enters Russia through (1903–14), 73; occupied by British troops (1918–19), 91, 92, 94, 146; United States famine relief for Russia arrives at (1921), 102; Soviet labour camps established near, 109, 110; and the Northern Sea Route, 112; allied aid enters the Soviet Union through (1941–45), 121; a German plan for (1941), 122; Soviet naval strength at (1970), 141

Ardahan: siege of (1829), 46; ceded to Russia by Turkey (1878), 48, 61; ceded to Turkey by Russia (1921), 104

Argun, River: tin mines near, 106

Arkhangelskii monastery: 19

Armavir: revolutionary outbreak at (1905), 76; claimed as part of the Ukraine, 97; occupied by the Germans (1942), 124

Armenia: Viking settlers reach, 11; annexed by Russia (1828), 48; and the proposed Union of Border States (1919–20), 100; its brief independence (1918–20), 104; a Soviet Republic, 144; declares independence (1991), 157; an independent Republic, 158; signs truce with Azerbaijan (1992), 160; signs Mutual Security Treaty (1992), 160; ethnic Russian minority in (1993), 161

Armenians: their settlement by 800 BC, 1; under Islamic influence, 10; converted to Eastern Catholicism, 15; their growing discontent with Russian rule (by 1905), 68, 76; protests by (1988), 151; violence by (1990), 155

Arms supplies: and the Cold War (1984–8), 148

Ashkhabad: annexed by Russia (1881), 61; linked to Moscow by railway (1915), 62; occupied by British forces (1918–19), 103; allied aid enters the Soviet Union through (1941–45), 121; becomes capital of independent Republic of Turkmenistan (1991), 158; joint Turkmenistan-Iran Chamber of Commerce established in (1992), 160; ethnic Russian and Kurdish minority in (1993), 161

Assyrians: their settlement by 800 BC, 1

Astara: annexed by Russia (1813), 48; anti-Bolshevik revolt in (1920–21), 104

Astrabad: Persian town, annexed by Russia (1723–25), 37

Astrakhan: the principal town of the Mongol Khanate of Astrakhan, 25; conquered by Ivan IV (1556), 26; and the river systems of European Russia, 27; in area of peasants' revolt (1670–71), 32; revolt of Streltsy at (1705–8), 37; Bolsheviks active in (1903–14), 73; strikes in (1905), 76; Bolsheviks seize power in (1917), 91; famine in (1921), 102; Soviet labour camps near, 110; allied aid enters the Soviet Union through (1941–45), 120, 121; a German plan for (1941), 122; Germans fail to reach (1941–43), 128

Atatürk, Kemal: his rejection of Armenian territorial claims gives him common cause with Lenin, 104

Athens: 3; raided by the Goths, 5; under Roman Catholic control, 24

Athos: raided by the Goths, 5

Attila the Hun: extends rule of the Huns to the Rhine, 6

Augustow: Germans occupy (1914), 81; Soviet Union annexes (1939), 114

Aurora (Russian cruiser): fires blanks at the Winter Palace, Petrograd (1917), 90

Auschwitz: German concentration camp at, 123

Austerlitz: Napoleon defeats the Russians at (1805), 49

Austria: Catherine the Great gives Russia a common frontier with, 41; a party to two partitions of Poland (1772, 1795), 42; Russia suppresses Hungarian revolt in (1849), 51; helps Russia suppress Polish revolt (1860), 53; signs trade agreement with Bolshevik Russia (1921), 101; helps to equip the Kara Sea Expedition (1921), 105; Russian refugees in (by 1930), 107; Soviet occupation zone in (1945–50), 133; and the East European exodus (1989), 152; asylum seekers in (1990), 154; and Stalin's crimes, 159

Austria-Hungary: and European diplomacy (1872–1907), 63, 64; and Russian policy in the Balkans (1876–1914), 78, 79; Lenin allowed to leave (1914), 87

Avars: their European conquests, 8; their demise, 9; settled along the middle Danube, 10

Azef; exposed as a police spy, 72

Azerbaijan: and the proposed Union of Border States (1919–20), 100; its brief independence (1918–20), 104; a Soviet Socialist Republic, 144; ethnic violence in (1988–91), 151, 155; votes to re-establish independence (1991), 157; an independent Republic, 158; signs truce with Armenia (1992), 160; ethnic Russian and Armenian minorities in (1993), 161

Azov: principal town of the Crimean Khanate, 25; a principal town of the Don Cossacks, 35; Don Cossacks defeated at (1708), 37; battle of (1736), 46

Azov, Sea of: Greek and Scythian settlements on shores of, 3; river routes across Russia from, 27; naval battle in (1737), 46; anarchist headquarters on the shore of (1918–20), 95; German occupation forces driven from (1943–44), 129

Babylon: area of Assyrian settlement in 800 BC, 1; reached by nomads from central Asia, 2

Bagdad: part of the Islamic world, 10, 15

Bahrein: comes under British control (1867), 61

Baibert: battle of (1829), 46

Baikal, Lake: largely within the Mongol dominions, 21; early Russian settlements on, 33; Chinese territory extended towards (1720–60), 40; and the Siberian exile system (1648–1917), 54; and Russian trade with China (1850–70), 59; and the Trans-Siberian railway, 62; forms the western boundary of the Far Eastern Republic (1920–22), 106; Soviet labour camp near, 111; industry in the region of (1970), 137

Baikonur: and Soviet-American space co-operation (1975), 147; riots in (1992), 160

Bakhchisaray: unsuccessful Russian attack on (1556–59), 26; battle of (1736), 46

Baku: Viking settlers reach, 11; temporarily annexed by Russia from Persia (1723–25), 37; large German community in (by 1914), 39; annexed by Russia (1806), 48; anarchists active in (1905–6), 55; industrial growth of (by 1860), 56; strikes in (before 1905), 68; industry in (by 1900), 71; political assassinations in, 72; secret Bolshevik printing press in, 73; revolutionary outbreak at (1905), 76; occupied by the Turks (1917–18), 85, 91; occupied by the British (1918–19), 92, 103, 104, 146; Soviet labour camps near, 110; United States aid reaches (1941–45), 120; a German plan for (1941), 122; its oilfields a major German military objective (1942), 124, 128; over half a million inhabitants (1959), 138; ethnic riots in (1990), 155; vote to re-establish independence in (1991), 157; becomes capital of independent Republic of Azerbaijan (1991), 158

Bakunin, Mikhail Alexandrovich: exiled to Siberia, 54; his view of anarchism, 55

Balkans: raided by the Slavs, 8; Slav settlements in, 9; Turkish rule of, 49; Bismarck demarcates Austro-Russian line of influence in, 63

Balkhash, Lake: on the eastern boundary of the lands of the Golden Horde, 21; and Russian trade with China (1850–70), 59; Ukrainian settlements in the region of (by 1937), 98; anti-Bolshevik revolt in region of (1917–20), 103; Stalinist deportation of national groups to (1941–45), 131; industry to the north of (1970), 137

Balta: annexed by Russia (1793), 43; anti-Jewish violence in, 69

Baltic Republics: become part of Russia (under Peter the Great and Catherine the Great), 37, 41; demand independence (1917), 89; independent (1918–39), 96, 100; Russian refugees in (by 1923), 107; annexed by Stalin (1940), 113, 116; occupied by Germany (1940–44), 123; re-incorporated in Soviet Union (1944–5), 133; Soviet Republics, 144; re-gain their independence (1990–1), 155, 156, 157; independent, 158, 160; Russian minorities in (1993), 161

Baltic Sea: Goths settle along, 4; Goths extend their control to the Black Sea from, 5; reached by the Huns, 6; reached by the Slavs, 7; reached by the Avars, 8; Slav control established along part of southern shore of, 9; Kievan Russian trade across, 14; extension of German control along southern shore of, 20; Lithuanians rule from shore of, to Black Sea, 23; its shores entirely controlled by Roman Catholic rulers, 24; Tsar Fedor re-establishes Russian control on, 26; river routes across Russia from, 27; Russian trade on, 34; Russian westward expansion along (1721–1945), 35, 47; Jews expelled from the coastline of (1828, 1830), 51

Baltimore (USA): Ukrainians at, 99

Balts: their area of settlement by 800 BC, 1; by 200 AD, 4; increasingly discontented with Russian rule (by 1905), 68, 76; four million in Russia (1897), 74

Bandar Shah (Persia): United States aid enters Soviet Union through (1941–45), 120

Bar: Jews murdered in (1648–52), 31

Baranovichi: annexed by Russia (1795), 43

Barcelona (Spain): Commonwealth of Independent States successful in Olympic Games at (1992), 160

Barguzin: founded (1648), 33; and the Siberian exiles, 54; in the Far Eastern Republic (1920–22), 106

Barnaul: Ukrainians at (by 1937), 98; industry at (1941–45), 121; a German plan for (1941), 122; Virgin Lands campaign extended to (after 1953), 136

Bashkirs: revolt against Russian rule (1708–11), 37; famine in homeland of (1921), 102; anti-Bolshevik uprising in (1917–20), 103; form an Autonomous Soviet Socialist Republic, 144

Basidu: British island near possible Russian railhead on Indian Ocean, 61

Batum: ceded to Russia by Turkey (1878), 48; anarchists active in (1905–6), 55; strikes in (before 1905), 68; Bolsheviks active in (1903–14), 73; revolution in (1905), 76; Turks advance on (1917), 85; Turks occupy (1918), 91; British occupy (1918–19), 92, 104, 146; Soviet aid to Republican Spain leaves from (1936–39), 101; a German plan to control (1941), 122

Baturin: revolt against Peter the Great in (1708), 37

Bavaria: German communists fail to seize power in, 108; East European asylum seekers in (1990), 154

Bayazit: occupied by Russia (1829), 46

Begovat: industry at (1941–45), 121

Belarus: new Republic of (1991-), 150, 157, 158, 160; ethnic minorities in (1993), 161

Belgium: Russian refugees from Bolshevism in (by 1930), 107; East European asylum seekers in (1990), 154

Belgorod: within area of peasants' revolt (1606–7), 29; trade fair at, 34; revolutionary outbreak at (1905), 76

Belgrade: Treaty of (1739), 46; and the defeat of Germany (1944–45), 130

Belopolye: Ukraine sets up customs barrier at (1991), 156

Belogorsk: and the Soviet-Chinese border (1970), 143

Belomor Canal: largely built by forced labour, 109

Belozersk: within Kievan Russia, 13; Orthodox monastery established at, 16; Ivan IV seizes land in region of, 28

Belzec (Belzhets): German concentration camp at, 123

Bender: proposed Russian railway to Persian Gulf at, 61

Bendery: siege of (1770), 46; fighting at (1992), 160

Berdiansk: attacked by anarchists (1918–20), 95; occupied by the Germans (1941–43), 128; Germans driven from (1943), 129

Berdichev: Jewish political activity in, 70

Berezov: founded (1593), 33

Bering Sea: Soviet labour camps on the shore of, 111

Berlin: colonized by the Germans, 20; Protocols of Zion published in (1911), 69; Russian students in, 70; Lenin in exile in (1907, 1912), 73; Treaty of (1878), 78; Lenin returns to Russia through (1917), 87; German communists try to seize power, but suppressed in, 108; entered by Soviet troops (1945), 113, 130; divided in Soviet, British, French and United States sectors (1945), 133; and the collapse of Communism in Eastern Europe (1989), 152

Berne (Switzerland): Lenin in exile in (1913–17), 73, 87

Bessarabia: annexed by Russia from Turkey (1812), 46, 50; peasant uprising in province of (1905), 75; Rumanian (from 1918), annexed by the Soviet Union (1940), 116; a German plan to control (1941), 122; Rumanian military government established in (1941), 123; reincorporated in the Soviet Union (1945), 133; a Soviet Republic, the Moldavian SSR (since 1945), 144

Bialystok (Belostok): Polish town, annexed by Prussia (1795), 43; becomes Russian (in 1815) and a centre of Polish revolt (1860), 53; anarchists active in (1905–6), 55; anti-Jewish violence in, 69, 75; political assassinations in, 72; and German war aims (1914), 80; Germans occupy (1915), 82; Red Army advances through, towards Warsaw (1920), 96; Soviet Union annexes (1939), 114; a part of Greater Germany, scene of a Jewish uprising, 123

Bikin: and the Soviet-Chinese border (1970), 143

Birobidzhan: capital of the Jewish Autonomous Region (since 1934), 135; and the Soviet-Chinese border (1970), 143

Bishkek: becomes the capital of the independent Republic of Kyrgyzstan (1991), 158; Russian ethnic minority in (1993), 161

Bismarck: and European diplomacy (after 1872), 63, 64

Bitlis: Russian troops occupy (1915–16), 85; Armenian claims to (1918), 104

Black Sea: nomads from central Asia reach the shores of, 2; Greeks and Scythians settle by, 3; Roman rule on shores of, 4; the Huns extend their rule to, 6; Slavs extend their control to, 7; Avars control part of the northern shore of, 8; Slavs re-establish their control of part of the northern shore of, 9; Khazars control northern shore of, 10; Kievan Russian rule extended to the shores of (by 1054), 13; Kievan Russian trade across, 14; and the spread of Eastern Catholicism, 15; Russia fails to establish control on, 26; river routes across Russia from, 27; Cossacks settle on eastern shore of, 35; Peter the Great fails to establish Russian control of, 37; Catherine the Great establishes Russian territory on, 41; and the wars between Russia and Turkey (1721–1829), 46; Russian territorial expansion along the eastern shore of (1803–78), 48; Jews expelled

Russian offensive against, unsuccessful (1917), 89; Red Army fails to capture (1920), 96; part of the West Ukrainian Republic (1918), 97; occupied by the Poles (1919), 100; annexed by the Soviet Union (1939), 114, 116; occupied by the Germans (1941), 118, 119; Jewish uprising against the Germans in, 123; Germans driven from (1944), 130; reincorporated into the Soviet Union (1945), 133

Maastricht: conference at (1991), agrees to emergency food aid to Russia, 160

Macedonia: and Russian policy in the Balkans (1876–85), 78

Magadan: principal town of the Kolyma River forced labour area, 111

Magdagachi: and the Soviet-Chinese border (1970), 143

Magnitogorsk: many Ukrainians settled at (by 1937), 98; a German plan for (1941), 122; over a quarter of a million inhabitants (1959), 138

Magyars: settle along the middle Danube, 12; converted to Roman Catholicism, 15

Maikop: annexed by Russia (1864), 48; revolutionary outbreak at (1905), 76; occupied by the Germans (1942), 124, 128

Maimaichin: under Chinese control, 40; and Russian trade with China (1850–70), 59

Majdanek: a German concentration camp, 123

Major, John: denounces anti-Gorbachev coup (1991), 157; signs Anglo-Russian Treaty (1992), 160

Makeyevka: coal strike in (1989), 151

Makhachkala: part of the Terek Peoples' SSR (1918–19), 104; Germans fail to reach (1941–43), 128

Makhno, Nestor Ivanovich: controls large area of southern Russia (1918–20), 95

Maklakovo: and the Northern Sea Route administration, 112

Malaya Vishera: Nicholas II's train halted at (1917), 86; Germans occupy (1941), 126

Malo Yaroslavets: under German military rule (1942), 123

Malta: Bush-Gorbachev summit in (1989), 150

Manchester (USA): Ukrainians at, 99

Manchuria: area of growing Russian influence (after 1895), 67; liberated from Japan by Soviet troops, and returned to China (1945), 142

Manfredonia (Italy): bombarded by the Russian fleet (1798–1800), 45

Mangalia: occupied by Russia (1810, 1828), 46

Mangazeia: founded (1601), 33

Mannerheim, General: active against the Bolsheviks (1918–19), 94; defeats Finnish Bolsheviks (1918), 100

Mannerheim Line: Finnish defences, broken by the Soviet Army (1940), 115

Manych, River: German advance to (1941–43), 128

Marienwerder: ruled by the Teutonic Knights, 20

Mariupol: occupied by German troops (1918), 91; attacked by anarchists (1918–20), 95; annexed to the Independent Ukraine (1918), 97; name changed to Zhdanov, 139

Marseilles: Russian students in, 70

Mary: a non-Slav tribe, revolting against Russian rule (1606–7), 29; famine in homeland of (1921), 102; an Autonomous Soviet Socialist Republic, 144

Masurian Lakes (East Prussia): Russians defeated by the Germans at (1914), 81

Mauritius: Soviet fishing agreement with (1970), 141

Mazepa, Ivan Stepanovich: leads Cossack Revolt (1708), 37

Mazovians: a Slav tribe north of the Pripet marshes, 12

Medes: their settlement by 800 BC, 1

Mediterranean Sea: reached by nomads from central Asia, 2; Vikings penetrate to, 11; Eastern Catholicism, Roman Catholicism and Islam established around, 15; Mongol conquests reach eastern shores of, 21; Roman Catholicism extends its control in east of, 24; Russian naval activity against France in (1798–1800), 45; and Soviet naval strength, (1970), 141

Medyn: Ivan IV seizes land in region of, 28

Megri: anti-Bolshevik revolt in (1920–21), 104

Melitopol: anti-Jewish violence in, 69, 75; annexed to the Independent Ukraine (1918), 97; occupied by Germany (1941), 123

Memel: ruled by the Teutonic Knights, 20; under communist rule (since 1945), 36, 133, 145

Memphis (Egypt): reached by nomads from central Asia, 2

Merv: annexed by Russia (1884), 61; linked to Moscow by railway (1915), 62

Mesembria: Greek colony on the Black Sea, 3

Meshed (Turkey): proposed Russian railway through, 61

Meskhetians: deported by Stalin to Siberia (1944), 131

Messina (Sicily): bombarded by the Russian fleet (1798–1800), 45

Mexico: Trotsky in exile in, and assassinated (1940), 113

Mezen, River: Soviet labour camps established at the mouth of, 110

Mezhdurechensk: coal strike in (1989), 151

Michael Romanov: crowned Tsar (1613), 29; liberates Moscow and Novgorod from Polish and Swedish control, 30

Midia (Turkey): occupied by Russia (1829), 46, 51; to have been part of a 'Big Bulgaria' (1878) 78; promised to Russia by Britain and France (1915), 85

Mikhailovsk: Russian settlement in Alaska (founded 1799), 44

Milan (Italy): a centre of Roman Catholicism in 1000 AD, 15; occupied by the Russians in the war against France (1798–99), 49

Military Colonies: established by Alexander 1, 50; revolts in, 52

Mineralnye Vody: revolution in (1905), 76; claimed as part of the Ukraine, 97

Minin and Pozharsky: organize Russian counter-attack against Poles (1611–12), 30

Minsk: conquered by the Lithuanians, 23; Jews murdered in (1648–52), 31; becomes part of Russia (1793), 41, 42, 43; anarchists active in (1905–6), 55; peasant discontent and serdom in (by 1860), 57, 58; trade unions in, infiltrated by Tsarist secret police (by 1903), 68; anti-Jewish violence in, 69, 75; Jewish political activity in, 70; agricultural workers strike in Province of (1905), 75; German army fails to reach (1915), 82; occupied by anti-Bolshevik forces (1918–19), 92; occupied by the Poles (1920), 96; occupied by the Germans (1941), 118, 119; a German plan for (1941), 122; Jewish uprising against the Germans in, 123; Germans driven from (1944), 130; over half a million inhabitants (1959), 138; general strike in (1991), 156; capital of an independent Republic (Belarus), 158; ethnic Russian minority in (1993), 161

Minusinsk: a town of exile in Siberia, 54, 72

Mir: annexed by Russia (1795), 43; occupied by Germany (1941), 123

Mitava (Mitau): under Roman Catholic control, 24; annexed by Russia (1795), 43; industrial growth of (by 1860), 56; Jewish political activity in, 70; industry in (by 1900), 71; and German war aims (1914), 80; German army enters (1915), 82